MCTS: Microsoft Silverlight 4 Development (70-506) Certification Guide

A compact certification guide to help you prepare for, and pass, the (70-506): TS: Microsoft Silverlight 4, Development exam

Johnny Tordgeman

[PACKT] enterprise 器

PUBLISHING   professional expertise distilled

BIRMINGHAM - MUMBAI

MCTS: Microsoft Silverlight 4 Development (70-506) Certification Guide

First published: June 2012

Production Reference: 1180612

Published by Packt Publishing Ltd.
Livery Place
35 Livery Street
Birmingham B3 2PB, UK.

ISBN 978-1-84968-466-8

www.packtpub.com

Cover Image by Artie Ng (artherng@yahoo.com.au)

Credits

Author
Johnny Tordgeman

Reviewers
Kunal Chowdhury

Evan Hutnick

Acquisition Editor
Kerry George

Development Editor
Susmita Panda

Technical Editor
Devdutt Kulkarni

Project Coordinator
Vishal Bodwani

Proofreader
Linda Morris

Indexer
Rekha Nair

Production Coordinator
Melwyn D'sa

Cover Work
Melwyn D'sa

About the Author

Johnny Tordgeman is a professional SharePoint, FAST, and frontend developer and trainer, who has over six years of experience in the development of web applications.

Johnny serves as the CTO at E4D Solutions where he specializes in building enterprise applications based on SharePoint and Silverlight, for the telecom, financial, and government industries.

Johnny is a frequent speaker at user groups and conferences on SharePoint and client-side technologies.

First, I would like to thank everyone at Packt Publishing, and especially Vishal Bodwani, for making this book a reality. Secondly, I would like to dedicate this book to my amazing wife Ayelet , my dear parents Itzik and Varda, my brothers Shirley and Yuval, and my friends Yossi, Idan, Leon, Niv, Itzik, Tal, and Zvi for believing in me in every step of the way..

Last, but not least, I would like to thank my academic mentor, Dr. Amnon Dekel, for giving me the confidence to know that even when things go wrong, someone is there for you.

About the Reviewers

Kunal Chowdhury is a Microsoft MVP (Silverlight), Telerik MVP, Codeproject MVP, and Mentor, and also a frequent speaker at various Microsoft events. Apart from being an author and passionate blogger, he is a software engineer by profession. He is very passionate about Silverlight, WP7, WPF, Windows 8 Metro UI, and LightSwitch. Kunal shares his findings at his technical blog — http://www.kunal-chowdhury.com/. He has also worked as a technical reviewer for the book, *Fun with Silverlight 4*.

He is the owner of http://www.silverlight-zone.com/. If you wish, you can follow him on Twitter (@kunal2383), or you can connect with him on his Facebook page — facebook.com/blog.kunal2383.

Evan Hutnick works as a Developer Evangelist and Solutions Consultant for Telerik, empowering customers to make the most out of the XAML platforms, as well as offering best practices, mentoring, and custom development services. Evan has previously provided a technical review for the *Silverlight 5 Data and Services Cookbook*, and also hosts a brand new XAML-based site named http://xamlwatch.com/, designed to deliver fresh and interesting content covering all of the XAML platforms.

> Last, but certainly not least, I would like to thank my wonderful wife and daughter, for supporting me in my development pursuits, and allowing me to geek it up on nights and weekends.

www.PacktPub.com

Support files, eBooks, discount offers and more

You might want to visit www.PacktPub.com for support files and downloads related to your book.

Did you know that Packt offers eBook versions of every book published, with PDF and ePub files available? You can upgrade to the eBook version at www.PacktPub.com and as a print book customer, you are entitled to a discount on the eBook copy. Get in touch with us at service@packtpub.com for more details.

At www.PacktPub.com, you can also read a collection of free technical articles, sign up for a range of free newsletters and receive exclusive discounts and offers on Packt books and eBooks.

PACKTLIB®

http://PacktLib.PacktPub.com

Do you need instant solutions to your IT questions? PacktLib is Packt's online digital book library. Here, you can access, read and search across Packt's entire library of books.

Why Subscribe?

- Fully searchable across every book published by Packt
- Copy and paste, print and bookmark content
- On demand and accessible via web browser

Free Access for Packt account holders

If you have an account with Packt at www.PacktPub.com, you can use this to access PacktLib today and view nine entirely free books. Simply use your login credentials for immediate access.

Instant Updates on New Packt Books

Get notified! Find out when new books are published by following @PacktEnterprise on Twitter, or the *Packt Enterprise* Facebook page.

Table of Contents

Preface

Microsoft Silverlight offers a robust development environment for rich, cross-browser, cross-operation system businesses, and rich, interactive media experiences. Microsoft's Silverlight MCTS exam is intended for developers, who wish to create these types of applications using the knowledge they already have as .NET developers.

This book will give you the essential knowledge to master the Silverlight MCTS exam, by first introducing you to the core concepts of developing with Silverlight, and gradually moving towards more advanced Silverlight concepts and techniques.

The book uses an example-driven approach that is easy to understand, and helps you master the material covered, by actually doing, and not only reading.

Each chapter contains sample practice questions at the end, based on actual exam questions, so you can test your knowledge, and get a feel for the actual exam, before taking it.

What this book covers

Chapter 1, Overview of Silverlight, is an introductory chapter to Silverlight that covers core concepts of the framework.

Chapter 2, Laying out Our User Interface, gives you an introduction to building user interfaces in Silverlight. The chapter covers core concepts, such as panels, navigation framework, and playing media files.

Chapter 3, Enhancing the User Interface, builds upon the foundations learned in the previous chapter, and arms you with advanced techniques, such as animations and behaviors, for building a better and richer user interface.

Chapter 4, Implementing Application Logic, deals mainly with adding logic to your UI. You will learn all about concepts, such as consuming services, and building dependency properties, which will help you make your application more than just a pretty face.

Chapter 5, Working with Data, introduces you to the world of handling data in Silverlight. You will learn all about binding, formatting, validating, and conversion of data.

Chapter 6, Interacting with the Host Platform, guides you through how to use the host of your Silverlight application to perform tasks, such as printing, copy/pasting, and more.

Chapter 7, Structuring Applications, covers how to make your code look cleaner, and behave better.

Chapter 8, Deploying Applications, packs things up by diving deep into configuring the Silverlight plugin, and reducing its size by dynamically loading resources.

What you need for this book

For this book, you will need Visual Studio 2010. In addition, you will need the Silverlight development tools, which can be downloaded from `http://www. silverlight.net/getting-started` for free, and a copy of Microsoft Expression Blend 4, which has a 60-day free trial version available at `http://www.microsoft. com/expression/try-it/`.

Who this book is for

This book is for anyone who wishes to learn the essential skills needed to pass the Microsoft Silverlight MCTS exam, and use these skills to build rich interactive applications using the Silverlight platform.

Conventions

In this book, you will find a number of styles of text that distinguish between different kinds of information. Here are some examples of these styles, and an explanation of their meaning.

Code words in text are shown as follows: " We have already seen the `Inline` properties when we declared our `Button` control—`Width`, `Height`, `Content`, and `x:Name` are all `Inline` properties."

A block of code is set as follows:

```
<Button Width="100" Height="40" x:Name="btnSubmit">
    <Button.Content>
        <Image Source="fun.png"/>
    </Button.Content>
</Button>
```

New terms and **important words** are shown in bold. Words that you see on the screen, in menus or dialog boxes for example, appear in the text like this: " Open Visual Studio 2010, click on **New Project…**, select **Silverlight** from the **Installed Templates** list on the left-hand side of the window, and click on **Silverlight Application**."

> Warnings or important notes appear in a box like this.

> Tips and tricks appear like this.

Reader feedback

Feedback from our readers is always welcome. Let us know what you think about this book — what you liked or may have disliked. Reader feedback is important for us to develop titles that you really get the most out of.

To send us general feedback, simply send an e-mail to feedback@packtpub.com, and mention the book title through the subject of your message.

If there is a topic that you have expertise in and you are interested in either writing or contributing to a book, see our author guide on www.packtpub.com/authors.

Customer support

Now that you are the proud owner of a Packt book, we have a number of things to help you to get the most from your purchase.

Downloading the example code

You can download the example code files for all Packt books you have purchased from your account at http://www.packtpub.com. If you purchased this book elsewhere, you can visit http://www.packtpub.com/support and register to have the files e-mailed directly to you.

Errata

Although we have taken every care to ensure the accuracy of our content, mistakes do happen. If you find a mistake in one of our books—maybe a mistake in the text or the code—we would be grateful if you would report this to us. By doing so, you can save other readers from frustration and help us improve subsequent versions of this book. If you find any errata, please report them by visiting http://www.packtpub.com/support, selecting your book, clicking on the **errata submission form** link, and entering the details of your errata. Once your errata are verified, your submission will be accepted and the errata will be uploaded to our website, or added to any list of existing errata, under the Errata section of that title.

Piracy

Piracy of copyright material on the Internet is an ongoing problem across all media. At Packt, we take the protection of our copyright and licenses very seriously. If you come across any illegal copies of our works, in any form, on the Internet, please provide us with the location address or website name immediately so that we can pursue a remedy.

Please contact us at copyright@packtpub.com with a link to the suspected pirated material.

We appreciate your help in protecting our authors, and our ability to bring you valuable content.

Questions

You can contact us at questions@packtpub.com if you are having a problem with any aspect of the book, and we will do our best to address it.

1
Overview of Silverlight

Just like everything in life, we start things off with an overview. If you have picked up this book on purpose, then I'm sure you have at least some idea what Silverlight is. But, if you just picked this book because the cover looked inviting, fear not, as this chapter will provide all the basics you'll need in your journey to become a certified Silverlight guru.

As Confucius once said, "A journey of a thousand miles begins with a single step", so let's take the first step now and get to know all the basics of Silverlight.

In this chapter we will cover the following topics:

- What is Microsoft Silverlight
- Introducing XAML
- The Silverlight application model
- Integrating Silverlight with HTML
- In and out-of-browser support
- Self-test (Q&A)

What is Microsoft Silverlight

Silverlight is Microsoft's cross-platform, cross-browser, and a .NET-based framework for building in and out-of-browser **Rich Internet Applications** (**RIAs**). In simple words, you can write Silverlight applications using a language you already know (be it C# or VB), and run it on all major operating systems (such as OSX, Windows, and Linux) and browsers (such as Internet Explorer, Chrome, Firefox, and Safari).

It's worth noting that the Linux variation of Silverlight is not developed or maintained by Microsoft. Moonlight, which is the name of the Linux variation, is developed by the Mono project with aid from Microsoft and Novell, and is primarily targeted for Linux and other Unix/X11-based operating systems. In addition, your Silverlight application doesn't have to stay inside the browser. Using the out-of-browser capabilities of Silverlight, you can take your application out of the browser and into the desktop, but we will learn more on that later.

Using Silverlight you can build just about anything — from a simple media player that streams movies from your server, to a complex **line of business (LOB)** application that fetches data from a database and uses some business logic to transform that data into a visually stunning executive dashboard with interactive charts and gauges.

Many companies nowadays are using Silverlight to enrich their applications. Take a look at Seesmic Desktop 2 for example (`http://www.seesmic.com/products/desktop`), which is a social media tool for Windows and Mac built entirely in Silverlight.

The main competition to Silverlight comes from Adobe Flash. Both are browser plugins targeting rich media applications. While not a direct competitor, HTML5 can also be considered as an alternative in some cases. While Silverlight has matured into a rich line of business platform that is getting increasingly popular for creating intranet applications, HTML5 offers greater reach, as it can be viewed on more devices. But, it is also much harder to develop the same level of business applications using HTML5 instead of Silverlight.

In addition, the HTML5 specifications are not finalized yet and, thus, not all the browsers implement it evenly. For example, while some browsers fully support the `Canvas` control, others support just some of its features, making it difficult to use the "code once, run everywhere" approach.

Whether you are an ASP.NET developer trying to decide if Silverlight is the right technology for your next project or you are a part of a development team in a big enterprise, here are some reasons to use Silverlight over other technologies:

- **Cross-browser and OS support**: The code you write will run exactly the same on every supported browser and OS, so you don't have to waste time with making your application supportable on other browsers than your own
- **Authoring tools**: Silverlight is developed on Visual Studio 2010, which you, as a .NET developer, already know and love
- **Plugins with a small size**: The Silverlight plugin weighs just a few megabytes, which is a small size compared to the entire .NET framework

- **.NET-based framework**: Silverlight is based on the .NET framework, which means that if you are already a .NET developer, learning Silverlight will be like a walk in the park

- **Out-of-browser support**: The ability to take your application out of the web world and into the desktop world opens a lot of opportunities to enrich the user's experience from your application

- **Enterprise-ready**: Silverlight can integrate with components such as Microsoft Enterprise Library 5 (http://msdn.microsoft.com/en-us/library/ff648951.aspx) and WCF RIA services (http://msdn.microsoft.com/en-us/library/ee707344%28v=vs.91%29.aspx), so you can complete the development of your LOB applications faster and more efficiently

- **Prism**: The Microsoft patterns and practices group has published Prism, which guides you on how to increase modularity and helps you to architect your application better

The adoption rate of Silverlight has recently reached the 70 percent milestone (http://www.riastats.com/), which means that almost every three out of four PCs already have Silverlight installed! With the rise in the adaptation rate comes the rise in the need for developers. A leading job-hunting site — http://www.dice.com/ — has recently found that Silverlight-related jobs experienced a 12.6 percent growth in demand over the last three months, while Adobe Flash-related jobs experienced just 2.2 percent growth over the same period of time (http://www.readwriteweb.com/enterprise/2011/05/it-hiring-and-salaries-up---wh.php). In addition, Silverlight is the language of choice to develop applications for Microsoft's newest mobile phone system — Windows Phone 7, which means that if you know Silverlight, you are not only a web and desktop developer, you are also a mobile developer!

If I have to sum up the last paragraph in simple words, I would say that you couldn't have picked a better time to become a certified Silverlight developer.

Now that you know what Silverlight is, what it can do, and why you should use it, let's move on to set up your development environment. Your development environment requires the following hardware and software components:

- A 1.6 GHz or faster CPU

- At least 1 GB RAM for 32-bit OS or 2 GB RAM for 64-bit OS

- 3 GB of available hard disk space

- A PC running Windows XP/Vista/7/Server 2003/Server 2008

Setting up your development environment

Setting up your development environment is as easy as it can get. The process consists of three downloads (two are mandatory and one is optional) and the installation of those components.

The first thing you need is Visual Studio 2010. If you have Visual Studio 2008 or an earlier version, you will need to upgrade it, as the Silverlight 4 developer tools don't support these versions. You can download a free version of Visual Studio 2010 from the Microsoft website at `http://www.microsoft.com/express/Downloads/`.

Once you have Visual Studio 2010 installed, you will need the Silverlight 4 developer tools. These tools add the support for developing and designing Silverlight 4 applications in Visual Studio 2010. If you have Service Pack 1 for Visual Studio 2010 installed, you already have the tools; if not, you can get them either by using the installed Microsoft/web platform located at `http://www.microsoft.com/web/gallery/install.aspx?appid=silverlight4tools;silverlight4toolkit;riaservicestoolkit` or downloading the Microsoft Silverlight 4 Tools for Visual Studio 2010 directly from `http://go.microsoft.com/fwlink/?LinkID=177428`.

The last thing you should download and install is the Silverlight 4 Toolkit from CodePlex. This toolkit adds new components and functionality to the developer tools, and it is highly recommended that you install it. This toolkit can be downloaded from `http://silverlight.codeplex.com/releases/view/43528`.

> While it is completely possible to develop Silverlight 4 applications without the Silverlight 4 Toolkit, it is highly recommended that you download it as it adds many frequently used components, such as an auto-complete box, to the arsenal of components that you can use in your applications.

Now you have a fully equipped development environment for Silverlight. With this accomplishment, we can move on and talk about the first major concept of working with Silverlight—XAML.

Introducing XAML

XAML is an acronym for **Extensible Application Markup Language**. Being a markup language, XAML isn't any different from your everyday-used XML or HTML. XAML is, at its core, an XML file that is used by Silverlight (and WPF) to create the user interface layer of your application. You can use just about any application to create XAML such as Visual Studio, Expression Blend, or even just plain old-school Notepad.

Not every XAML file is used by Silverlight for rendering the user interface layer. In every Silverlight project you will create, you'll notice a file named App.xaml. This file doesn't have any controls added to it, nor does it have the ability to host any controls. Instead, this file is used to host the application-level style resources (such as a Resource Dictionary, which we will talk about in a later chapter) and all of the application lifecycle events' receivers (such as the startup or exit events).

XAML gives us the ability to separate the **user interface** (**UI**) layer from the code layer. A XAML element will always represent a .NET element, so every attribute we set on the UI layer using XAML actually corresponds to a property within that .NET element it represents. This direct representation is also the reason why everything you can do with XAML on the UI layer, you can do in code (using C# or VB) as well.

To see how XAML makes our life easier when working with user interface components, let's examine the following line of code:

```
<input type="button" style='width:100px;height:40px;' value="Submit"/>
```

The preceding line of code should look familiar to you as it's the basic HTML syntax for adding a button to the screen.

Now, let's add the same button using the ASP.NET syntax:

```
Button btn = new Button();
btn.Width = Unit.Pixel(100);
btn.Height = Unit.Pixel(40);
btn.Text = "Submit";
```

Finally, let's add this button using XAML:

```
<Button Width="100" Height="40" Content="Submit"/>
```

As you can see, using XAML cuts down our code from four lines in ASP.NET to one short line of code.

Button, among other controls, also known as content controls, allow us to add a child control to display the control's content. If we take our button as an example, we can add an image as its content instead of the usual text:

```
<Button Width="100" Height="40">
    <Button.Content>
        <Image Source="fun.jpg"/>
    </Button.Content>
</Button>
```

Content controls

Content controls are used very often in Silverlight and we will dig more into them later on, but the one key concept to remember about content controls is that they can only hold one child control as content. This limitation may look strange to you right now, but as we discuss layout controls, such as the Grid control in *Chapter 2, Laying out Our User Interface*, you will see that this limitation is hardly a limitation at all.

The easiest way to work with XAML controls is to drag them out of the toolbox and into the design surface. We can do this using both Visual Studio 2010 or a more designer-oriented application, for example Microsoft Expression Blend 4.

The following screenshot shows what the controls toolbox looks like in Visual Studio:

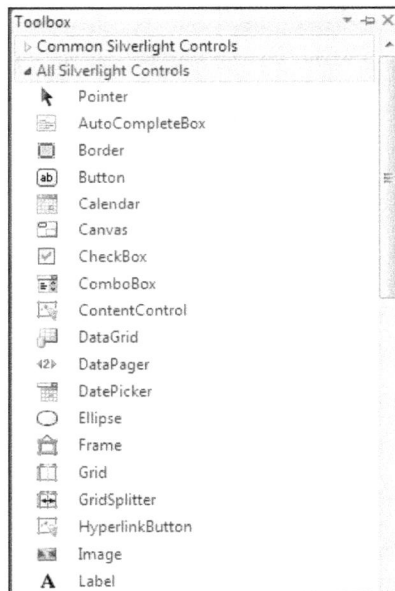

The following screenshot shows what the **Controls** toolbox looks like in Microsoft Expression Blend 4:

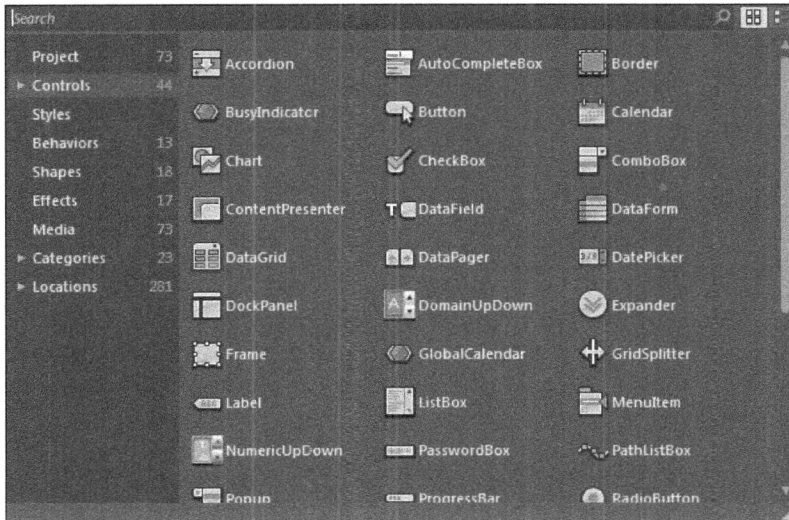

Namespaces

Just like many other programming languages, XAML uses namespaces to organize related controls into groups. Each namespace represents a group of controls and in order to use any of those controls, the namespace must be added to the XAML file (either at the root element level which affects the entire page, or at a lower-level container control which affects only the children of that control).

As we will probably need more than one group of controls within our application, XAML supports multiple namespaces within a single application. To differentiate the different namespaces, each is assigned a prefix value. That prefix value will later be used when we want to add a control from that specific group.

Of course, a declaration of a namespace without reference to the assembly file that actually has the control is useless, so make sure you reference the correct assembly file before adding the namespace.

Let's examine the basic `MainPage.xaml` file, which gets created whenever you create a new Silverlight project:

```
<UserControl x:Class="SilverlightApplication2.MainPage"
xmlns="http://schemas.microsoft.com/winfx/2006/xaml/presentation"
xmlns:x="http://schemas.microsoft.com/winfx/2006/xaml"
xmlns:d="http://schemas.microsoft.com/expression/blend/2008"
xmlns:mc="http://schemas.openxmlformats.org/markup-compatibility/2006"
mc:Ignorable="d"
d:DesignHeight="300" d:DesignWidth="400">
...
</UserControl>
```

From the preceding code snippet, we can see that `http://schemas.microsoft.com/winfx/2006/xaml/presentation` is the default namespace that the page will use (we can tell it's the default namespace as it has no prefix). This namespace hosts a bunch of the core controls you can add to your Silverlight application.

Another namespace that gets declared by default is `http://schemas.microsoft.com/winfx/2006/xaml`. Unlike the default namespace, this namespace gets declared with a prefix (x). That means that whenever we wish to use a control or a property from this namespace, we will have to first mention its prefix value, followed by the name of the property. This namespace provides functionality that is common across our application. We can also add our own namespaces to our application. We will discuss all about namespaces in *Chapter 2, Laying out Our User Interface*.

Naming your objects

If we look back at the button we defined previously in this chapter, we will notice that it has no name/ID attribute, which means that we won't be able to access this object in our code behind by name, but we will have to use more complicated methods such as the `FindChildByType` or `FindName` methods of the visual tree object to access it. To give an object a name in Silverlight, we can use either the `x:Name` attribute (can you guess where the x prefix came from?) or just the plain `Name` attribute. The following line of code shows the XAML code for our button with the newly added property:

```
<Button Width="100" Height="40" Content="Submit" x:Name="btnSubmit"/>
```

If you play around a bit with adding controls in Visual Studio, you will notice that many of the controls you add from the toolbox will automatically add a reference to the right assembly and declare the correct namespace for you. We will discuss in detail how to reference namespaces in the next chapter of this book.

Setting properties

XAML allows us to set properties of our objects in two ways—Using the `Inline` property and using the `Element` property. We have already seen the `Inline` properties when we declared our `Button` control—`Width`, `Height`, `Content`, and `x:Name` are all `Inline` properties. When we wish to set a simple property of our element, we will usually use the `Inline` properties as they are fast and easy to set, but if we want to set an image as the content of our button, we would need a way to represent a more complex value for the property. To set an image as the content of a button, we will set an `Element` property. An `Element` property of the content will look like this:

```
<Button Width="100" Height="40" x:Name="btnSubmit">
    <Button.Content>
        <Image Source="fun.png"/>
    </Button.Content>
</Button>
```

Notice the syntax for the content `Element` property in the following line of code:

```
<ControlType.PropertyName>some-value</ControlType.PropertyName>
```

You don't have to remember this syntax by heart, as Visual Studio's IntelliSense will help you write it.

With this we conclude our overview of XAML, but obviously there is a lot more in the language than what we've covered. As XAML is a key concept in Silverlight, we will deal with it a lot more in the coming chapters, so even if you didn't understand everything we talked about so far, you definitely will, once we get to use it more.

The Silverlight application model

A Silverlight application, once compiled, will end up as a XAP (pronounced as zap) file. That XAP file, which is actually a ZIP file renamed, will contain your compiled code in the form of a DLL file, which is a manifest file named `AppManifest.xaml` that describes your application to the Silverlight runtime engine and possibly some resources such as images, web service connection information, or any other type of content your application might need.

Due to the fact that a XAP file contains more than just compiled code, there may be times when we need to edit its content, which is where knowing the fact that "the XAP files are basically the ZIP files" comes in handy.

Consider the following scenario:

You are developing a Silverlight application that needs to access a database in order to display data from it. To access the database, you will connect to a WCF web service that grabs the data and sends it back to your application in the XML format. In most cases, the WCF web service won't be hosted on the same machine in both development and production environments and, thus, will have a different IP address on each. As we have mentioned earlier, the XAP file contains, among other things, the web service connection information for our application inside a file called `ServiceReferences.ClientConfig`. So, before we move our application from a development to a production environment we need to edit this file and change the address of the WCF web service from a testing environment address to the production address.

In order to run our Silverlight application, the browser will download our XAP file to the client computer, which means file size may be an issue for users with limited bandwidth or a slower connection. We may try to reduce the size of our XAP file by re-zipping it using a stronger compression rate. But, this will come at the expense of slower decompression of the XAP file on older machines, and the slower the decompression rate is, the longer it will take for your application to start running.

A better method to decrease the size of your XAP file would be using the "application library caching" option. The application library caching, also known as **assembly caching**, is a packing method, which avoids packing the DLL files into your XAP file, and instead zips them into individual files alongside it. Using assembly caching may greatly reduce the size of your XAP file, providing faster initial loading time for your application.

To use assembly caching, right-click on the project name in Visual Studio 2010 and select `Properties`. In the new dialog box, select the **Reduce XAP size by using application library caching** option, as shown in the following screenshot:

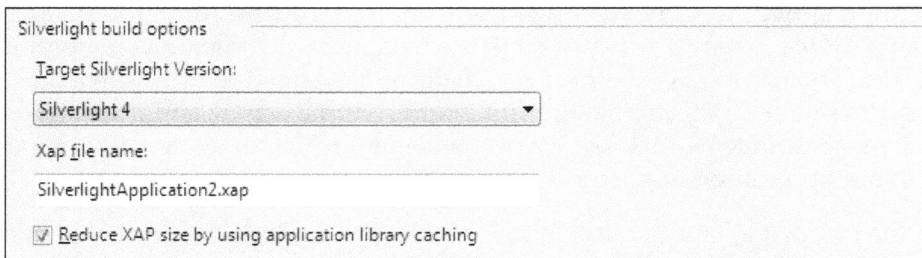

Silverlight build options

Target Silverlight Version:

Silverlight 4

Xap file name:

SilverlightApplication2.xap

☑ Reduce XAP size by using application library caching

You cannot use assembly caching if you are building an out-of-browser application. We will discuss the out-of-browser applications later on in this chapter.

You may be wondering at this point how the Silverlight runtime engine knows that we used the assembly caching option, and that it needs to download a list of external DLL files. The answer to this question is simpler than you might imagine — the `AppManifest.xaml` file.

We have mentioned the `AppManifest.xaml` file earlier when we discussed the content of a XAP file and now we can elaborate more about it. The `AppManifest.xaml` file has one important role — it is responsible for describing our application to the Silverlight runtime engine. Whenever you create a new Silverlight project, Visual Studio 2010 creates this file as part of the project and updates it throughout the project lifetime if necessary. As Visual Studio is responsible for updating this file, it would be rare that we need to update this file by hand ourselves.

Visual Studio 2010 will generate the content of the file, once you compile your Silverlight project. Let's take a look at a basic example of an `AppManifest.xaml` file:

```
<Deployment xmlns="http://schemas.microsoft.com/client/2007/
deployment" xmlns:x="http://schemas.microsoft.com/winfx/2006/xaml" Ent
ryPointAssembly="SilverlightApplication2" EntryPointType="SilverlightA
pplication2.App" RuntimeVersion="4.0.60310.0">
    <Deployment.Parts>
        <AssemblyPart x:Name="SilverlightApplication2"
        Source="SilverlightApplication2.dll" />
        <AssemblyPart x:Name="System.Windows.Controls.Navigation"
        Source="System.Windows.Controls.Navigation.dll" />
        <AssemblyPart x:Name="System.Xml.Linq"
        Source="System.Xml.Linq.dll" />
    </Deployment.Parts>
</Deployment>
```

As can be seen from the preceding code snippet, the `Deployment` element has three attributes as follows:

- `EntryPointAssembly`: This attribute will always point to the name of the assembly. We will always see this same assembly referenced under the `Deployment.Parts` section as well.

- `EntryPointType`: This attribute will always point to the class that should be used to start the application (we will discuss the `App.xaml` file later in this book).

- `RuntimeVersion`: This attribute will tell the runtime engine which version of Silverlight the application was built with.

Under `Deployment` lies the `Parts` section. This section houses one or more `AssemblyPart` entries, each of which point to a DLL file that our application is using. The first entry is usually our compiled Silverlight application, which also contains the entry point class that was specified under the `EntryPointType` attribute of the parent `Deployment` tag.

Other than `Parts`, the `Deployment` element may also contain an `ExternalParts` section. This section will be visible only if we have used the application caching option. This section tells the Silverlight runtime engine which files it needs to download, other than the XAP file, in order to run the application. The `ExternalParts` section will contain one or more `ExtentionPart` entries, each of which point to an external ZIP file.

An example of the `ExternalParts` section may look like the following code snippet:

```
<Deployment.ExternalParts>
    <ExtensionPart Source="System.Windows.Controls.Navigation.zip" />
    <ExtensionPart Source="System.Xml.Linq.zip" />
</Deployment.ExternalParts>
```

In our sample, the Silverlight runtime engine will have to download two external files to get the application running.

Integrating Silverlight with HTML

Now that we know how the Silverlight application model works, let's see how Silverlight interacts and integrates with HTML to actually display the application to the user.

There are two ways to add a Silverlight application to your HTML page as follows:

- Using the `object` tag
- Using the JavaScript helper files

Using the object tag

The object tag method is the easiest way to add a Silverlight application to your page. Using this method, you won't need to use any external JavaScript files for adding a Silverlight application to your page. This method is also supported by all the browsers that are supported by Silverlight. A basic Silverlight object tag will look as follows:

```
<object data="data:application/x-silverlight-2," type="application/x-
silverlight-2" width="100%" height="100%">
        <param name="source" value=" MyCoolApp.xap"/>
        <param name="onError" value="onSilverlightError" />
        <param name="background" value="white" />
        <param name="minRuntimeVersion" value="4.0.60310.0" />
        <param name="autoUpgrade" value="true" />
        <a href="http://go.microsoft.com/fwlink/?LinkID=
        149156&v=4.0.60310.0" style="text-decoration:none">
                <img src="http://go.microsoft.com/
fwlink/?LinkId=161376"
                alt="Get Microsoft Silverlight" style="border-
                style:none"/>
        </a>
</object>
```

The object tag has four mandatory attributes as follows:

- data: While not used by most browsers in the context of Silverlight, it is recommended by Microsoft to have the value of this attribute set to "data:application/x-silverlight-2," to prevent decreased performance in some browsers. You can think of this attribute as a sort of MIME type.

- type: This attribute actually represents the MIME type. It identifies the object tag as a Silverlight object, which will cause the browser to initiate the Silverlight plugin in order to render the object.

- width and height: They specify the width and height of the Silverlight application. You can specify the measurements in pixels or percentages.

Inside the `object` tag we have several `param` entries, as listed in the following table:

Name	Description	Required	Default
source	This specifies the URI to the XAP file. It can be a relative or absolute URI.	Yes	None
onError	This specifies a JavaScript function to call when an error occurs while loading the Silverlight application.	No	None
background	This specifies the background color for the `object` tag rectangular area that displays the Silverlight application. It can accept color names (such as Red) or hexadecimal values with or without alpha (#ff000000 or #000000).	No	white
minRuntimeVersion	This specifies the earliest Silverlight version required to run the application.	No	Currently installed version
autoUpgrade	This specifies whether or not to automatically update to the specified version in the `minRuntimeVersion` attribute if the currently installed version is an older version.	No	true
initParams	This specifies user-defined initialization parameters using comma-separated key-value pairs, for example, UserName=JohnnyT	No	None

There are many more parameters you can use with your Silverlight `object` tag, and you can read more about them at Microsoft's MSDN web page—http://msdn. microsoft.com/en-us/library/cc838259(v=vs.95).aspx.

If the browser fails to render the Silverlight application, it will fall back to the content inside of the `object` tag. The default content of a Silverlight `object` tag will look like the following screenshot:

You can always change the content of the `object` tag to your liking by simply removing all the content the `object` tag currently has (remember, don't delete the `param` entries!) and writing your own HTML code instead.

Using the JavaScript helper files

If you need greater control on the `object` tag or the installing/upgrading process, you can use the JavaScript method.

The JavaScript method makes use of a helper file called `Silverlight.js`, which can be found in the `Tools` directory under the `Silverlight` SDK folder usually located at `C:\Program Files (x86)\Microsoft SDKs\Silverlight\v4.0\Tools`.

Once referenced, the `Silverlight.js` file creates a class called `Silverlight`, which will provide you with different methods and properties related to Silverlight, such as `Silverlight.CreateObject`, `Silverlight.IsInstalled`, and more.

Adding Silverlight using JavaScript is out of the scope of this book, but you can find all the information you need for it on MSDN at `http://msdn.microsoft.com/en-us/library/cc265155(v=vs.95).aspx`.

Silverlight's interaction with JavaScript certainly doesn't end here. In *Chapter 6, Interacting with the Host Platform*, we will discuss many features of Silverlight-JavaScript-HTML integration, such as calling a JavaScript method from Silverlight, calling a Silverlight method from JavaScript, manipulating the **Document Object Model (DOM)** from Silverlight, accessing cookies, and more.

As you might recall, we have mentioned earlier in this chapter that Silverlight isn't limited to running inside the browser anymore. This new concept, called out-of-browser applications, was introduced back in Silverlight 3 and got heavily enhanced in Silverlight 4, so introducing it now would be the perfect way to finish off this chapter.

In and out-of-browser support

Silverlight started its life as an in-browser technology offering rich UX, media playing capabilities, and animation. Starting with Version 3, Silverlight gained the ability to run applications outside the browser, as sandboxed desktop applications. In Silverlight 4, the out-of-browser feature gained a serious boost with the introduction of "elevated trust". Not only can you now access local files and folders on the user's computer (pending his/her approval for your application to run in elevated trust mode) but you can also use COM automation to connect to other applications, for example Microsoft Office. Other important features of out-of-browser applications are toast notifications (a notification API), full screen mode support (for kiosk-based applications), and complete control over the application window. A great example for an out-of-browser Silverlight application is Seesmic Desktop 2, which you can see in the following screenshot:

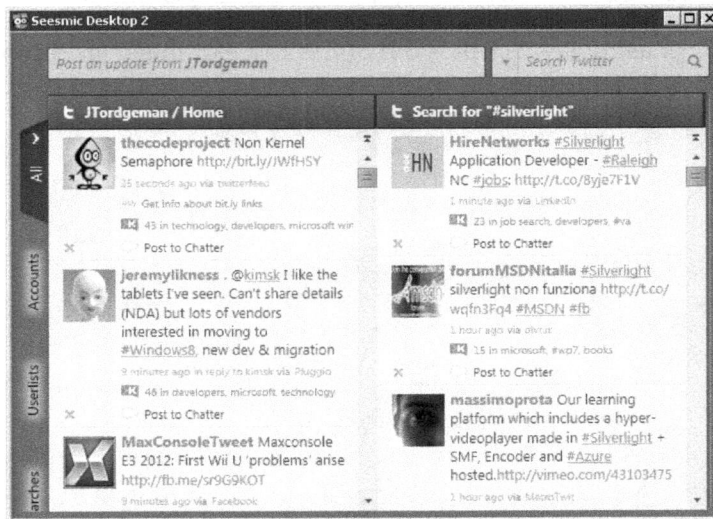

While we won't go into detail here on how to create and work with out-of-browser applications, as we have a chapter dedicated to this subject later on, we will address some of the differences between in and out-of-browser applications as follows:

- In-browser applications have 1 MB of isolation storage quota, as opposed to 25 MB quota for out-of-browser applications. Both quotas can be extended upon a request from the user.

- Out-of-browser applications cannot interact with JavaScript and the HTML DOM (they don't have any HTML DOM to interact with as they aren't running inside a browser).

- Out-of-browser applications can interact with the Windows 7 taskbar using COM automation in elevated trust mode and they can be pinned to the taskbar in Windows 7 while in-browser applications cannot.

- Out-of-browser applications have no initial parameters like in-browser applications.

- In order to update an out-of-browser application, the developer is required to implement a check for a newer version in his code, whereas in browser applications, it is done automatically.

The installation process of an out-of-browser application is quick and painless; the user either right-clicks on the application surface or chooses install, as shown in the following screenshot:

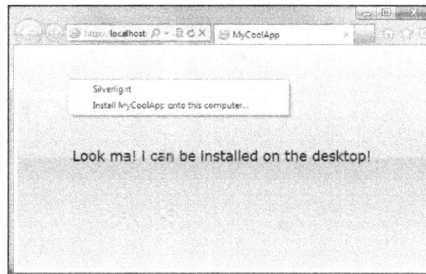

To make things easier for the user, we can create an installation button that will initiate the installation process. We will discuss this method in *Chapter 6, Interacting with the Host Platform* of the book.

There is a lot more in the subject of out-of-browser applications and while this chapter only provided a glimpse of the possibilities of the features, *Chapter 6, Interacting with the Host Platform*, will dive much deeper into it.

Summary

With this we will end the introductory chapter of this book. We've learned about what Silverlight is and what we can do with it. We've set up a development environment for Silverlight. We've learned about XAML—what it does and how to use it. We've also looked into the Silverlight application model and learned what a XAP file is and what it contains, and we finished off with an introduction to the integration of Silverlight with HTML and the concept of out-of-browser applications.

I hope that you gained as much as possible from this chapter and grasped all the basics of Silverlight, as we are now ready to move on to laying out a user interface, which is the topic of our next chapter.

Laying out Our User Interface

2

We will continue our journey to become a Silverlight guru by covering the different aspects of laying out a user interface in Silverlight. In this chapter we will get some hands-on experience of laying out, displaying, and creating different controls. We have a lot to cover, so let's get going and write some code!

In this chapter we will cover the following topics:

- Arranging content with panels
- Using core and content controls
- Creating user controls
- The navigation framework
- Displaying a collection of items
- Playing media files
- Test your knowledge

Arranging content with panels

Imagine the following scenario:

You are responsible for building your company's new BI dashboard. You get the requirements from your superior, and you notice one of the requirements is that your application must support all of the different screen resolutions in the office. This is exactly the point of knowing the different panels that Silverlight offers and how they come into play. Silverlight, being a rich UI framework, offers six different kinds of layout panels for different causes, and as nothing beats seeing things for yourself, we will now create our first Silverlight application to see how the panels differentiate from one another.

Downloading the example code

You can download the example code files for all Packt books you have purchased from your account at http://www.packtpub.com. If you purchased this book elsewhere, you can visit http://www.packtpub.com/support and register to have the files e-mailed directly to you.

Creating your first Silverlight application

To begin, you will need to complete the following steps:

1. Open Visual Studio 2010, click on **New Project...**, select **Silverlight** from the **Installed Templates** list on the left-hand side of the window, and click on **Silverlight Application**. Name the new application as **Chapter2-Layouts**. Your screen should look similar to the following screenshot:

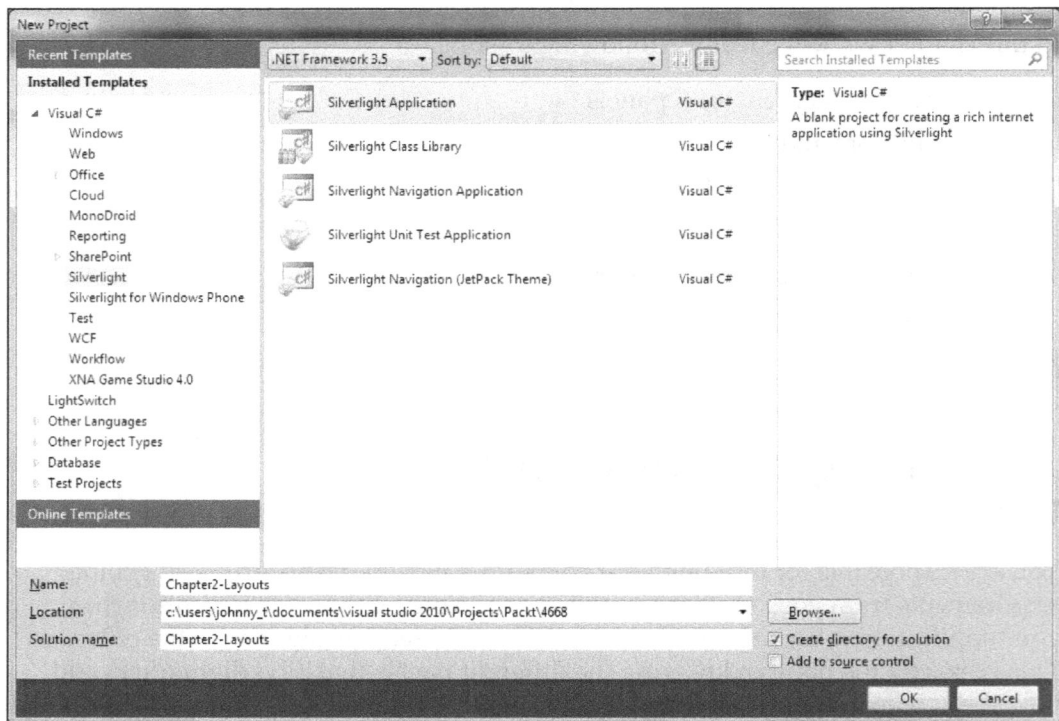

2. To actually create the project, click on the **OK** button. You'll get a pop-up window asking you if you would like to host your Silverlight application within an ASP.NET website. Hosting your application in such a website makes it easier for us to debug and display the application, so don't change anything in this window and just click on **OK**.

3. We have just created our first Silverlight application! Your visual studio should look similar to the following screenshot:

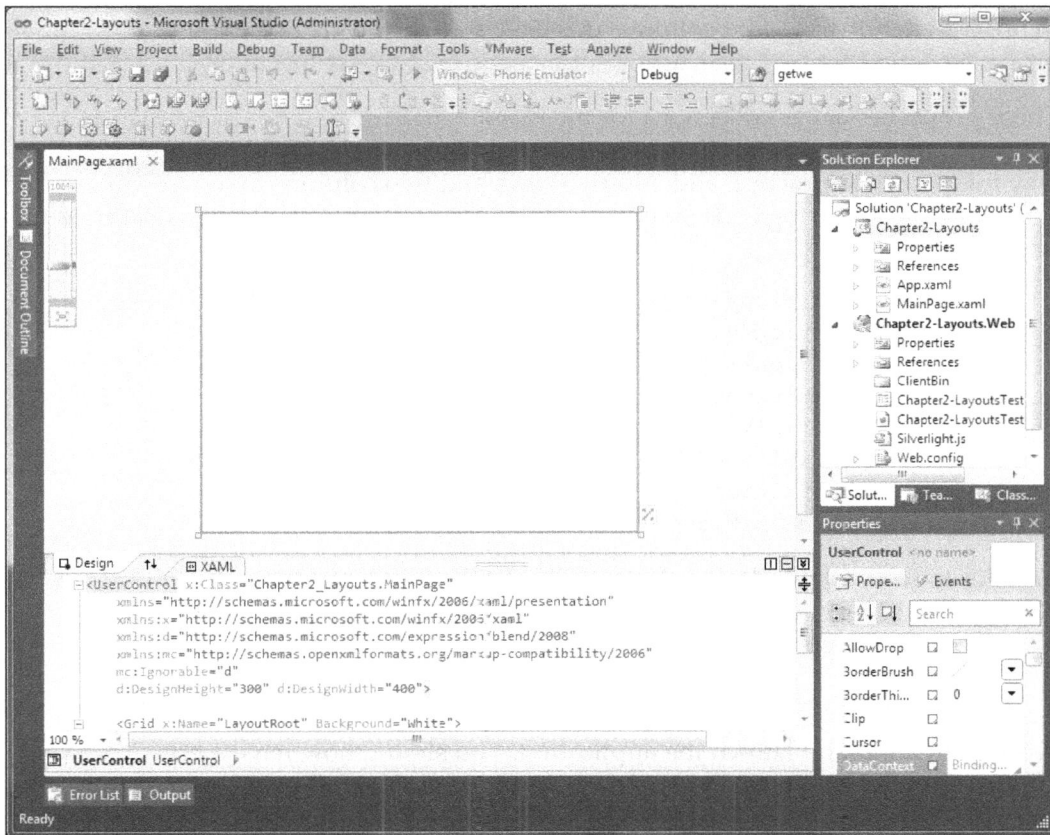

Right now, our new application might look like a blank white box, but under the hood you might notice the first layout panel we are going to discuss—Grid.

Grid

The `Grid` control can be considered as Silverlight's equivalent to the good old HTML table element. Just like the HTML table, the `Grid` control allows you to arrange controls in rows and columns, span a control across multiple rows or columns, and define different heights and widths for each row or column. `Grid` is the control you're most likely to use the most. Not only is it the default root element control for the `UserControl` and page templates, but it is also the best control to use when you want your content to extend/shrink according to the space available for it. In order to define rows and columns in a grid, we use the grid's `Element` properties — `RowDefinitions` and `ColumnDefinitions` — respectively.

These properties act as collections for the `RowDefinition` and `ColumnDefinition` elements, which as you might have guessed, define a single row or column. Let's take this theory to practice, and add two rows and two columns to our `LayoutRoot` grid. Add the following code snippet between the starting and closing tags for your `LayoutRoot`:

```
<Grid.RowDefinitions>
    <RowDefinition/>
    <RowDefinition/>
</Grid.RowDefinitions>
<Grid.ColumnDefinitions>
    <ColumnDefinition/>
    <ColumnDefinition/>
</Grid.ColumnDefinitions>
```

In order to see the boundaries of each cell, add the inline property — `ShowGridLines` — to the `Grid` element, and give it the value of `True`, so your `Grid` element should look as follows:

```
<Grid x:Name="LayoutRoot" Background="White" ShowGridLines="True">
```

Press *F5* to build and launch the application. You should now have a grid divided into two columns and two rows, as shown in the following screenshot:

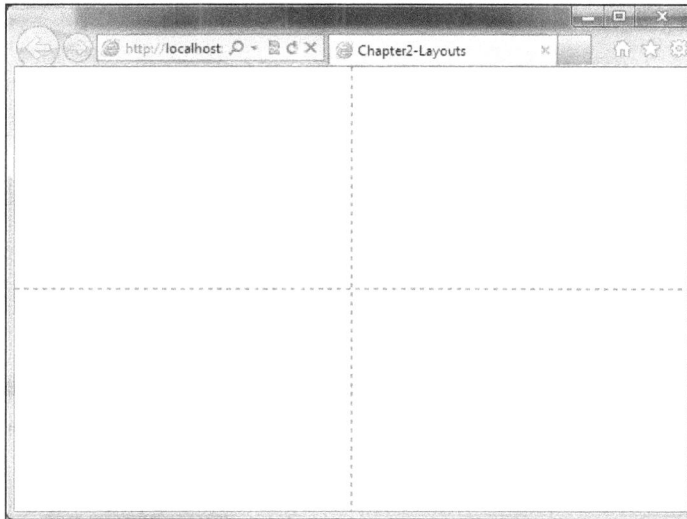

As we didn't specify fixed values for the grid's dimensions, the grid will resize itself according to the space available to it. If you resize the window where the grid is rendered, you will see that the grid resizes itself according to the new window's size.

Setting the dimensions of a grid or almost any other Silverlight control, is done by specifying a fixed number of pixels to the Width and Height properties; setting these properties for a RowDefinition or ColumnDefinition element is quite different.

Unlike most Silverlight controls, the Width and Height properties of ColumnDefinition and RowDefinition are represented as the GridLength values. GridLength allows you to select between three different ways to allocate the available space, and as the default selection is star sizing we will start with it.

Star sizing

Star sizing is used when you wish to distribute the available space of the grid equally between its rows or columns. Star sizing is calculated based on the amount of space a grid has; but if a grid also uses other forms of the GridLength values, they will take precedence when the space is calculated.

But, what if you want one column to always have, for example, twice the space as another column? This is when multiplier star sizing comes into the picture. Take a look at the following code snippet:

```
<Grid.ColumnDefinitions>
    <ColumnDefinition Width="2*"/>
    <ColumnDefinition Width="*"/>
</Grid.ColumnDefinitions>
```

Can you notice the first column has a number before the star? That means it would take *n* times the space as the other column. You aren't limited to whole numbers when using a multiplier with star sizing. You can also define a column to be half the size of other columns by using 0.5 as the multiplier. Using a multiplier with star sizing is the perfect way to make sure a specific area of the grid is always *n* times larger or smaller than the other star-sized areas of the grid.

The following screenshot shows the result of our grid using the `ColumnDefinitions` property from the preceding code snippet:

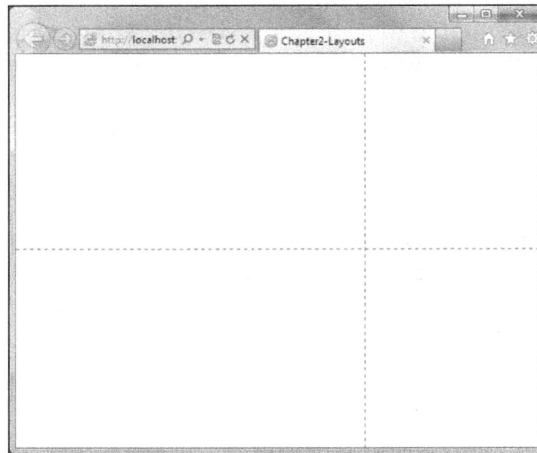

Absolute sizing

Absolute sizing, as the name implies, is used when you wish to give a column or a row a fixed size in pixels. The pixel value is of the double type, which means you are not limited to a value of a whole number, and you can use a floating point as your value as well. The value you set using the absolute sizing is fixed, and it won't change regardless of whether the content of the row or column is larger in size than the space you allocated to it. If, for example, you put a button with the height of 40 pixels into a fixed-size row with the height of 20 pixels, the button will get cut off. Absolute sizing takes precedence over the other two sizing options and it is always the first one to get calculated.

The following code snippet demonstrates how to set up a row with the height of 40 pixels using absolute sizing:

```
<Grid.RowDefinitions>
    <RowDefinition Height="40"/>
    <RowDefinition Height="*"/>
</Grid.RowDefinitions>
```

Auto sizing

Auto sizing is the last of the three possible options of `GridLength`. When a row or column size is set using the auto sizing option, the size of the row or column will be primarily dictated by the content within it. Why primarily? Because other than content, the following factors take part in calculating a row or column that is auto sized:

- In an auto-sized row or column, the largest element in that row or column dictates its height or width.
- Unless you specifically state a sizing option for the last row of a grid, all the remaining space will be allocated to it.

To use auto sizing, all you have to do is assign a value of `Auto` to the `Height` or `Width` properties of a row or column in your grid. In the following screenshot, two rows were defined with the auto sizing option. Notice how the larger button dictates the height of the row and how the remaining space is just allocated for the last row of the grid, regardless of the content inside of it:

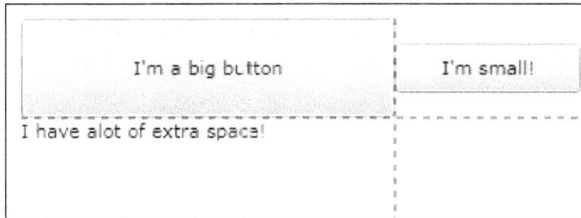

Placing content into a grid

Now that we have understood how to size up our grid, it's time to put some content into it. Before we begin, make sure the code for your grid is as follows:

```
<Grid x:Name="LayoutRoot" Background="White" ShowGridLines="True">
    <Grid.RowDefinitions>
        <RowDefinition Height="Auto"/>
        <RowDefinition Height="30"/>
    </Grid.RowDefinitions>
    <Grid.ColumnDefinitions>
```

```
            <ColumnDefinition Width="*"/>
            <ColumnDefinition Width="*"/>
        </Grid.ColumnDefinitions>
    </Grid>
```

If you are unsure about any of the sizing in this code, please refer to the previous section.

Positioning an element within a grid is done by using the following four attached properties:

- Row: The grid row in which the element will be positioned
- Column: The column in which the element will be positioned
- RowSpan: The amount of rows an element will be spanned over
- ColumnSpan: The amount of columns an element will be spanned over

> **Attached properties** are a specialized kind of properties that give a child element the ability to specify a value for a property that is actually defined in another element, which is mostly their parent element. Attached properties have a very easy-to-spot syntax—TypeName. AttachedProperty. The primary use of attached properties is for layout purposes, but attached properties can also be found in Silverlight's animation engine and other places within the Silverlight framework. An example of an attached property can be Grid.Row, where Grid is the type and Row is the name of the attached property.

Numbering of rows and columns begins at 0, and if you don't specify any value to an element within the grid, it will default to the first row (0) and the first column (again, 0).

Let's add an image to the first row of our grid but on the second column (remember: our grid is divided into two rows and two columns with different-sized schemes). Copy the following line of code to your project, just below the closing Grid. ColumnDefinitions tag:

```
<Image Source="http://www.packtpub.com/sites/default/files/banners/
Learning%20jQuery%201.3.jpg" Grid.Row="0" Grid.Column="1" />
```

Recognizing the attached properties? Using Grid.Row and Grid.Column, we told our new image element that we want to position it in the first row and the second column. The result should look like the following screenshot:

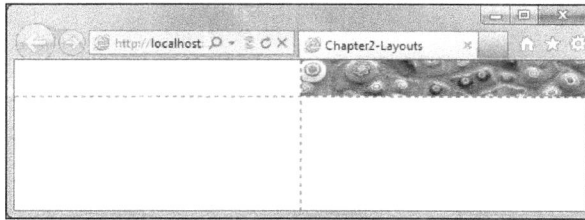

To stretch the image across both columns we simply replace the Grid.Column attached property with the Grid.ColumnSpan attached property and provide it with the number of columns we wish to span across as the value. Setting the Grid. ColumnSpan property with the value of 2 will give the result, as shown in the following screenshot:

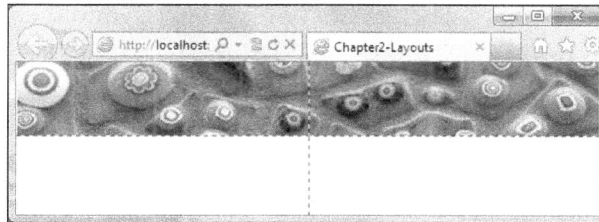

To demonstrate the RowSpan property, change the value of the first row's height from Auto to 30, so it will have a valid height; and change the Image element as follows:

```
<Image Source="http://www.packtpub.com/sites/default/files/banners/
Learning%20jQuery%201.3.jpg" Grid.RowSpan="2" Stretch='UniformToFill"
/>
```

The preceding line of code sets the image to span over two rows and sets its stretching mode to UniformToFill, so it would fill all the available space. This change will result in the following screenshot:

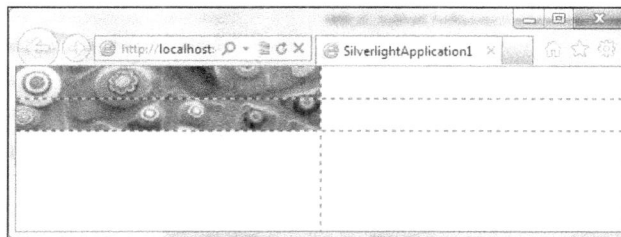

Our image now spans over two rows, each having 30 pixels of height, and as we have set its Stretch property to UniformToFill, it also fills up all the available space.

Changing the grid layout dynamically

When we were introduced to XAML in the previous chapter, we looked at everything that could be done with it and also how it could be done in code, which is not as easy. While designing our grid is usually done in XAML, there may be times when you wish to add rows or columns dynamically using code. The process involves exactly two lines of code—one for defining the RowDefinition or ColumnDefinition object, and the other for actually adding that new definition to our grid. Let's add a new row to our grid (which is named LayoutRoot) dynamically. In Visual Studio 2010, right-click on **MainPage.xaml** and click on **View Code**. Add the following code snippet right after InitializeComponet() in the MainPage constructor method:

```
RowDefinition myNewRow = new RowDefinition();
LayoutRoot.RowDefinitions.Add(myNewRow);
```

The first line of code defines a new RowDefinition object and the second line adds the new row definition to the grid's row definitions collection using the Add method.

Build and run the application, and you should see the new row added to your grid.

> Adding a column definition works exactly the same way, but instead of defining a RowDefinition object, we define a ColumnDefinition object. The same goes for adding it to the grid; instead of adding the new column to the RowDefinitions collection, we add it to the ColumnDefinitions object.

To remove a row or column, we use the same scheme. First, we declare a row or column we wish to remove, and then we tell the grid control to remove it from the collection. The following code snippet will remove the last row from a grid:

```
int lastRowIndex = LayoutRoot.RowDefinitions.Count - 1;
RowDefinition rowToDelete = LayoutRoot.RowDefinitions[lastRowIndex];
LayoutRoot.RowDefinitions.Remove(rowToDelete);
```

The first line of code specifies which row we wish to delete. As we want to delete the last row of the grid, we can count the number of rows in the grid and subtract 1 (remember, collections start with index 0). Once we have the index number, we get the desired RowDefinition object from the collection, and finally we remove that RowDefinition object from the collection using the Remove method.

StackPanel

StackPanel is one of the easier layout controls to use. The StackPanel control is used when you wish to position the elements in a horizontal or vertical layout spanning across a single row or column. Using StackPanel is very straightforward. The following code snippet demonstrates how to use it:

```
<StackPanel>
    <Rectangle Fill="#ff80bca3" Height="20" />
    <Rectangle Fill="#fff6f7bd" Height="20" />
    <Rectangle Fill="#ffe6ac27" Height="20" />
</StackPanel>
```

The preceding XAML code demonstrates the use of a StackPanel control with three 20-pixel high rectangles inside of it. It will render as follows:

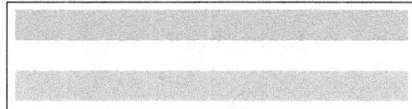

The StackPanel control's default orientation is to vertically align its child controls, but by specifying the orientation to horizontal, StackPanel is capable of arranging its controls horizontally. The following code snippet changes the orientation of StackPanel:

```
<StackPanel Orientation="Horizontal" Height="60">
<Rectangle Fill="#ff80bca3" Width="33"  />
<Rectangle Fill="#fff6f7bd" Width="33" />
<Rectangle Fill="#ffe6ac27" Width="33" />
</StackPanel>
```

The preceding code snippet will render as follows:

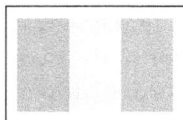

Nesting layout controls is an important concept that you should always keep in mind. While there is no shame in nesting a StackPanel control inside other StackPanel controls, you should always make sure there is no better suited layout control for your desired layout.

Canvas

Imagine yourself sitting in art class. A blank drawing board is positioned in front of you. As an artist you have the freedom to draw (or position) anything you want anywhere on the drawing board. This is what the Canvas layout inspires to mimic. The Canvas layout is the highest performing layout panel in Silverlight, and its purpose is to provide you with a freeform layout environment for your UI needs. Using the Canvas control will look familiar to anyone, who's been doing HTML. We control how far from the left and how far from the top an object will be placed.

In your Silverlight application, replace the LayoutRoot node with the following code snippet:

```
<Canvas x:Name="LayoutRoot" Background="White">
    <TextBlock Text="Look ma! I'm at the default position!"/>
</Canvas>
```

Build and run your application, and you should see that the text is positioned at the top-left corner.

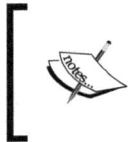

> Unless specified, the Canvas element will position the added child controls to the top-left corner, as this is the beginning of the positioning scheme. We will shortly discuss how to move an element further to the right, left, top, or bottom.

Controlling the position of an element inside the canvas is done by using the following three attached properties:

- Left: This is a value, in pixels, that specifies how far an element should be positioned from the left border of the canvas. A positive value moves the element away from the left border (in other words, it moves an element to the right), a negative value moves the element closer to the left border.

- Top: This is a value, in pixels, that specifies how far an element should be positioned from the top border of the canvas. A positive value moves the element away from the top border (down) while a negative value moves the element closer to the top border (up).

- ZIndex: This controls the stacking order of elements. The bigger an element's ZIndex value is, the closer that element is to the foreground. In simple words, if two elements are positioned in the same place, the element whose ZIndex property is higher will be on top of the other element.

It's important to know that even though ZIndex is an attached property of Canvas, it works with other panels such as Grid as well. Keep in mind that ZIndex is only relative to the panel that it is set upon and not the entire application.

To demonstrate the use of the Canvas properties, replace the content of your canvas with the following code snippet:

```
<Rectangle Height="60" Width="60" Fill="Blue"/>
<Rectangle Height="60" Width="60" Fill="Red" Canvas.Left="10" Canvas.
Top="20"/>
```

Build and run your application, and you should get the result, as shown in the following screenshot:

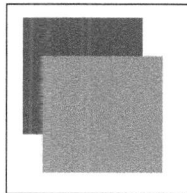

As expected, the red rectangle is 10 pixels to the right-hand side of the left border and 20 pixels down from the top border of the blue rectangle. The red rectangle is on top of the blue one, because it was declared after the blue rectangle. To draw the blue rectangle on top of the red one, change the blue rectangle declaration as follows:

```
<Rectangle Height="60" Width="60" Fill="Blue" Canvas.ZIndex="2"/>
```

Build and run your application, and you should see the blue rectangle is now on top of the red one. Because, the blue rectangle's ZIndex property has a higher value than the red one (which uses the default 0), it is drawn on top of it.

Setting the Canvas properties from code behind

While this topic is out of the scope of this book, it is entirely possible to set an element's Top, Left, or ZIndex properties using code as well. When you wish to set one of the Canvas properties on an element from code behind, you should use the Canvas static class and then either the SetLeft, SetTop or SetZIndex methods. The following code will move an element 20 pixels to the right using code:

```
Canvas.SetLeft(blueRectangle, 20);
```

The syntax is quite simple. The first argument we pass is the name of the UI element we wish to set the property to, for example `blueRectangle`. The second argument we pass is the value (or amount) we wish to set. In our example, we use the `SetLeft` method of the `Canvas` static class to set the `blueRectangle` element `20` pixels to the right. Wish to set it 20 pixels to the left? No problem! Just set the value of the second argument to -20. Because, the value property is of the double type, we are not limited to whole numbers only.

Border

The `Border` control is one of the simplest layout controls, and its job is to add a border to its child element. The `Border` control can hold exactly one child element at a time and while this seems limiting, just remember that this one child element can also be another layout panel, such as `Grid` or `StackPanel`. Using the `Border` control usually involves the `BorderBrush` and `BorderThickness` properties. `BorderBrush` dictates the color of the border, which can be one of the color enumerators (`Red`, `Green`, and so on) or the hex value of a color (ARGB—`Alpha`, `Red`, `Green`, and `Blue`). You could also use `LinearGradientBrush` for your `BorderBrush` value, but that means that you will have to use `BorderBrush` as an `Element` property. To see an example of this approach, have a look at Silverlight Show's border article located at `http://www.silverlightshow.net/items/Using-the-Border-control-in-Silverlight-2-Beta-1-.aspx`. The `BorderThickness` property dictates how wide the border will be. If you set one value for this property (for example, 4), then all four sides of the border will have the width of 4 pixels, but if you wish to have a different width for each side of the `Border` control, you need to supply four values for this property, separated with a space. To demonstrate this, replace the `Canvas` element in your Silverlight application with the following code snippet:

```
<Border BorderBrush="Black" BorderThickness="4 10 4 10" >
    <Image Source="http://www.packtpub.com/sites/default/files/banners
    /Learning%20jQuery%201.3.jpg" Stretch="UniformToFill"/>
</Border>
```

Build and run your application, and you should see the result, as shown in the following screenshot:

The left and right borders of the image are 4 pixels wide while the top and bottom are 10 pixels wide.

ScrollViewer

The `ScrollViewer` control has one purpose in life; to scroll content. Imagine you have built a gorgeous dashboard application for your office. On your 23-inch wide screen, the dashboard is shown well, but the boss's secretary's monitor is smaller and uses a lower resolution and, thus, your gorgeous dashboard is cut off and looks weird. To make sure your application will fit all screen sizes, you can use the `ScrollViewer` control. With the `ScrollViewer` control in hand, you have the full control on both the horizontal and vertical scroll bars. Controlling the scroll bars is done via two properties — `HorizontalScrollBarVisibility` and `VerticalScrollBarVisibility`. Possible values for these properties are — `Auto`, `Disabled`, `Hidden`, and `Visible`. To demonstrate the `ScrollViewer` control, replace the code for `Border` with the following code snippet:

```
<ScrollViewer HorizontalScrollBarVisibility="Auto"
VerticalScrollBarVisibility="Auto">
    <Image Source="http://www.packtpub.com/sites/default/files/banners
    /Learning%20jQuery%201.3.jpg" Stretch="UniformToFill" Width="1000"
    Height="1000"/>
</ScrollViewer>
```

Build and run your application. If your browser's window dimensions are smaller than 1000 pixels, you should get the result, as shown in the following screenshot:

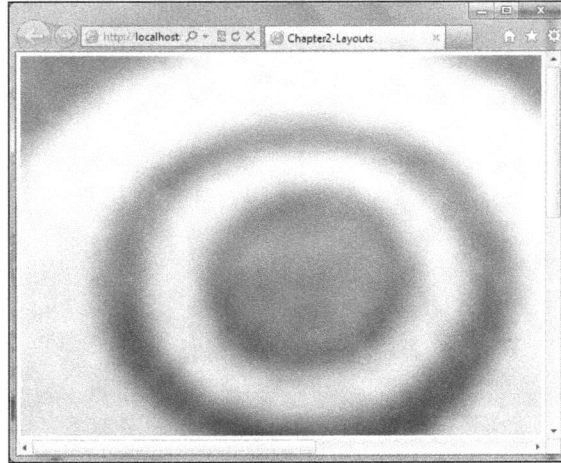

If you play around with the browser's dimensions, you will see that the scroll viewer automatically adjusts its scroll bars as well.

The larger the window size is, the shorter the scroll bars are, and vice versa of course.

Let's assume we wish to hide the vertical scroll bar, no matter what the size of the window is. All we have to do is change the value for the VerticalScrollBarVisibility property from Auto to Hidden.

ViewBox

If you're coming from a WPF background, the ViewBox control should look familiar to you, as it's been part of WPF since the beginning. If not, don't worry; you'll know all about ViewBox in a second. The main purpose of the ViewBox control is to scale its child control's content to the full available space that the ViewBox control itself is occupying. That means that if the ViewBox control is occupying the width of 300 pixels and height of 300 pixels, any control we will place inside of it will also scale to occupy the same dimensions. If at any point, we resize the ViewBox control, the content inside of it will resize as well. To demonstrate the control, replace the code for ScrollViewer with the following code snippet:

```
<Viewbox>
    <TextBlock Text="Look ma! I can stretch!"/>
</Viewbox>
```

Build and run your application. As you play around with the browser's window size, you will notice that the text inside the `TextBlock` control is always positioned at the center of the window, and that the text shrinks and grows as you change the size of the window, as shown in the following two screenshots:

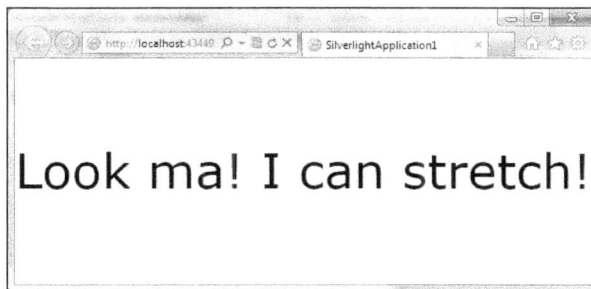

Controlling the visibility

Every UI element in Silverlight, be it `TextBox`, an image, or even a layout control have the ability to be visible or hidden. We control the visibility of an element using the `Visibility` property. `Visibility` has two possible values—`Visible` (default) or `Collapsed`. It is important to remember that if an element's visibility property is set to `Collapsed`, that element will not render on the page and, thus, won't take up any space. To read more about visibility, please visit the *UIElement.Visibility Property* page on MSDN at `http://msdn.microsoft.com/en-us/library/system.windows.uielement.visibility%28v=vs.95%29.aspx`.

Using core and content controls

Silverlight's control library is constantly growing. Some controls are living in the assemblies and included in the Silverlight plugin install by default. These controls are usually referred to as the **core controls**. These core controls include all-time favorites such as TextBox, Button, CheckBox, and so on. But the power of Silverlight doesn't come from its core components alone; you can always reference other assemblies that have other controls living in them and add them to your project. When you add such "outside" control to your page, you need to reference its namespace in your page.

Using core controls

Among Silverlight's core controls, there are controls we already know (and love) from other frameworks. Let's discuss the usage and properties of those controls. What is the first control that comes to your mind when you're thinking about text input? Most developers will answer—the TextBox control.

TextBox

The well-known TextBox control has one purpose; to get text input from the user. Silverlight's TextBox control can render itself in two modes—single line of text and multiline text area. The TextBox control is very flexible, and its properties range from simple properties such as dimensions (height and width), font colors, and font size to more complex properties such as background or text wrapping. The following table lists the most frequently used properties of TextBox:

Name	Description	Possible Values
Text	The text that will be displayed inside the textbox. It can be used in code behind to both get and set the text.	Any text input.
Height	This dictates the height of the textbox.	A number.
Width	This dictates the width of the textbox.	A number.
VerticalAlignment	This dictates the vertical alignment of the text.	Bottom, Center, Stretch, Top.
HorizontalAlignment	This dictates the horizontal alignment of the text.	Bottom, Center, Stretch, Top.

Name	Description	Possible Values
Background	This sets the background color of the textbox. It can be used as an element property as well, which gives the property some extra flexibility with brushes such as `ImageBrush` or `LinearGradientBrush` (brushes will be discussed later in this book).	Color name or hexa-decimal value of a color (ARGB), for example, #FF0000FF.
FontFamily	This sets the font family that will be used to render the text.	A selection of fonts.
FontSize	This sets the size of the font.	A number.
Foreground	This sets the color of the text.	Color name or ARGB value.
FontWeight	This sets the weight of the font.	A list of selection ranging from `Thin` to `ExtraBold`.

The basic syntax for a `TextBox` control is as follows:

```
<TextBox Text="Look ma! I'm a TextBox! "/>
```

Using the basic syntax, your `TextBox` will render using the default black color and in the default font size and font family (Portable User Interface).

TextBlock

The `TextBlock` control is like the `TextBox` control's little brother. While `TextBox` is used to get user input, `TextBlock` is used to display text to the user. `TextBlock` controls share the same properties as the `TextBox` control, with the addition of two special properties, as shown on the following table:

Name	Description	Possible Values
TextTrimming	This is used to trim a string up to a certain width. If set to `WordEllipsis`, the text will be trimmed at a word boundary and an ellipsis (...) will replace the remaining text.	None (default) or `WordEllipsis`
Run	The `Run` element lets you mix different formatting of text within the same `TextBlock` control. Run will be demonstrated in the next paragraph.	Negative

An example for using the `TextBlock` control is as follows:

```
<TextBlock Text="Look ma! I can be trimmed!" Foreground="Red"
TextTrimming="WordEllipsis"/>
```

The preceding `TextBlock` will render the text in red and trim it if the text is too long to fit in its allocated space.

An example of using the `Run` element within a `TextBlock` control is as follows:

```
<TextBlock FontSize="25">
    <Run FontFamily="Comic Sans MS" Foreground="Red" Text=
    "Hey there! I'm Red!"/>
    <Run FontFamily="Arial" Foreground="Blue" Text=" And I'm Blue!"/>
</TextBlock>
```

The preceding code snippet will render as follows:

Hey there! I'm Red! And I'm Blue!

Two completely different styles share the same `TextBlock` element.

Buttons

The `Button` control represents a button (big surprise here right?). In Silverlight, you have more than one `Button` control. Other than regular `Button` controls, you can use `HyperlinkButton`, `ToggleButton`, `CheckBox` (that's a button, too!), and `RadioButton`.

We will start by introducing the `Button` control and then move on to the other types of buttons.

Button

Just like most of the controls in Silverlight, you can set all the 'usual' properties on a button: you can specify its width, its height, its vertical and horizontal alignment, and font settings (weight, color, family, and so on). What makes the button a button is the fact that it has three basic states — normal, hover, and pressed. We will discuss the states later in this book but as a short introduction, states represent a control's look at a specific point in time, and can be used to animate the control's look. In the button's case, when you hover over a button, you will see that the button changes its color to blue. That's the hover state in action. The Button control has two important properties — Click and ClickMode. The Click property's value represents the name of the code behind method that will fire when a user clicks on the button. Let's demonstrate this. In your Silverlight application, add a button using the following line of code:

```
<Button Content="Click me!" Height="30" Width="130" />
```

> The content of a button doesn't have to be just text. As a button inherits the ContentControl class, it can hold other controls as its content as well. We will discuss this in detail later.

If you build and run your application now, and click on the button, you'll notice that nothing happens. This is because we haven't set the Click property. Right after the value of width, start typing Click= and once you see <New Event Handler>, click the Enter button. Your button code should look like the following code snippet:

```
<Button Content="Click me!" Height="30" Width="130" Click="Button_
Click" />
```

Switch over to your code behind file (MainPage.xaml.cs), and you'll notice there is a method called Button_Click there. Visual Studio created it when you set the Click property value. Add the following line of code to the Button_Click event handler:

```
MessageBox.Show("I GOT CLICKED!");
```

Build and test your application. You'll get a nice message box each time you click the button.

The ClickMode property sets when the Click event should occur. This property has the following three possible values:

- Hover: The Click event will occur every time you hover over the button.
- Press: The Click event will occur as soon as you click on the button.
- Release: This is the default value. The Click event will occur as soon as you release the mouse button.

Try to set your button's ClickMode property to all three values and watch how your button changes its behavior.

HyperlinkButton

The `HyperlinkButton` control is really a button that acts as a hyperlink. The `HyperlinkButton` control's most important property is `NavigateUri`. `NavigateUri` gets or sets the URL that the button should navigate to once clicked. No hyperlink will be complete without a property to specify its target. The `HyperlinkButton` control has that property and it is named `TargetName`. You can set the value for `TargetName` the same as you would for a regular HTML `<a>` tag target property such as _blank, _parent, and so on. For a list of all possible values, check out the MSDN documentation for *HyperlinkButton.TargetName Property* at `http://msdn.microsoft.com/en-us/library/system.windows.controls.hyperlinkbutton.targetname%28VS.95%29.aspx`.

The following line of code demonstrates the use of a `HyperlinkButton` control:

```
<HyperlinkButton NavigateUri="http://www.packtpub.com" Content="My
Publisher"/>
```

ToggleButton

`ToggleButton` is the base class for the `CheckBox` and `RadioButton` controls, but it can also be used as a standalone control as well. `ToggleButton`, as the name suggests, is used in the scenarios where states need to be toggled around. `ToggleButton`, being a button itself, has all the properties and events of a regular button, in addition to two very conceptual events—`Checked` and `Unchecked`. `Checked` occurs when the state of the `ToggleButton` has changed to checked, while `Unchecked` occurs when the state has changed to unchecked. Another property that is special to the `ToggleButton` control is `IsThreeState`. This Boolean property, when set to `True`, adds a state to `ToggleButton` named `Indeterminate`. Let's examine how to use the `ToggleButton` control with three states:

```
<StackPanel>
    <ToggleButton IsThreeState="True"
    Indeterminate="ToggleButton_Indeterminate"
    Unchecked="ToggleButton_Unchecked" Checked="ToggleButton_Checked"
    Content="Click me!"/>
    <TextBlock x:Name="tbState"/>
</StackPanel>
```

The preceding code snippet adds `ToggleButton`, which has three states. Each state is represented by an event handler. A `TextBlock` is added to display the `ToggleButton` control's current state.

Switch over to the `MainPage.xaml.cs` file, and add the following code snippet below the constructor:

```
private void ToggleButton_Indeterminate(object sender, RoutedEventArgs
e)
{
    tbState.Text = "Indeterminate";
}
private void ToggleButton_Unchecked(object sender, RoutedEventArgs e)
{
    tbState.Text = "Unchecked";
}
private void ToggleButton_Checked(object sender, RoutedEventArgs e)
{
    tbState.Text = "Checked";
}
```

Each event handler will change the text property of `tbState` to the state's name.

Build and run the application, and you'll notice that every click on the button changes the text according to the state the button is currently in.

> **Checking the ToggleButton state programmatically**
>
> You can always check what state `ToggleButton` is in, from code behind using the `IsChecked` property. If the `ToggleButton` control is checked, the property will return `true`, if unchecked `false`, and if indeterminate the `ToggleButton` control will return null.

CheckBox

The Silverlight `CheckBox` control is similar to any other checkbox control you know from other platforms. As the `CheckBox` control's base class is `ToggleButton`, it uses the same events and properties as its parent class. To mark a `CheckBox` control as checked, we set the `IsChecked` property to `true` and to react to checked and unchecked events, we set the `Checked` and `Unchecked` events handlers. A commonly used `CheckBox` control's line of code will look as follows:

```
<CheckBox Content="Check me!" Checked="CheckBox_Checked"
Unchecked="CheckBox_Unchecked' />
```

In your code behind file, you will have two event handlers as follows:

```
private void CheckBox_Checked(object sender, RoutedEventArgs e)
{
    MessageBox.Show("I'm checked!");
}
private void CheckBox_Unchecked(object sender, RoutedEventArgs e)
{
    MessageBox.Show("I'm not checked!");
}
```

Build and run the application. The result of the preceding code snippet will render a checkbox with the content Check me!, which will pop up a message box with some text once checked or unchecked.

RadioButton

Just like the CheckBox control, the RadioButton control also derives from ToggleButton. The main difference between the RadioButton control and the CheckBox control is that only one radio button can be selected within a given group. To specify a group, the RadioButton control uses the GroupName property. Using the RadioButton control is relatively simple. Its use can be outlined by the following code snippet:

```
<StackPanel Orientation="Horizontal">
    <RadioButton GroupName="Group1" Content="Choose me!"/>
    <RadioButton GroupName="Group1" Content="No! Me!"/>
    <RadioButton GroupName="Group2" Content="I don't belong here..."/>
</StackPanel>
```

The preceding code snippet adds three radio buttons, two from the same group and one from a different group. Build and run the application, and you'll notice that you can only select one radio button from the first pair, but the last radio button can be selected regardless of the others.

Using content controls

Take a journey down memory lane and try to remember the last time you've used the HTML button control. That button control knew how to work with just one specific type of content, text. To make a button use different content, such as an image, you have to use **Cascading Style Sheets** (**CSS**) and position a background image. But, what if you wanted that button to be a movie clip for example? You simply couldn't. Silverlight (and WPF) introduced a much more flexible model to work with controls' content. A Silverlight control can indicate whether or not it supports the inclusion of any type of control (text, image, or even a layout control) or just the inclusion of a predefined known item type.

Every content control is based upon the ContentControl class, which in turn is based on the Control class. As the base class of ContentControl is Control, any content control element features all of the properties, events, and methods that any normal control has.

The content of a content control can be any arbitrary object. If Silverlight cannot natively add the content to the visual tree, the ToString method of the object will be called and its result will be displayed. This is the reason why a content control can have either simple text or a complex element as its content. To demonstrate how to set the content for a content control, let's add two buttons to our project:

```
<StackPanel>
    <Button Width="200" Height="100" Content="I'm a text based
button!"/>
    <Button Width="200" Height="100">
    <Button.Content>
        <StackPanel>
            <TextBlock Text="I'm a video playing button!"/>
            <MediaElement Source="/demo.wmv" Height="70" Width="100"
            Stretch="Uniform"/>
        </StackPanel>
    </Button.Content>
    </Button>
</StackPanel>
```

The preceding code snippet renders two buttons—one with simple text content, and the other with a movie and text as its content. The resulting UI will look like the following screenshot:

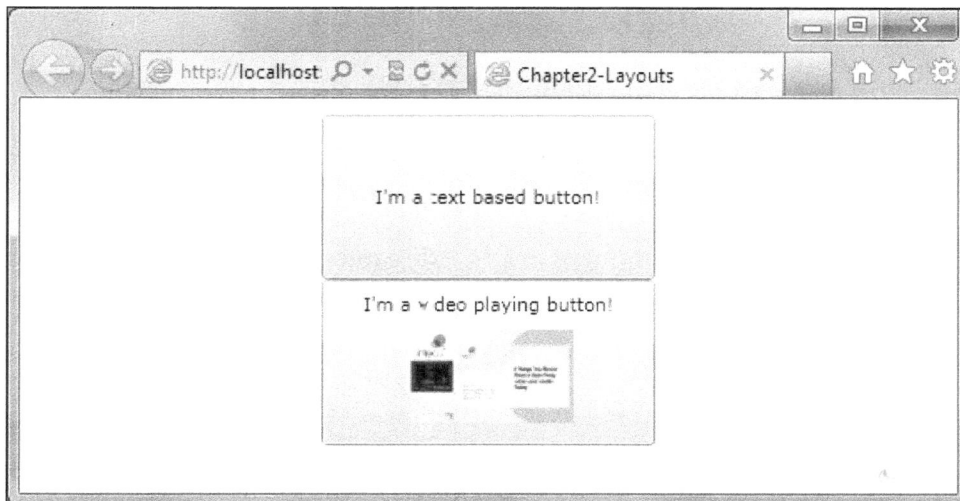

As we can see from the preceding example, the content of a button, which is a content control, can be anything from a simple line of text to just about any UI control Silverlight has!

The magic that makes all of this happen is the ContentPresenter element. The ContentPresenter element holds the logic that the control needs in order to render any object passed on to it. ContentPresenter uses TemplateBinding to bind an element in XAML to a dependency property in the control's implementation. We will discuss TemplateBinding and ContentPresenter in much more detail later in this book.

Creating user controls

Silverlight, being a rich UI framework, provides us with many controls ready to be used out of the box. But, no matter how rich the toolbox may be, there will come a time when you wish to create your own controls. Creating your own controls in Silverlight can be done by creating either a user control or a custom control. As creating the user controls is easier than creating the custom controls, we will introduce this method first.

A **user control**, in its core, is nothing more than a combination of existing controls that can be reused throughout your application. Once we learn about dependency properties later on in the book, we'll see how user controls can be extended with data binding and templating.

Creating your first user control

To walk you through creating your first user control, we will create a simple control that combines a TextBlock control and a Button control. Each time the button is clicked, the TextBlock control's text will indicate the number of clicks of the button. We will add three of these controls to the main page of the application, each in a grid row of its own. The first step you need to take is to create a new Silverlight application within Visual Studio 2010 and name it **Chapter2-MyFirstUserControl**. If you don't remember how to create a new project, refer to the earlier section — *Creating your first Silverlight application* — in this chapter.

As soon as Visual Studio finishes creating your application, you are faced with the MainPage.xaml file. As the default container is a grid, all we have to do now is split it into three rows. As we have already discussed how to work with the Grid element, the following code snippet should look familiar to you. Add the following code snippet inside your Grid element:

```
<Grid.RowDefinitions>
    <RowDefinition Height="100"/>
    <RowDefinition Height="100"/>
    <RowDefinition Height="100"/>
</Grid.RowDefinitions>
```

Now we will move on to creating the user control itself. Right-click on the **Chapter2-MyFirstUserControl** project and select **Add** and **New Item**. Locate the Silverlight user control template and name it **ClickCounter.xaml**.

We are now looking at our brand new user control! True, it is a bit empty at the moment, but we will fill it up shortly. We mentioned earlier that our user control should contain `Button` and `TextBlock`. We also want our user control to have a fixed height and width so that every instance of it will look the same, no matter where it was added. To give the user control a fixed height and width, locate the following line of code:

```
d:DesignHeight="300" d:DesignWidth="400"
```

Replace the preceding line of code with the following line of code:

```
Height="60" Width="200"
```

> Whenever you see `d:Design`, it means that the property (in this case being height and width) is only used for design preview purposes. When defining your application size, keep in mind that if you want your application to use fixed sizing, remove the d prefix. If you keep it and not define a fixed width and height for your root layout control, then your application will take up all the available space when rendered.

Next, we need to add the button and textblock. Our user control is quite simple in UI terms and all it needs is a textblock with a button next to it. The perfect layout control for such a scenario is `StackPanel` with a horizontal orientation. Replace the `LayoutRoot` Grid element with the following code snippet:

```
<StackPanel Orientation="Horizontal" x:Name="LayoutRoot"
Background="White">
    <TextBlock VerticalAlignment="Center" Text="I was clicked 0
times!"
    x:Name="countTb"/>
    <Button Height="40" Content="Click me!" Margin="10,0,0,0"
    x:Name="countButton" Click="countButton_Click"/>
</StackPanel>
```

The resulting UI should look as follows:

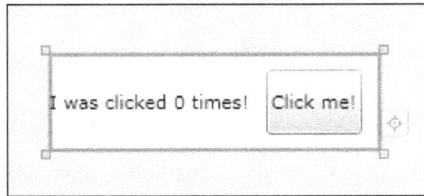

The only thing left to do in the user control is hook up the `Click` event handler so that it will increase the number in the `TextBlock` control. As we have already defined the name of the event handler in XAML (`countButton_Click`), all that's left to do is to add its logic in the code behind file. Open `ClickCounter.xaml.cs` and add the following `private` global variable above the constructor method:

```
private int _counter = 0;
```

We will use this variable to count the number of times a button was clicked. Now it's time to add the event handler's logic. Add the following method right after the constructor method:

```
private void countButton_Click(object sender, RoutedEventArgs e)
{
    _counter++;
    countTb.Text = string.Format("I was clicked {0} times!", _
counter);
}
```

Quite simple, isn't it? Every time a button is clicked, the counter variable goes up by one and the text property of the `TextBlock` control is being set.

We are now finished with our user control. To see it in action, we need to add it to the page, but before we can do anything with it we have to build the application first. Right-click on the **Chapter2-MyFirstUserControl** project and select **Build**. Switch over to the `MainPage.xaml` file. As our user control resides in a namespace that isn't referenced in the file, we have to add a reference to it. We've discussed namespaces in the previous chapter so if you don't feel comfortable with the subject, please refer back to the *Namespaces* section from *Chapter 1, Overview of Silverlight*. Add the following declaration code inside the `UserControl` node:

```
xmlns:local="clr-namespace:Chapter2_MyFirstUserControl"
```

Your `UserControl` node should now look as follows:

```
<UserControl x:Class="Chapter2_MyFirstUserControl.MainPage"
    xmlns="http://schemas.microsoft.com/winfx/2006/xaml/presentation"
    xmlns:x="http://schemas.microsoft.com/winfx/2006/xaml"
    xmlns:d="http://schemas.microsoft.com/expression/blend/2008"
    xmlns:mc="http://schemas.openxmlformats.org/markup-
    compatibility/2006"
    xmlns:local="clr-namespace:Chapter2_MyFirstUserControl"
    mc:Ignorable="d"
    d:DesignHeight="300" d:DesignWidth="400">
```

We have added a new namespace called `local`, which points to the namespace of our application. If we create another user control in our application now, we won't need to add another reference as the namespace is already referenced in our file.

Scroll down to the closing element of the `RowDefinitions` property and add the following line of code below it:

```
<local:
```

IntelliSense has picked up the namespace, and we can select our new user control!

Now we will add three instances of our newly created user control to the page, each will reside in its own row in the grid:

```
<local:ClickCounter Grid.Row="0"/>
<local:ClickCounter Grid.Row="1"/>
<local:ClickCounter Grid.Row="2"/>
```

That's it! Build and run your application. The finished application will look like the following screenshot:

As you can see, each user control is independent and clicking on one changes only the text next to it.

To get a deeper understanding of the user control, it is encouraged that you read the MSDN documentation—*UserControl Class*—at `http://msdn.microsoft.com/en-us/library/system.windows.controls.usercontrol%28v=vs.95%29.aspx`.

The navigation framework

The navigation framework was first introduced in Silverlight 3. This framework is based on the concept of having a frame that displays pages and takes care of the whole navigating process from one page to another. The navigation framework supports many of the modern concepts of navigation, such as back and forward navigation, journal histories, and deep linking. The easiest way to create an application that uses the navigation framework is to select the **Silverlight Navigation Application** template while creating a new Silverlight project. Go ahead and create a new Silverlight project with the **Silverlight Navigation Application** template and name it **Chapter2-Navigation**.

As you look at the solution explorer, you may notice that the structure of this application is different from the one we are used to. It has a **Views** directory, which holds several XAML files, and the `MainPage.xaml` file already has some code inside of it. In a navigation application, the `MainPage.xaml` file, which we are used to working with as the main page of our application is nothing more than a `Frame` control and a `Grid` control to host the upper banner. You can think of this upper banner area as an ASP.NET master page—no matter what page you navigate to on your site, the upper part stays the same, so your application has a consistent feeling and style among all its pages. Before we explore the new `MainPage.xaml` page, go ahead and build the application. Once you have finished, run the application, and you should get the result, as shown in the following screenshot:

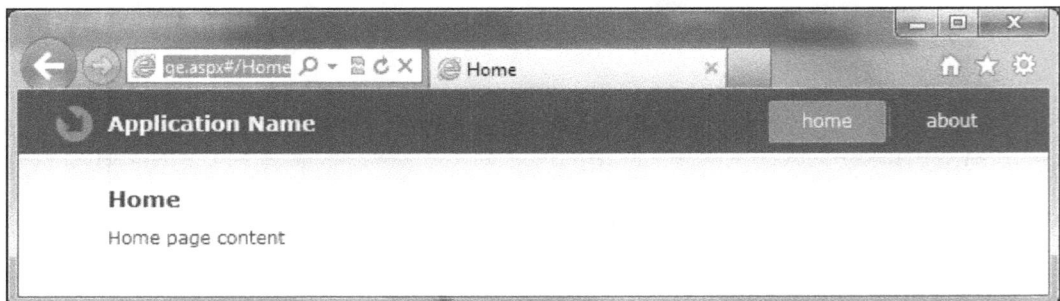

A few things to notice about this application are as follows:

- The end of the URL address corresponds to the currently selected page
- The navigation buttons on the right-hand side are also synchronized with the URL and page

Click on the **about** button on the right-hand side of the navigation menu. You should see how the ending of the URL now points to the **about** page and the title in the browser tab changes to **about**. If we click on the browser's back button at this point, we will go back to the previous page we watched (**home**) just like any regular website. As you can see from this simple example, Silverlight's interaction with the browser navigation is quite tight!

Adding new pages

Currently our application has only two pages—**about** and **home**. For the vast majority of cases, you will want to add additional pages to the application containing additional logic and information. Adding a page to the application requires two steps:

1. Add a new page (view) to the views folder.
2. Add a link to that page in the navigation menu.

While the first step is as easy as adding a new item, the second step involves some work on the MainPage.xaml file.

To add a new page to your application, right-click on the **Views** directory, click on **Add**, and then click on **New Item**.

In the **New Item** dialog box, select the **Silverlight Page** template and name it **NewPage.xaml**. The page template derives from the navigation:Page class, and in its core is UserControl with some added support for the navigation framework.

At this moment, our new page is nothing more than a blank grid, but we will get back to it later. Right now, our users have no way to reach the new page, and in order to solve that issue, we will use a control we discussed before, the HyperlinkButton control.

Open up MainPage.xaml and look for the LinksBorder border control. As you can see, we have two HyperlinkButton controls, and a rectangle, which acts as the divider between the two buttons. To add a new button here, all we have to do is add another HyperlinkButton and Divider. Add the following code snippet just below the Divider1 rectangle:

```
<HyperlinkButton x:Name="NewPageLink" Style="{StaticResource
LinkStyle}" NavigateUri="/NewPage" TargetName="ContentFrame"
Content="new page"/>
<Rectangle x:Name="Divider2" Style="{StaticResource DividerStyle}"/>
```

There are a few interesting things to notice about our newly added
HyperlinkButton as follows:

- The NavigateUri property points to /NewPage when the actual page is
  stored at /Views/NewPage.xaml. This is handled by UriMapper, which
  we will discuss in a bit.

- The TargetName property points to ContentFrame. We've mentioned this
  property when we discussed the HyperlinkButton control earlier in the
  chapter, and here you can see that other than the usual _self or _blank
  values, it can also accept a Frame control name. If you scroll up a bit in the
  MainPage.xaml file, you'll see a Frame element named ContentFrame that
  is used to host the pages.

- The Style property, although not limited to the navigation framework, is
  used to style the different components of the page. We will discuss styling
  in Silverlight later on in this book.

Build and run your application, and you should see our new HyperlinkButton
control in the navigation bar. Clicking on the new HyperlinkButton control will
switch the active viewing page to our newly created NewPage.xaml.

Navigation events

The navigation:Page class includes four navigation-related events, as shown in the
following table:

Event name	Description
OnFragmentNavigation	This event triggers when a fragment inside the application is navigated to. An example for such a case would be /Views/Customers.xaml#CustID1023. This can be considered as Silverlight's equivalent to HTML's hashtag navigation.
OnNavigatedFrom	This event triggers when a page is no longer the active page in the frame. This event is usually used when you wish to perform a final cleanup for a page.

Event name	Description
OnNavigatingFrom	This event triggers just before a page is swapping with another page. If the criteria you specify isn't met, you can use this event to cancel navigation to a page or remind the user to save the content before continuing.
OnNavigatedTo	This event triggers when a page becomes the active page in a frame. This event is usually used instead of the Loaded event in regular non-navigational pages.

If you take a look at MainPage.xaml.cs, you'll see that you already have the event handler for OnNavigatedTo ready to be used in your page. This is the most commonly used event for page navigation as you get to work with caching retrieval, as well as perform any page initialization setup.

NavigationService

The NavigationService class is used when you wish to work with the navigation system of the hosting frame from code behind. The NavigationService class provides five useful methods for controlling navigation, as shown in the following table:

Method name	Description
GoBack	This method navigates to the previous entry in the currently active history journal. If no entry is available, an exception will be thrown.
GoForward	This method navigates to the next entry in the currently active history journal. If no entry is available, an exception will be thrown.
Navigate	This method is used to navigate to any given URI.
Refresh	This method reloads the current page.
StopLoading	This method is used to cancel any asynchronous navigation action that hasn't been processed yet.

The GoBack and GoForward methods are typically used in the full-screen applications where you might want to build your own UI for controlling navigation. The Refresh and StopLoading methods are similar to the browser's refresh and stop/cancel buttons. Navigate is used to navigate to a different page in your application. Navigating using the Navigate method will fire the navigation events at their appropriate time.

As an example of going backward using the `NavigationService` class, add a button to `NewPage.xaml` using the following line of code:

```
<Button Content="Back!" x:Name="backButton" Click="backButton_Click"
Width="100" Height="20"/>
```

Switch over to the `NewPage.xaml.cs` file, and add the following event handler:

```
private void backButton_Click(object sender, RoutedEventArgs e)
{
    if (NavigationService.CanGoBack)
    {
        NavigationService.GoBack();
    }
}
```

In order to prevent an exception, we first check if it's possible to go back (`CanGoBack`) and if so, perform the action.

Build and run your application, click on the **New Page** button on the top-right navigation bar and then click on the new back button. You'll get right back to the page you were coming from.

Other than these methods, the `NavigationService` class also exposes some useful events. Three of these events are equivalent to the page navigation events we've mentioned earlier. `FragmentNavigation` is equivalent to `Page.FragmentNavigation`, `Navigated` is equivalent to `Page.OnNavigatedFrom`, and `Navigating` is equivalent to `Page.OnNavigatingFrom`.

It is more common to use the events directly exposed from the `Frame` class than the `Page` one, but it is perfectly fine to use the ones in `Page` if it fits your purpose better.

Other than the three equivalent methods, an additional two methods are exposed, as shown in the following table:

Event name	Description
NavigationFailed	This event is raised when the frame fails to navigate to the requested page. It provides exception information.
NavigationStopped	This event is raised when the navigation is stopped.

The UriMapper class

The `UriMapper` property of the `Frame` class is responsible for translating real URLs of views such as `/Views/NewPage.xaml` to a more user-friendly URL such as `/NewPage.xaml`.

The `UriMapper` class exposes the `UriMapping` objects, which represent a single pair of URIs to be mapped. Each of these `UriMapping` objects must contain the `Uri` property, as well as the `MappedUri` property.

Let's look at the default `UriMapper` that our page currently has:

```
<navigation:Frame.UriMapper>
    <uriMapper:UriMapper>
        <uriMapper:UriMapping Uri="" MappedUri="/Views/Home.xaml"/>
        <uriMapper:UriMapping Uri="/{pageName}"
        MappedUri="/Views/{pageName}.xaml"/>
    </uriMapper:UriMapper>
</navigation:Frame.UriMapper>
```

The `Uri` property is what the `UriMapper` class will activate upon and the `MappedUri` property sets the full path to the value of the `Uri` property. In our example, the first `UriMapper` maps any blank page entry to the home page. Assuming our application resides at `http://MyNavApp.com/Application.aspx`, if the user visits that address, the first `UriMapping` will come into play and redirect the user to the home page. On the other hand, if a user visits `http://MyNavApp.com/Application.aspx#/MyNewPage`, the second `UriMapping` will come into play and redirect the application to the `Views` directory and the `MyNewPage.xaml` file. Mappings are read top to bottom, and completed when a match is hit. Also, note that `UriMapping` will only work when the hashtag fragment is presented in the URL address.

A common use of the `UriMapper` classes is to pass data from one page to another. In HTML's world, the common pattern of passing parameters is the use of query strings. A **query string** is basically a name/value set that comes after a question mark sign in a URL address. While we can use the same approach in Silverlight, we have got used to showing a friendlier URL to the user. Instead of showing `http://MyNavApp.com/Application.aspx#/MyNewPage?UserID=50123`, we can map this address to `http://MyNavApp.com/Application.aspx#/MyNewPage/50123`.

To do such a thing, we need to add the following `UriMapper` class to our application:

```
<uriMapper:UriMapping Uri="/MyNewPage/{UserID}" MappedUri="/Views/
MyNewPage.xaml?UserID={UserID}"/>
```

Retrieving the `UserID` parameter in the target page is done using the `NavigationContext` object. The `NavigationContext` object has a `QueryString` property, which can be used to retrieve the query string parameter from the URL. The most common place to retrieve the query string parameter is in the `OnNavigatedTo` event handler. This is the first event that gets fired once the page is navigated to, so if the query string parameter is used to initialize some content on the page (for example, showing the details of a user whose ID is 50123), this would be the perfect place to retrieve it.

The code for retrieving the `UserID` property is as follows:

```
protected override void OnNavigatedTo(NavigationEventArgs e)
{
    if (NavigationContext.QueryString.ContainsKey("UserID"))
    {
        string id = NavigationContext.QueryString["UserID"];
    }
}
```

The journal

In Silverlight, a journal is used to save the browsing history of the user, just like your browser does when you visit the pages with it. You can always go back and forth on the pages you visited during the current user session. The `Frame` class has a property called `JournalOwnership`, which lets you decide who should own the history journal. The default value of the `JournalOwnership` property is `Automatic`. This value will set the journal to the browsers if the frame is both the top-level frame and running in the browser. If the application is running out of browser or the frame is not the top-level one, the frame itself will be in charge of maintaining the history journal.

Unless you want to build a specific navigation logic that will be used with your frame, keeping the `JournalOwnership` property to its default value will be sufficient in most cases.

Implementing caching

Whenever you navigate to a page using the navigation framework, a new instance of the page will be created, even if you use the back button for example. If you want Silverlight to cache a certain page, you'll have to enable caching at the page level (the `navigation:Page` node at the top of the XAML file) using the `NavigationCacheMode` property. The default value of this property is `Disabled`, which means no caching will be happening. Other than `Disabled`, you can set the `NavigationCacheMode` to `Required` or `Enabled`. `Required` will always use the cached version of a page once it's been cached. `Enabled` will also cache the page, but when the `Frame` instance's cache limit (we will discuss more on that in a second) is reached, the cache will be discarded.

The `Frame` instance is responsible for caching the pages it loads. By default, the size of the cache limit is set to 10 pages, but it can be changed very easily using the `CacheSize` property. The cache is ordered in a queue—new pages are added on top of old pages and when the limit is reached, the oldest page in the queue will no longer be cached and it will be taken off the queue to make space for the cached version of the new page. Only the pages that are marked with the `Enabled` value for the `NavigationCacheMode` property are counted for the `CacheSize` limit. The pages marked with `Required` will always cache, no matter the limit size. When a cached page is dropped from the cache, it will reload from the server the next time the user hits it. In order to save logic or inputs from a page, you should override the `OnNavigatedFrom` event. This event fires as soon as the user navigates from one page to another page. Even if your page is cached, the navigation events will fire, so you should handle all kinds of initialization or saving processes inside those events without having to worry whether or not the page is cached.

Displaying a collection of items

Displaying a collection of items can be considered as one of the highlights of using Silverlight. Silverlight contains many controls whose purpose is to display a list of items ranging from simple listboxes to a datagrid, which can be used to display an Excel-like representation of data. One of the most important aspects of displaying a collection of items is templating. With templating, we can change the way our items will render. The items of a collection can be either bound to the control or added manually through XAML or code. We will discuss the concept of binding later in this book, so don't be discouraged if you don't understand what it means right now. It's time to start exploring the items controls of Silverlight, and so we start with the `ItemsControl` control.

ItemsControl

`ItemsControl` is the base class for the `ListBox`, `ComboBox`, and `TabControl` controls. Other than the usual properties, you might expect to find in a regular control that the `ItemsControl` class contains some items-specific properties as well, as shown in the following table:

Property	Description
Items	This is a collection of items that the control will render.
ItemsSource	This is the source of the items. Usually, it is used with binding in XAML.
ItemsPanel	This is the panel used to display the items. It can be templated to represent different kinds of panels (such as `Grid`, `StackPanel`, and so on.)
ItemTemplate	This is the data template, which is used to render an item.

The key concept you need to keep in mind when working with the `ItemsControl` control (or any control that is derived from it) is that you have to template your items. As we go further in this subject, we will discuss this concept even further.

Before we discuss this topic further, create a new Silverlight application in Visual Studio 2010 and name it **Chapter2-Collections**.

ListBox

One of the most commonly used controls to display a collection of items is the `ListBox` control. Using this control, you can show a collection of items at the same time on the screen, exposing the selected item and enable scrolling if not enough room is available for the control to show all the items at once. The `ListBox` control uses the `Items` property to load its collection of items at runtime. An example of this can be seen in the following code snippet:

```
<ListBox x:Name="MyFirstListBox">
    <ListBox.Items>
        <ListBoxItem Content="Item 1"/>
        <ListBoxItem Content="Item 2"/>
        <ListBoxItem Content="Item 3"/>
        <ListBoxItem Content="Item 4"/>
        <ListBoxItem Content="Item 5"/>
    </ListBox.Items>
</ListBox>
```

When we run the preceding code snippet, we will get the result as follows:

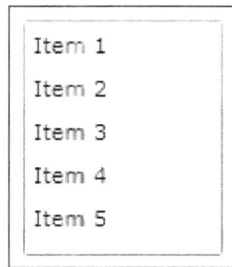

```
Item 1
Item 2
Item 3
Item 4
Item 5
```

As we can see from the preceding code snippet, each item of the ListBox control is represented as a ListBoxItem element. ListBoxItem is a ContentControl type of control and as such, doesn't have to be just text. We can use almost any control we like as the content of ListBoxItem. The ListBox control allows us to set a data template to style our items as well, but this is a more advanced topic, and we will discuss it in detail in the next chapter. In order to work with the items of ListBox, the control exposes a number of properties and events. The SelectedIndex and SelectedItem properties allow you to either get the index number, or the object of the currently selected item, or set an item as the currently selected item by specifying its index or object. When using the SelectedIndex property, it is important to remember that it is zero based and, as such, begins its count with 0. To know if the user has selected an item or changed his/her selection, we can use the SelectionChanged event. Every time a user changes his/her selection, the SelectionChanged event fires, letting you perform some business logic.

ComboBox

The ComboBox control should be familiar to you from just about any other language you use. The ComboBox control provides the user with the ability to select a single option from a list of predefined choices. These choices are visible to the user as long as ComboBox is open. In most cases, you will need to give the user the ability to open or close ComboBox, but if you want more control over this, you can use the IsDropDownOpen property from code behind to either get or set the ComboBox drop-down portion. An example of a simple ComboBox can be seen in the following code snippet:

```
<ComboBox x:Name="MyFirstComboBox" Width="100" Height="30">
    <ComboBox.Items>
        <ComboBoxItem Content="Item 1" IsSelected="True"/>
        <ComboBoxItem Content="Item 2"/>
        <ComboBoxItem Content="Item 3"/>
        <ComboBoxItem Content="Item 4"/>
```

```
              <ComboBoxItem Content="Item 5"/>
          </ComboBox.Items>
      </ComboBox>
```

The preceding code snippet will render `ComboBox` with predefined dimensions, set a list of the `ComboBoxItem` elements, and set the first item as the currently selected one. (Quick quiz: what would be the value of `MyFirstComboBox.SelectedIndex` right now?)

The preceding `ComboBox` would look as follows once rendered:

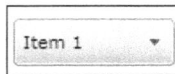

And it would look as follows when in an open state:

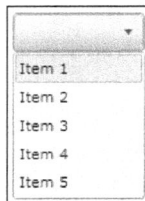

Just like the `ListBox` control, each of the `ComboBoxItem` controls is of the `ContentControl` type, and as such, their content can be set to just about almost any Silverlight control.

Just like the `ListBox` control, the `ComboBox` control exposes the `SelectedIndex` and `SelectedItem` properties, but it also exposes the `MaxDropDownHeight` property, which allows you to set the maximum possible height for the drop-down portion of `ComboBox` once opened. If the maximum height is not enough to fit all the items, a vertical scroll bar will appear. In addition, the `ComboBox` control exposes two events — `DropDownOpened` and `DropDownClosed`. These events fire when the user (or you, using the `IsDropDownOpen` property) opens and closes the drop down.

TreeView

The `TreeView` control allows you to display hierarchical data in a tree structure. In addition to that, the `TreeView` control has the ability to expand or collapse an item displayed in it. The `TreeView` control inherits from `ItemsControl`, which means that you can use the `Items` or `ItemsSource` properties to set its content. Using the `TreeView` control is quite straightforward. It can be seen from the following code snippet:

```
<sdk:TreeView x:Name="MyFirstTreeView">
    <sdk:TreeViewItem Header="Products">
    <sdk:TreeViewItem Header="Books"/>
    <sdk:TreeViewItem Header='Movies'/>
    <sdk:TreeViewItem Header='Books'/>
</sdk:TreeViewItem>
    <sdk:TreeViewItem Header='NoItems'/>
    <sdk:TreeViewItem Header='Rectangles' IsExpanded="True">
        <Rectangle Width="10" Height="10" Fill="Beige"/>
        <Rectangle Width="10" Height="10" Fill="Azure"/>
        <Rectangle Width="10" Height="10" Fill="Bisque"/>
</sdk:TreeViewItem>
</sdk:TreeView>
```

The preceding code will render as follows:

As can be seen from the preceding code, the TreeView control lies in the sdk namespace. The easiest way to add a TreeView control to your page is to simply drag it off from Visual Studio or Blend's toolbox. By doing that, Visual Studio or Blend will add the required references and namespaces to your project. The scheme for using the TreeView control is quite simple. You have a parent TreeView control, which hosts a bunch of the TreeViewItem elements. Each TreeViewItem element can also nest the TreeViewItem elements inside of it. As TreeViewItem is also of the ContentControl type, you can use just about anything you like as its content, just like the last TreeViewItem control in our example, which nests three rectangles. TreeViewItem has two important properties as follows:

- Header: This is the text to display as the header for the node

- IsExpanded: This is a Boolean property, which determines whether the node should be opened or closed when the application first runs

> The header can be more than just text!

The header of your `TreeViewItem` isn't limited to being just text. As the header is also of the `ContentControl` type, you can very easily display other controls as the header for your `TreeViewItem`. By changing the `NoItems` node to the following code snippet, we can also display an image next to the text:

```
<sdk:TreeViewItem>
<sdk:TreeViewItem.Header>
<StackPanel Orientation="Horizontal">
<Image Source="Images/xicon.png"/>
<TextBlock Text="No Items!"/>
</StackPanel>
</sdk:TreeViewItem.Header>
</sdk:TreeViewItem>
```

The `NoItems` node will now render as follows:

DataGrid

The `DataGrid` control is used to show information in a tabular form. One of the coolest features of the `DataGrid` control is its ability to allow users to add, edit, delete, select, and sort items that are bounded to it. The `DataGrid` control uses its `ItemSource` property to bind data for display. Another important aspect of the `DataGrid` control is its usage of a feature known as **UI virtualization**. UI virtualization ensures that while the `DataGrid` control handles all its items in memory, only the required UI elements needed to display the items are actually created. Imagine the performance gained from this feature when you have a collection of a million items. If `DataGrid` didn't use this feature, it would load all the million items to the memory and create all the required UI elements for all the million items, but with UI virtualization, even though `DataGrid` holds the million items in memory, only the data that the user can actually see is displayed on the screen. The `ListBox` control we discussed earlier also supports this feature. As we haven't discussed the concept of data binding yet, it may look odd to you. Don't worry if you don't get it right away; it will be greatly explained in *Chapter 5, Working with Data*. For now, just follow the code and try to understand the `DataGrid` control's properties and schemes.

Displaying data in DataGrid

The easiest way to get a DataGrid control to display data is to set its AutoGenerateColumns property to True. Doing that will tell DataGrid that you are not interested in templating the data you wish to display and you want everything to be done automatically. As a basic example, let's assume we have a list of objects named Food, which represents foods and contains two properties—the name of the food and a link to the image that represents it. Add a DataGrid to your page by dragging it out of the toolbox, and set its properties, as shown in the following line of code:

```
<sdk:DataGrid x:Name="MyFirstGrid" AutoGenerateColumns="True" />
```

Now switch to the code behind file (MainPage.xaml.cs), and add the following line of code inside the constructor method:

```
List<Food> foods = GetFoods();
MyFirstGrid.ItemsSource = foods;
```

> The GetFoods method returns a list of the Food objects to the local foods list. The code for this method can be found in the book code pack that you can download from the Packt website under the Chapter2-Collections project.

Run the application, and you should get the following result:

Name	Image
Cake	Images/cake.png
Bread	Images/bread.png
Cookie	Images/cookie.png
Hamburger	Images/hamburger.png
Pizza	Images/pizza.png

We've bound a list of objects to our DataGrid control, and because we told it to autogenerate the columns itself, we've got a nice textual representation of our object!

If you try to double-click on any of the DataGrid control's cells, you'll notice you can edit the text. Click on one of the headers and the DataGrid control will sort the data in ascending or descending order. You can react to these types of events using the CellEditEnded and CellEditEnding events. The first one fires after the edit has ended, and the second one fires just before the edit will end.

You can also implement your own logic for adding new items or deleting old ones.

DataGrid templating

Watching that sample, you will notice that DataGrid renders our object with text. This happens because the default column type that DataGrid uses when set to automatically generate the columns is DataGridTextColumn. This type of column is used to display text, and because of that, the column will call the bound object's ToString method in order to display it. The one exception to this rule is Boolean values. When the DataGrid control tries to render a Boolean property, it will use DataGridCheckBoxColumn. This type of column will render a CheckBox control to represent the true/false values.

When we want to have more control over the rendered content of DataGrid, we set the AutoGenerateColumns property to False and define our own template for the cell. As we haven't discussed templating yet, this feature will not be explained in much detail here. To control how a cell renders its content, we can use the DataGridTemplateColumn element. This type of column allows us to set a data template (a template for the data we wish to display) for the bound data. Change your datagrid according to the following code snippet:

```
<sdk:DataGrid x:Name="MyFirstGrid" AutoGenerateColumns="False">
    <sdk:DataGrid.Columns>
        <sdk:DataGridTextColumn Header="Name" Binding="{Binding Name}"
        Width="Auto"/>
            <sdk:DataGridTemplateColumn Header="Image">
            <sdk:DataGridTemplateColumn.CellTemplate>
                <DataTemplate>
                    <Image Source="{Binding Image}"/>
                </DataTemplate>
            </sdk:DataGridTemplateColumn.CellTemplate>
            </sdk:DataGridTemplateColumn>
    </sdk:DataGrid.Columns>
</sdk:DataGrid>
```

The preceding code will render as follows:

Once we set the `AutoGenerateColumns` property to `False`, we have to define each and every column we wish to display manually. For the **Name** column, we've used the `DataGridTextColumn` type of column as we only wish to display text. We bind that column using the `Binding` property to the `Name` property of the `Food` class. For the **Image** column, we've used the `DataGridTemplateColumn` type of column as we need to define a template for that column, so instead of text it will render an image with the source bound to the `Image` property of the `Food` class.

As mentioned earlier, the cells of the `DataGrid` control can be edited by the user. If you wish to prevent such editing, set the `IsReadOnly` property of `DataGrid` to `False`. If you do use editing in your `DataGrid`, you have a set of events aimed at helping you control the editing process. The `BeginningEdit` event fires just as soon as the cell enters the editing mode. Using this event, you can do things, such as preventing a user from editing the cell. The event exposes a Boolean property named `Cancel` within its `EventArgs`, which, when set to `True`, stops the event from running. If the `BeginningEdit` event successfully completes, the `PreparingCellForEdit` event fires next. This event gives you the ability to override any changes made in the `BeginningEdit` event. When these two events finish running successfully, the previously mentioned `CellEditEnding` and `CellEditEnded` events fire.

Sorting

The last concept of `DataGrid`, which we will discuss is sorting. `DataGrid` has built-in support for sorting collections of items that implement the `IList` interface. This interface is used almost everywhere in Silverlight, due to the fact that it allows `DataGrid` to sort almost any collection of items immediately. Each `DataGrid` column type has a property named `SortMemberPath`, which allows you to set the name of the collection that this column will be sorted with. Take our **Image** column for example. If you click on it right now, it won't sort anything, because the column doesn't know how to sort images, but if you click on the **Name** column, the grid will sort itself by that column. To give the **Image** column the same ability, set the `SortMemberPath` property of the image's `DataGridTemplateColumn` to any of the property's name of the `Food` class. In our example, it doesn't matter which property you set as the names of the images and foods is the same.

As you can see, `DataGrid` is a powerful control, which can be of great help when you want to create applications that let a user view and edit data. It is strongly encouraged that you play with the control a bit more to fully grasp all its power. As for binding, don't worry if you didn't understand the concept fully. We will dig much deeper into the subject when we reach *Chapter 5, Working with Data*.

Playing media files

The final subject we will discuss in this chapter is the media capabilities of Silverlight. As it was first introduced, Silverlight was always a media-focused framework. Silverlight has the ability to play audio and video files (HD content), stream media, and use **Digital Rights Management** (DRM) to protect the displayed media. The heart of all of these is the MediaElement control.

The MediaElement control

The MediaElement control is a rectangular control that can contain audio or video as its content. Silverlight supports many codes for audio and video and a full list of supported codecs can be found on the MSDN website—http://msdn.microsoft.com/en-us/library/cc189080%28v=vs.95%29.aspx.

Using the MediaElement control is quite straightforward. Create a new Silverlight project in Visual Studio and name it **Chapter2-Media**. Copy a video file to your web project ClientBin directory (you can find a few in Windows 7 operating system's Sample Videos folder), and copy the following line of code to your MainPage.xaml file:

```
<MediaElement x:Name="MyFirstMediaElement" Source="Wildlife.wmv" />
```

That's it! Build and run the application, and you should see that the movie starts playing in your browser.

Controlling the MediaElement control is done in code behind using a couple of methods. To demonstrate this, wrap the newly added MediaElement in StackPanel, and add two buttons below it— Play and Stop. Your code should look something similar to the following code snippet:

```
<StackPanel>
    <MediaElement x:Name="MyFirstMediaElement" Source="Wildlife.wmv"
/>
    <Button Content="Play" Width="100" x:Name="playBtn"
    Click="playBtn_Click"/>
    <Button Content="Stop" Width="100" x:Name="stopBtn"
    Click="stopBtn_Click"/>
</StackPanel>
```

Switch over to the MainPage.xaml.cs file and add the missing playBtn_Click and stopBtn_Click methods:

```
private void playBtn_Click(object sender, RoutedEventArgs e)
{
    MyFirstMediaElement.Play();
```

```
}
private void stopBtn_Click(object sender, RoutedEventArgs e)
{
    MyFirstMediaElement.Stop();
}
```

Build and run the application. You can now control the media playing using the two new buttons.

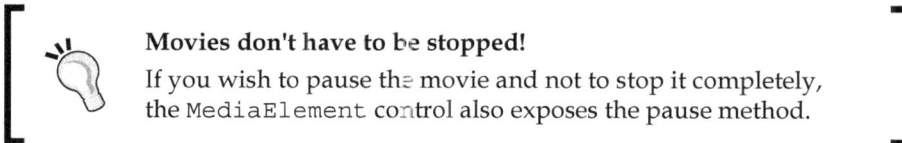

> **Movies don't have to be stopped!**
> If you wish to pause the movie and not to stop it completely, the MediaElement control also exposes the pause method.

The MediaElement control exposes a few handy properties as well. AutoPlay is a Boolean property that sets whether the current media should be automatically played when the control is loaded or not. CanPause is used to determine whether or not a user can pause the playing media and CurrentState returns the current state of the playing media.

Other than these properties the MediaElement control offers us the properties to know its current location and the total length of the movie. NaturalDuration returns a Duration element, which states the total length of the playing media. Using the Position property, you can read the current position of the playing media, and if CanSeek is set to True, you can also set the position programatically. CanSeek is a read-only property and it is set when the media is loaded to the MediaElement control. If you are playing a streamed media (from a streaming service for example), then CanSeek will be set to False, otherwise it is set to True.

The MediaElement control is fun, and it's a simple control, and you are encouraged to play a bit more with it and read about it on the MSDN website—http://msdn.microsoft.com/en-us/library/ms611595%28v=VS.95%29.aspx—before moving on to the next subject.

Digital Rights Management

Integrating **Digital Rights Management** (DRM) into your Silverlight application allows you to better protect and secure your media content. The most common use for the DRM mechanism is to protect media. Streaming sites that use progressive download (a streaming method in which the media plays as it downloads) or sites that offer the user, downloads of media files for offline watching, usually use DRM to protect their assets from being passed freely from one user to another. DRM is a wide and complicated subject, and as such it is beyond the scope of this book.

If you wish to know more about DRM, you should visit MSDN's documentation on *Digital Rights Management (DRM)*, which explains in detail how the process works and offers a few code samples. MSDN's documentation can be found at http://msdn.microsoft.com/en-us/library/cc838192%28v=vs.95%29.aspx.

Working with audio files

The MediaElement control can be used for more than just playing video. This control offers several audio-specific properties that give the user a greater listening experience. AudioStreamCount, AudioStreamIndex, Balance, Volume, and IsMuted are the properties responsible for controlling the audio.

AudioStreamCount and AudioStreamIndex

AudioStreamCount and AudioStreamIndex give you access to the individual audio tracks of a media file if there is more than one. Imagine a recording of a band playing a song—there is one track for the guitar, one for the singer, and one for the drums. You can use these properties in code behind, just as soon as the media is opened and the MediaOpened event is fired. The AudioStreamCount property holds the number of available tracks in this media file, while the AudioStreamIndex property specifies which of the available tracks is currently playing. By default, this property will be set to 0, so the MediaElement control will play the first of the available audio tracks.

Balance

The Balance property enables you to shift the sound from one speaker to the other. This property accepts a double type of value between -1.0 and 1.0. If you set the value to -1.0, the sound will project only from the left speaker; and if you set the value to 1.0, the sound will project only from the right speaker. For the balanced point between the two speakers, the value of 0 should be used.

Volume

The Volume property is used for controlling the volume. This property accepts a double type of value between 0.0 and 1.0. Setting the volume to 0 means the sound is inaudible, and 1 is the maximum possible volume. By default, this property's value will be set to 0.5.

IsMuted

Last, but not least, we have the `IsMuted` property. This property simply determines whether the audio of the media playing is audible or not. Setting this property to `True` means that the media will play fully but won't have any audio at all, regardless of the user's volume settings. For better control between completely inaudible and audible, you should use the `Volume` property.

Displaying closed captioning

Silverlight supports the concept of "closed captioning" through the use of timelined events. Other than just playing the media, the `MediaElement` control also enables you to interact with the timeline of the playing media for various uses. These can range from displaying subtitles to showing content-specific advertisements or just about anything else you think is relevant to the currently displayed content. The `TimeLineMarker` object is the one responsible for this interaction. The `Text` property of the `TimeLineMarker` object is a string that represents the value of the object. The `Type` property is used to specify the marker type of `TimeLineMarker`, and the `Time` property accepts a `TimeSpan` type of value, which represents the position of the marker within the playing media we wish to interact with.

There are two different types of `TimeLineMarker`. The first type is the `Basic` type. It's used when you wish to provide fixed information (for example, subtitles). The second type is known as the `Script` type, and it can be used when you wish to run some code when the marker reaches the time specified in the `TimeLineMarker` object.

To interact with the timeline, we use code behind and build a collection of the `TimeLineMarker` objects. Then we add the `MarkerReached` event to the `MediaElement` control. This event gets fired whenever one of the `TimeLineMarker` objects' `Time` property is reached. Let's add subtitles to our current project. We already have a `MediaElement` control added that plays a WMV file, so all we have to do is add the `MarkerReached` event to it. Change your `MediaElement` control as follows:

```
<MediaElement x:Name="MyFirstMediaElement" Source="Wildlife.wmv" Marke
rReached="MyFirstMediaElement_MarkerReached" />
```

Because, the collection of markers gets built once the media is loaded, we have to add a call to the `MediaOpened` event handler. Add it to your `MediaElement` control so that it looks like the following code snippet:

```
<MediaElement MediaOpened="MyFirstMediaElement_MediaOpened"
x:Name="MyFirstMediaElement" Source="Wildlife.wmv" MarkerReached="MyFi
rstMediaElement_MarkerReached" />
```

Don't forget to change the Source property to the name of your video file.

We also need a control to display the subtitles. Add a TextBlock control just below the MediaElement control and name it MySubs:

```
<TextBlock x:Name="MySubs"/>
```

Now we need to add some TimeLineMarker objects to the MediaElement control. The only place to add markers to the MediaElement control is the MediaOpened event handler. In your code, add the following MediaOpened method:

```
private void MyFirstMediaElement_MediaOpened(object sender,
RoutedEventArgs e)
{
    List<TimelineMarker> markers = GetMarkers();
    foreach (TimelineMarker marker in markers)
    {
        MyFirstMediaElement.Markers.Add(marker);
    }
}
```

The preceding code snippet creates a list of the TimeLineMarker objects from the GetMarkers method. The code for the GetMarkers method can be found in the downloadable source from the Packt website under the **Chapter2-Media** project directory. Once we have the list of objects, we will need to go over it using the foreach loop and add the marker to the Markers collection of the MediaElement control.

To actually make the subtitle shown on the page, we need to change the MarkerReached event handler. Change the event handler to the following code snippet:

```
private void MyFirstMediaElement_MarkerReached(object sender,
TimelineMarkerRoutedEventArgs e)
{
MySubs.Text = e.Marker.Text;
}
```

What all the preceding code snippet does is to set the Text property of the previously added TextBlock to the Text property of the reached marker.

Build and run the application, and you should notice that when the movie starts playing, a subtitle is shown as follows:

The subtitle's text is changed when MediaElement reaches the second marker, 4 seconds later.

The MediaElement control is the heart and soul of every media-related project done in Silverlight. It can be extended to subtitles, buttons, and just about anything your imagination thrives to.

Test your knowledge

1. You are tasked to develop a Silverlight 4 based application. The application contains the following code snippet:

```
<Grid x:Name="LayoutRoot" Background="White">
    <Grid.RowDefinitions>
        <RowDefinition Height="200"/>
        <RowDefinition Height="*"/>
    </Grid.RowDefinitions>
</Grid>
```

You need to add a horizontally oriented `StackPanel` control into the second row. Which XAML fragment should you use?

a. `<StackPanel Orientation="Horizontal" Row="1"></StackPanel>`

b. `<StackPanel Orientation="Horizontal" Grid.Row="1"></StackPanel>`

c. `<StackPanel Orientation="Horizontal" Grid.Row="2"></StackPanel>`

d. `<StackPanel Orientation="Vertical" Grid.Row="1"></StackPanel>`

2. You are developing a Silverlight-based media player application. You need to add a `MediaElement` control that is able to handle an event when a media starts playing and when it fails. Which XAML fragment should you use?

a. ```
<MediaElement x:Name="MyMediaElement"
MediaOpened="MyMediaElement_MediaOpened"
MediaFailed="MyMediaElement_MediaFailed"/>
```

b. ```
<MediaElement x:Name="MyMediaElement"
MediaOpened="MyMediaElement_MediaOpened"
MediaEnded="MyMediaElement_MediaEnded"/>
```

c. ```
<MediaElement x:Name="MyMediaElement"
MediaStarted="MyMediaElement_MediaStarted"
MediaFailed="MyMediaElement_MediaFailed"/>
```

d. ```
<MediaElement x:Name="MyMediaElement" MediaOpenedAndFailed="MyMediaElement_MediaOpenedAndFailed"/>
```

3. You are developing a Silverlight application based on `Grid`. You need to ensure that the `Grid` control has four evenly spaced rows that will fill the height of `Grid`. Which XAML fragment should you use?

a. ```
<Grid x:Name="LayoutRoot" Height="400" Width="400">
<Grid.RowDefinitions>
<RowDefinition Height="1"/>
<RowDefinition Height="1"/>
<RowDefinition Height="1"/>
<RowDefinition Height="1"/>
</Grid.RowDefinitions>
</Grid>
```
```

b.
```
<Grid x:Name="LayoutRoot" Height="400" Width="400">
<Grid.RowDefinitions>
<RowDefinition Height="0.25"/>
<RowDefinition Height="0.25"/>
<RowDefinition Height="0.25"/>
<RowDefinition Height="0.75"/>
</Grid.RowDefinitions>
</Grid>
```

c.
```
<Grid x:Name="LayoutRoot" Height="400" Width="400">
<Grid.RowDefinitions>
<RowDefinition Height="0.25*"/>
<RowDefinition Height="0.25*"/>
<RowDefinition Height="0.25*"/>
<RowDefinition Height="0.25*"/>
</Grid.RowDefinitions>
</Grid>
```

d.
```
<Grid x:Name="LayoutRoot" Height="400" Width="400">
<Grid.RowDefinitions>
<RowDefinition Height="100*"/>
<RowDefinition Height="100*"/>
<RowDefinition Height="*"/>
<RowDefinition Height="*"/>
</Grid.RowDefinitions>
</Grid>
```

4. You are developing a navigation-based Silverlight 4 application. In your `MainPage.xaml` file, you have a `Frame` element named `ContentFrame` and a `URIMapper` element named `ContentMapper`. You need to add a `HyperlinkButton` control to the application, which navigates to your newly created `ContactUs` page. Which XAML fragment should you use?

a.
```
<HyperlinkButton NavigateUri="/ContactUs"
TargetName="ContentFrame" Content="Contact Us"/>
```

b.
```
<HyperlinkButton NavigateUri="/ContactUs"
TargetName="ContentMapper" Content="Contact Us"/>
```

c.
```
<HyperlinkButton NavigateUri="/ContactUs" TargetName="_
blank" Content="Contact Us"/>
```

d.
```
<HyperlinkButton NavigateUri="/ContactUs.aspx"
TargetName="ContentFrame" Content="Contact Us"/>
```

5. You are tasked with developing a Silverlight 4 application that uses a `DataGrid` control. The `DataGrid` control needs to be aware of when a user finishes editing a cell. Which XAML fragment should you use?

   a. `<sdk:DataGrid x:Name="MyFirstGrid" AutoGenerateColumns="False" CellEditEnding="MyFirstGrid_ CellEditEnding"></sdk:DataGrid>`

   b. `<sdk:DataGrid x:Name="MyFirstGrid" AutoGenerateColumns="False"></sdk:DataGrid>`

   c. `<sdk:DataGrid x:Name="MyFirstGrid" AutoGenerateColumns="False" CellEditEndingFinished="MyFir stGrid_CellEditEndingFinished"></sdk:DataGrid>`

   d. `<sdk:DataGrid x:Name="MyFirstGrid" AutoGenerateColumns="False" CellEditEnded="MyFirstGrid_ CellEditEnded"></sdk:DataGrid>`

Summary

This has been a long ride, hasn't it? We have covered a lot of ground in this chapter. We started with creating our first Silverlight application, and by using it, we learned all about the layout panels and what each and everyone of them is used for. Then we moved on to using the core and content controls, a topic which has a fair amount of questions in the Silverlight certification exam. The next subject we discussed was the navigation framework. We learned how to navigate between pages, use query strings and other related subjects, without which no line of business application can be completed. We then moved on to displaying a collections of items — a set of controls aimed at helping us display a large amount of data while using binding, templating, and more. We concluded the chapter with the ever fun `MediaElement` control — the heart and soul of working with media in Silverlight.

In the next chapter, we are going to extend our knowledge of the Silverlight UI. We will work with animation, modify controls, manipulate visuals, and much more!

3
Enhancing the User Interface

Armed with the knowledge from the previous chapter, we will continue to dive deep into the user interface layer of Silverlight. While the previous chapter dealt with the core concepts of laying a user interface in Silverlight, in this chapter we are going to discuss some of the more 'fun' features of Silverlight, such as templates, animations, and behaviors. Just like before, we have a lot to cover, so let's get started!

In this chapter, we will cover the following topics:

- Creating or modifying the control styles
- Creating control templates
- Creating or modifying data templates
- Manipulating visuals
- Animating visuals
- Implementing behaviors
- Managing the visual state

Creating or modifying the control styles

Just like in real life, first impressions mean a lot. When your users need to fill out a form for example, which is more likely to get their attention, the plain old vanilla form or a customized styled form? The answer in most cases is a customized one.

Take a look at the following screenshots, which show the comparison between an unstyled (left) form and a styled (right) form in Silverlight:

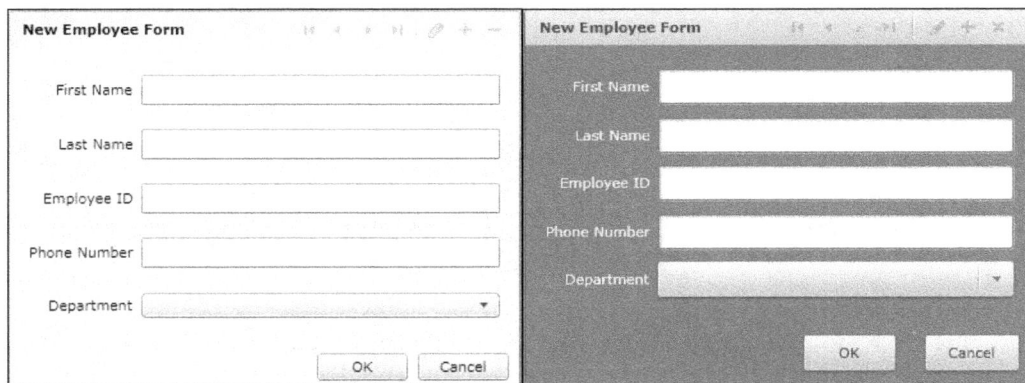

The styling controls in Silverlight are very similar to the styling controls in HTML using **Cascading Style Sheets** (**CSS**). While it is possible (and valid) to add the style tag on almost any HTML elements and set all kinds of properties such as direction, font-weight, color, and so on; it can get messy (and not very readable) very fast. CSS was invented to help separate the visual code from the functional code, instead of setting the same style over and over again, for elements (like the textboxes in our form example) you can create a class once and just set it on all the desired elements. If you ever want to change the style of the elements, all you have to do is to change the class's properties in one centralized place. Once done, all the elements that use that class will change accordingly. This will change their look. Silverlight styling works in a very similar model — you can set a style on the element level (just like the style attribute), the page level, and the global level. Let's discuss each of them in detail while styling the `DataForm` control from the preceding screenshots. Go ahead and open the **Chapter3-Styling** project from the downloaded project files from the Packt website in Visual Studio 2010.

Styling at the element level

Setting a style on the element level simply means that only this specific element will be affected by that style. To style an element on the element level, we simply add the desired property setting, such as `FontSize`, directly within the element declaration line. Let's change the font size of the first `TextBox` control. Locate the following line of code in your `MainPage.xaml` file:

```
<TextBox Text="{Binding FirstName, Mode=TwoWay}"/>
```

Change the preceding line of code as follows:

```
<TextBox Text="{Binding FirstName, Mode=TwoWay}" FontSize="22"/>
```

Build and run your application, and you will notice the font size of the first `TextBox` control is much bigger than the rest of the `TextBox` controls. Let's change the color of the text inside the textbox as well. Add the following line of code right after the `FontSize` property in your `TextBox` declaration line:

```
Foreground="BlueViolet"
```

Build and run your application, and you'll see that the text now has a blue-violet color.

Lastly, let's make the text in the `TextBox` control bold. Add the following line of code right after the `Foreground` property in your `TextBox` declaration line:

```
FontWeight="Bold"
```

Build and run your application. The end result should look similar to the following screenshot:

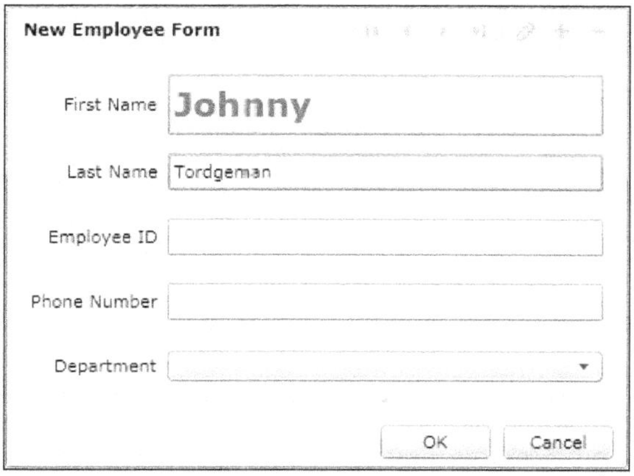

While this type of styling is fine for setting the design properties on a single element, it gets quite messy when multiple elements of the same kind need to have the same style properties. Think about our form for example, if we wanted to make all the `TextBox` elements have a red font, we would need to copy the style declaration of the foreground color over and over again to every one of the `TextBox` controls in the form. And what if you suddenly need to change the font color to green? You'll then have to fix the same font style declaration on each and every one of the `TextBox` controls. That might be ok if you have two or three controls to design, but what if you have fourteen or a hundred? To tackle this problem you can use page-level styling and that is what we are going to talk about next.

Styling at the page level

In its core, the page-level styling is the same as the element-level styling, but instead of being applied on a single element, the style will be applied on all the elements of the same type in that specific page. A page-level style is defined under the top parent element (in our case, UserControl as we are editing MainPage.xaml) by using the attached property—Resources. An empty page-level styling will look as follows:

```
<UserControl.Resources>

</UserControl.Resources>
```

Inside the Resources elements, we define any style we wish to share among the different elements of the page.

There are three types of page-level styling—explicit, implicit, and BasedOn. Up until Silverlight 4, explicit styling was the only way to set a style in Silverlight but ever since Silverlight 4 introduced the concept of implicit styles, it became quite a popular addition. We will start our journey of page-level styling with explicit styles, move on to implicit styles, and finish up with the BasedOn styling mechanism.

Explicit styling

An **explicit style** is a style that has its TargetType property set. To apply an explicit style to an element, you must define the style name as a static resource in the element's Style property.

Once you declare a style, you can define the content of the style (the styles you are applying) using the Setter elements. The Setter element contains two properties as follows:

- **Property**: This gives the name of the property you wish to style (for example, FontSize)
- **Value**: This is the styling value (for FontSize, it can be 22, 24, or any other font size you wish)

Let's take the TextBox style, which we defined in the previous example and transform it into an explicit style at the page level. The code for that style will look as follows:

```
<UserControl.Resources>
<Style x:Key="TextBoxStyle" TargetType="TextBox">
    <Setter Property="FontSize" Value="22"/>
    <Setter Property="Foreground" Value="Violet"/>
        <Setter Property="FontWeight" Value="Bold"/>
```

```
</Style>
</UserControl.Resources>
```

In the preceding example, we have defined a style called `TextBoxStyle`, which will target elements of the `TextBox` type and format them to have a font size of 22, a foreground color of violet, and a bold weight.

Copy and paste the preceding code snippet to your `MainPage.xaml` page just under the `UserControl` element (above the `LayoutRoot Grid` element). If you compile and run your application now, you will see that no textbox has changed its style according to what we wrote. The reason for that is explicit styles need to be explicitly set on elements. For every `TextBox` control on your page, add the following line of code before the closing bracket:

```
Style="{StaticResource TextBoxStyle}"
```

By binding the `Style` property to the name of style we have just created, we explicitly set the style of the element to the style we defined.

> It's important to remember to only bind a style to an element of the same type of the style's `TargetType` property. Binding a style to an element of the wrong type will result in a compilation error.

Build and run your application, and you should see that all the textboxes are now styled based on our definition:

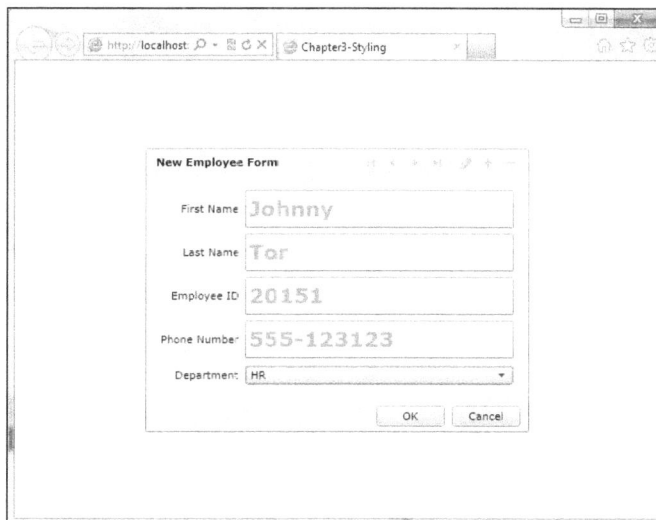

The big advantage of using page-level explicit styling is that you can now edit the style in one central location, and all the elements that inherit it will change accordingly. Let's make the font size of our textboxes smaller. In your style definition, change the value of the FontSize setter to 15. The complete style should look as follows:

```
<UserControl.Resources>
<Style x:Key="TextBoxStyle" TargetType="TextBox">
    <Setter Property="FontSize" Value="15"/>
        <Setter Property="Foreground" Value="Violet"/>
        <Setter Property="FontWeight" Value="Bold"/>
</Style>
</UserControl.Resources>
```

Build and run your application and you'll notice the font size of the TextBox elements is smaller now.

Another advantage of using explicit styling comes into play when you want to have different styles for the same type of element. Nothing stops you from defining another TextBox style on your page and using it with the selected TextBox elements. Let's add another style for the TextBox element on our page. Copy and paste the following code just below the closing element of our previous style:

```
<Style x:Key="TextBoxStyleRed" TargetType="TextBox">
<Setter Property="FontSize" Value="15"/>
<Setter Property="Foreground" Value="Red"/>
</Style>
```

Next, find the TextBox elements of **Phone Number** and **Employee ID**, and change the binding of the Style property from TextBoxStyle to TextBoxStyleRed. Build and run your application, and you should get the result, as shown in the following screenshot:

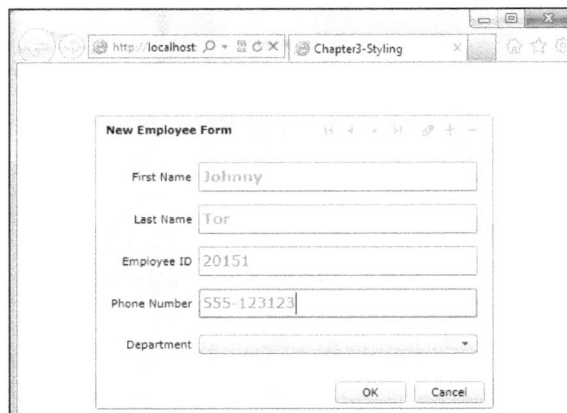

Explicit styling is great when you wish to have different styles for the same type of element within a selected page. Unlike element-level styling, you have one central place to edit the styles of all the elements, your code looks much cleaner, and you can define different styles for the same type of element within the same page.

Implicit styling

We've just seen how explicit styling works and what its advantages are, but think about what happens when you are dealing with a large-scale application that has hundreds of controls. Going through each one and setting its style property can be tiresome and very error-friendly. This is where implicit styling kicks in. Implicit styles were first introduced in Silverlight 4, and they are very similar to their explicit counterpart with one exception—they don't have a key. If you look back at the *Explicit styling* section, you'll see that each explicit style we defined had the key property. That property was mandatory, and the elements that wanted to use that style had to specify it. With implicit styling you define the style exactly the same, but as you omit the key property, the TargetType property becomes the key, and the style implicitly affects all the elements of that type with one exception—if the element we target already has a defined style, the implicit style won't affect it.

Let's revisit the explicit style's example and make it implicit. Go over the code and remove all the Style attributes from the TextBox elements. Next, remove the x:Key property from the first TextBox style on your page. Build and run your application, and you should get a result similar to the following screenshot:

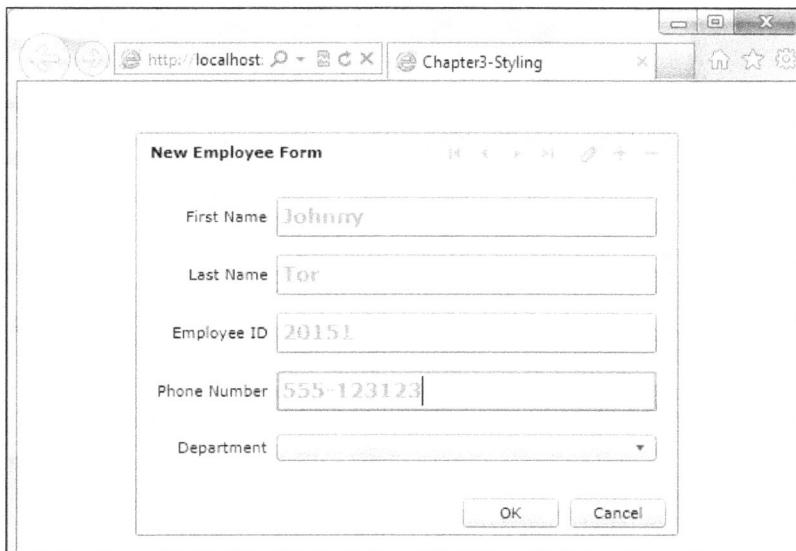

By removing the key property of a style, we've changed its nature from needed to be explicitly called by an element to implicitly affect all elements of the style's type.

BasedOn styling

Implicit styling is useful for sure, but what happens when you define more than one implicit style for the same element in a page? Well, you get a runtime error, that's what.

If you want to emulate CSS, which can cascade styles, you can use the BasedOn system for your styling. Using BasedOn, you can create a base style for your page (for example, all the textboxes will have the font size of 15) and then create an addition style based on it.

BasedOn styling is not unique to implicit or explicit styling and, in fact, it uses a combination of both. To understand BasedOn styling better, let's see an example of how to use it. Delete all the styles inside your `UserControl.Resources` element and then add the following code:

```
<Style x:Key="BaseTextBoxStyle" TargetType="TextBox">
<Setter Property="FontSize" Value="15"/>
</Style>
```

There is nothing you haven't seen before in the preceding code. It's an explicit style named `"BaseTextBoxStyle"` aimed at the `TextBox` element, which sets the `FontSize` property to `15`. But, this is only the first half of our BasedOn style. Now, we can create a style that will be based on our base style. Add the following code below the closing element of the previous style:

```
<Style TargetType="TextBox" BasedOn="{StaticResource
BaseTextBoxStyle}">
<Setter Property="Foreground" Value="Red"/>
</Style>
```

This looks like any other implicit style we defined in the previous part except for one major difference—it has a property called `BasedOn`, which is bound to the base style we defined just a minute ago. Build and run your application, and you should get something similar to the following screenshot:

We have just created an implicit style that is based on a base style. BasedOn styles are great time savers and let you create a clearer, better-understood code when you have styles that are very similar in nature but differ in their properties.

Styling at the global level

Up until now, we have dealt with element-level styling and page-level styling. The last level of styling that Silverlight offers us is the global level. Styles in the global level are styles that can be used throughout your application and not just on a single page. Explicit, implicit, and BasedOn styles do not have to be defined at the page level. These kinds of styles can happily be set at the global level, too. With global-level styling, we are basically talking about defining styles in the App.xaml file. If you open up your App.xaml file right now, you should see only the following lines of code:

```
<Application.Resources>

</Application.Resources>
```

If this looks familiar to you, then it is no coincidence. If you look back at the page-level styling, you will see that all the styles were written under the UserControl. Resources node. Application.Resources defines resources that are to be used at the application (global) level and, thus, have to be written under a global scope. Let's consider the following scenario:

You are building an application that uses a wizard form where users can go from one page to another. If you define all the styles for that application on the element level, you would have a big mess on your hands. If you define all the styles on the page level, you would basically have duplication of code, because for each style you define on page one, you have to define another on page two. The solution here is global-level styling. You define the styles once at the global level and both pages (and others that you might add in the future) can use it. All your code is centralized and easily maintainable.

As styles on the global level are just like their sibling on the page level, you can take all the styles we wrote in the previous part and move them right into the App.xaml file. If you build and run your application once the change is done, you will see that the user interface is exactly the same.

Styles hierarchy

Just like most things in life, styles have a clear order of hierarchy. Knowing about this hierarchy can help you when you wish to override certain styles or even modify a global style on a specific element. The style hierarchy in Silverlight strongly resembles the hierarchy of styles/CSS in HTML. First, you have the global styles; these styles are the weakest in the style hierarchy and can be overridden by both page-level styles and element-level styles. To demonstrate this hierarchy, open a new Silverlight application project in Visual Studio 2010, and add a Button control to MainPage.xaml. Once the button is in place, edit the App.xaml file, and add the following style between the opening and closing of the Application.Resources element:

```
<Style TargetType="Button">
<Setter Property="Background" Value="Green"/>
</Style>
```

If you run your application now, you'll see that the button has picked up the global style and its background is now greenish. Now, add the following code in your MainPage.xaml just under the top-level UserControl element:

```
<UserControl.Resources>
<Style TargetType="Button">
   <Setter Property="Background" Value="Red"/>
   </Style>
</UserControl.Resources>
```

Run your application now, and you'll notice that the button has a red flavor. What just happened is usually referred to as style overriding. Because the page-level styles are higher in the style hierarchy than the global level ones, they override the settings.

The same applies for element-level styling. Element-level styling is on top of the hierarchy and, thus, can override any other style. To recap, the main idea of this topic is that global-level styles are always at the bottom of the styles hierarchy, which means any style higher in the hierarchy will override them. Next in the styles hierarchy are page-level styles. Sitting at the top of the hierarchy are element-level styles. If you define a style to an element using its `Style` property directly, nothing will override it.

Creating control templates

In today's world, professionals want to use a wide array of controls such as `Button`, `TextBox`, `Slider`, and so on. In many cases, you don't want to reinvent the wheel but just use the basic control in a way that fits your design. How many times did you want to have a round button? Or a control that does the exact same action as a slider but looks completely different? To answer these kinds of issues the concept of templates was introduced. **Templating**, as the name implies, allows you to completely change the way a control looks without sacrificing its behavior. To template a control, you first need a control. Let's create a new Silverlight application project, name it **Chapter3-Templates** and leave all the default options. Once the project is ready, add a button to the page using the following code:

```
<Button Width="100" Height="100" Content="Round" Click="Button_Click">
</Button>
```

Switch over to the code behind file (`MainPage.xaml.cs`), and add the following event handler:

```
private void Button_Click(object sender, RoutedEventArgs e)
{
MessageBox.Show("I'm clicked!');
}
```

Here, there is nothing that we haven't seen before. We've added a button, whose content is `"Round"`, and once you click on it, a message box pops out saying **I'm clicked!**

To make things interesting (the button is called **Round** after all), we are going to template the button to look like a round button. One way to template a control is to use its `Template` attached property. Change your button code, so it will look like the following code snippet:

```
<Button Width="100" Height="100" Content="Round" Click="Button_Click">
<Button.Template>
    <ControlTemplate>
        <Ellipse Height="100" Width="100" Stroke="Blue"
StrokeThickness="1" Fill="Pink"/>
    </ControlTemplate>
  </Button.Template>
</Button>
```

By using the `Template` attached property of `Button`, we can set the `ControlTemplate` property, which tells the Silverlight engine how to render the UI of the control. In our example, we've created a simple `Ellipse` shape, which is perfectly rounded as its width and height are set to the same value. If you run your application now, you would see that the button has changed the way it looks to a pink circle with a blue stroke but retained its buttonly behavior. If you click on it, the following message box will pop:

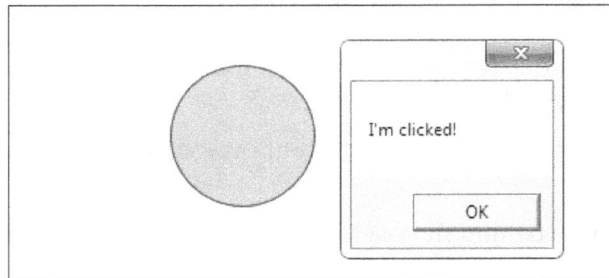

TemplateBinding

As nice as the template we've just created is, it has a big flaw. Its height and width values are hardcoded. With hardcoded width and height, the button loses its ability to resize according to its properties, and we are basically left with a fixed-size button. To solve this issue, we have the `TemplateBinding` mechanism. `TemplateBinding` is part of the data binding family, and it can only be used within `ControlTemplate`. The source of `TemplateBinding` is the control to which the `ControlTemplate` it resides in refers to.

Let's change our fixed-size `Width` and `Height` properties to use the `TemplateBinding` mechanism. Change your `Ellipse` element in your `ControlTemplate` as follows:

```
<Ellipse Height="{TemplateBinding Height}" Width="{TemplateBinding
Width}" Stroke="Blue" StrokeThickness="1" Fill="Pink"/>
```

By replacing the fixed size values and using the `TemplateBinding` mechanism, we are telling Silverlight that whatever width and height we set on the parent element (`Button` in our case), the same values should also be used in our template. Change the values of the `Width` and `Height` properties in the `Button` element, and then build and run your application. You'll notice that whatever values you put in these properties affect the size of your button template. `TemplateBinding` isn't limited to the `Width` and `Height` properties. In your template, you can set `TemplateBinding` to just about any other property such as `Background`, `Foreground`, `FontSize`, and so on.

Showing the content

You may have noticed that something is still missing in our button template—the content of the button! When creating a template for a control, we have to tell Silverlight where we want to place our content. In order to accomplish this task, Silverlight provides us with two specially designed elements—`ContentPresenter` and `ItemPresenter`. Each of these elements has a very distinct job when it comes to show content, and for that reason, we will discuss them right now.

The ContentPresenter element

The `ContentPresenter` element is nothing more than a placeholder for the content. Its job is to take the content of the element—be it some text, an image, another control and so on—and place it in your template. To best demonstrate this control, change your `ControlTemplate` element as follows:

```
<Grid>
<Ellipse Height="{TemplateBinding Height}" Width="{TemplateBinding
Width}" Stroke="Blue" StrokeThickness="1" Fill="Pink"/>
<ContentPresenter HorizontalAlignment="Center"
VerticalAlignment="Center"/>
</Grid>
```

By placing the `Ellipse` element inside a `Grid` and adding the `ContentPresenter` element, we've added the content back to the button. The content itself comes from the `Content` property of the parent control and presents wherever we place `ContentPresenter` in our template. In our example, the content will be shown in the center of the `Ellipse` element, because the `ContentPresenter` element's `HorizontalAlignment` and `VerticalAlignment` properties are set to center.

Play around with the `Content` property of the button, and then build and run your application. You'll notice the content—no matter if it's text or anything else—is always presented in the middle of the button:

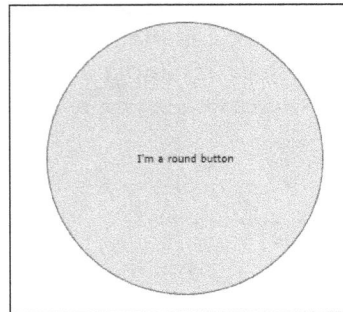

The ItemPresenter element

While the `ContentPresenter` element is perfect for showing content, if you are templating a control based on `ItemsControl`, such as `ListBox`, you're better off using the `ItemPresenter` element. The `ItemPresenter` element's job is to place the items in your template but not templating the items themselves. We will deal with item templating later in this chapter. To demonstrate the `ItemPresenter` element, replace your `Button` control with the following `ListBox` control:

```
<ListBox x:Name="myTemplatedListBox" Height="300" Width="300">
<ListBox.Template>
    <ControlTemplate>
        <Border CornerRadius="20" BorderThickness="15"
BorderBrush="Cyan" Padding="5">
            <ItemsPresenter></ItemsPresenter>
        </Border>
    </ControlTemplate>
</ListBox.Template>
    <ListBoxItem Content="Item 1"/>
    <ListBoxItem Content="Item 2"/>
    <ListBoxItem Content="Item 3"/>
</ListBox>
```

Build and run your application, and you'll be presented with the following result:

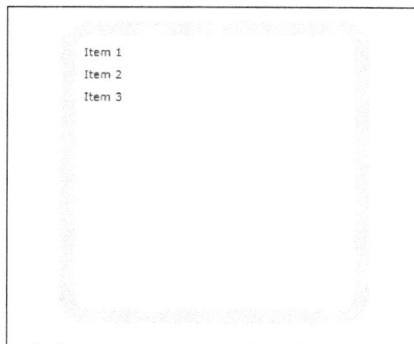

By templating the `ListBox` control, we've added a nice rounded cyan-flavored border around the control itself. The `ItemPresenter` element was used to place the `ListBox` control's items inside that border. Play around with the template, and add your own controls inside of it. Templating is all about your creativity after all.

Attaching the style

Up until now, we've only created templates on the element level. Just like styling however, we can create templates on larger scales such as the page and global levels.

Consider the following scenario:

You are in charge of templating a form in Silverlight that contains three comboboxes and two buttons. If you try to template these controls like we did so far in this chapter, you'll end up using duplicate, messy, and error-prone code. Each of the controls will have its own template, which is a duplication of the other control template. To solve this mess, we will use either the page-level or the global-level templating. Let's change the `ListBox` template we have just created from element level to global level. The process of such a change is quite simple. First, delete the `ListBox` template, which we've previously created for the `ListBox` element, from your `MainPage.xaml` file. Once done, open the `App.xaml` file, and create a new implicit style using the following line of code:

```
<Style TargetType="ListBox"></Style>
```

Template is a property just like any of the other properties we've seen while creating a style. To set a control's template in a style, examine the following code snippet:

```
<Setter Property="Template">
<Setter.Value>
    <ControlTemplate>
```

```
            <Border CornerRadius="20" BorderThickness="15"
    BorderBrush="Cyan" Padding="5">
                <ItemsPresenter></ItemsPresenter>
            </Border>
        </ControlTemplate>
    </Setter.Value>
</Setter>
```

We are defining a `Setter` element with the property of `Template` and by using attached properties we are setting the `Value` of that property to the template we've already created in the previous exercise. As this is an implicit style, `ListBox` on the `mainpage.xaml` page will be affected by it immediately. Build and run your application, and you should see that the `ListBox` control still retains its cyan border.

> If we were to create an explicit-style template, all we would have to change in our code is the binding name of the style that holds the template to the `Style` property of the control we wish to template.

Creating or modifying data templates

Creating a **line of business** (**LOB**) application usually deals with data, controls that show data, controls that manipulate data, and so on. So far in this chapter, we have dealt with templates and styling of controls. But, there is another aspect of styling and templating, and that is styling and templating of data. When displaying a collection of items in Silverlight, using controls like `ListBox` or `ComboBox`, the data is rendered using data template. A **data template** is used to define how raw data will be presented to a user. To demonstrate the idea of data template, think about a menu hung on the wall of a donut shop. While it is easy to just have prices and names, a better visualization of the menu would be, each donut having a small image next to it. Appetite does start with the eyes after all. This visual organization of data is what data template is all about. Data templates are most commonly used with a control based on `ItemsControl`, and while it is possible to use data templates with `ContentControl` as well, we won't deal with it in this book as it's hardly used.

Creating your first data template

Open Visual Studio 2010, and load the **Chapter3-DataTemplates** project from the downloadable content of the book at `www.packtpub.com`. The application is a small menu for a cakes factory and its content is quite simple—you have a `Grid` control with a background as the host of the application, a `TextBox` control for the header, a `ListBox` control for the content, and another `TextBox` control for the footer. The

ListBox control is bound to ObservableCollection of CakeEntities, which contains a title, an image URL, and a price. If you run the application right now, you'll get the result, as shown in the following screenshot:

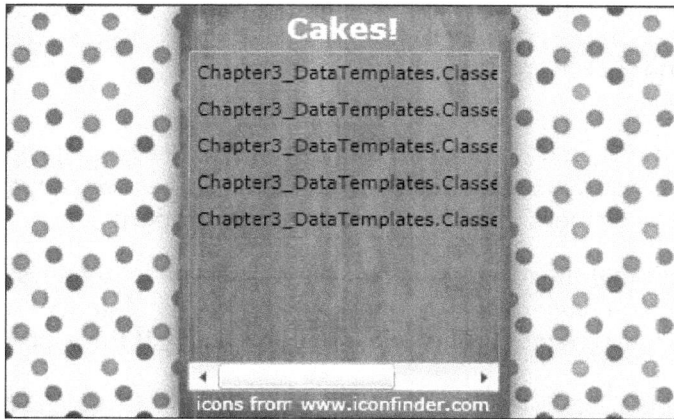

As the ListBox control doesn't have a template, it uses its default ToString method, and the result is the name of the entity we are binding to ListBox. As this is obviously not what we are after, it's time to define a data template for this application.

As we don't have any other ListBox controls in this application, we will define the data template on the element level. Open the MainPage.xaml file and look for opening the ListBox element. Add the following code snippet below it:

```
<ListBox.ItemTemplate>
<DataTemplate>
        <StackPanel Orientation="Horizontal">

        </StackPanel>
    </DataTemplate>
</ListBox.ItemTemplate>
```

By using the ItemTemplate attached property, we are telling the ListBox element that it has a data template to look into before it renders the items in ListBox. As with every template, we have to define the root element for the template, and in our case we are using a horizontally-oriented StackPanel. If you run the application right now, you'll notice that ListBox doesn't show anything. The reason for that is that we defined a data template for ListBox that is currently empty. No binding has been done for the content and, thus, Silverlight has got nothing to show. Let's add some content to our template by adding the following code snippet inside the template's root StackPanel:

```
<Image Source="{Binding ImageUrl}" Width="17" Height="17"
Margin="0,0,4,0"/>
<StackPanel>
        <TextBlock Text="{Binding Name}" Style="{StaticResource
CakeName}"/>
            <TextBlock Text="{Binding Price,StringFormat='Price: {0}$'}"
Style="{StaticResource CakePrice}"/>
    </StackPanel>
```

The template contains an image, which is bound to the `ImageUrl` property of the `CakeEntity` class, a `TextBlock` element bound to the `CakeName` property, and another `TextBlock` element bound to the `CakePrice` property.

Always remember that the most important thing in a data template is binding. Without binding, you have no way of showing any kind of data. We will dive deep into binding in a later chapter of this book, so don't worry if the concept isn't familiar to you.

Build and run your application, and you should get the result, as shown in the following screenshot:

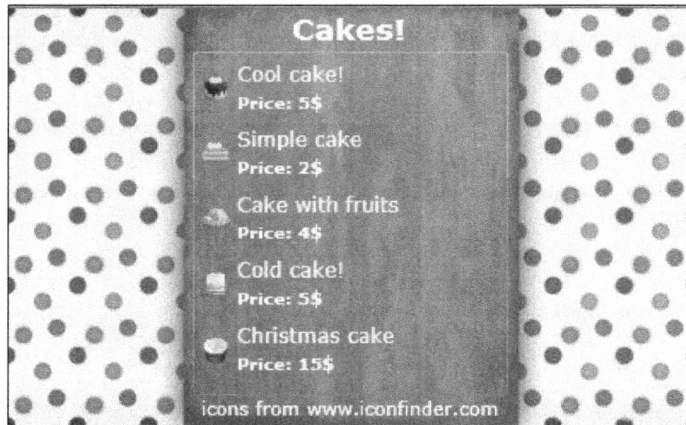

This is the true power of data templates—taking textual properties, and using binding and XAML, transforming them into a rich graphical representation.

DataForm templates

The `DataForm` control was introduced to Silverlight in order to allow easy creation and manipulation of rich data forms. The `DataForm` control enables you to display, edit, and update data by using different data templates for each operation. While we are going to focus on templating `DataForm` in this chapter, we will discuss it in more detail later in this book. In order to use the `DataForm` control, you have to drag it from the toolbox.

Open the **Chapter3-DataForm** project from the companion downloadable projects of this book at www.packtpub.com.

Within the project, we have a simple `DataForm` control that is bounded using code behind the collection of the `NewFormEntity` objects.

Build and run the project, and you should get the result, as shown in the following screenshot:

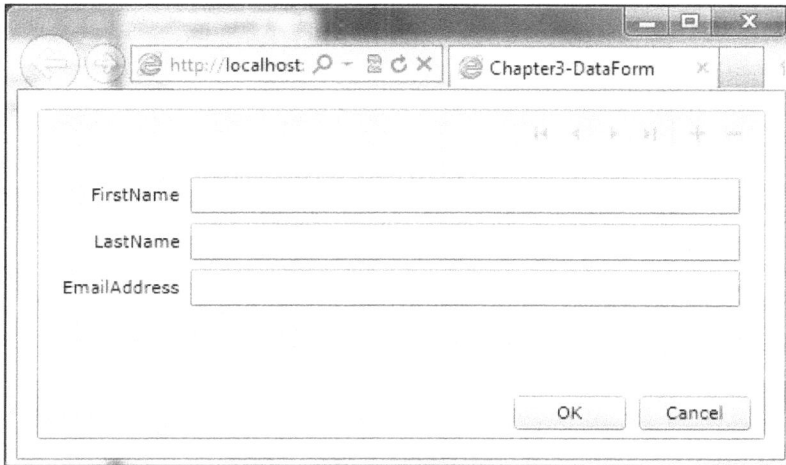

This is the default look of the data template. It can also be called `NewItemTemplate` or `CreateTemplate`, because it is used when a user wishes to add a new item using `DataForm`. Let's make some changes to `CreateTemplate`. Open `MainPage.xaml`, and look for the `DataForm` element. Under that element, add the following code snippet:

```
<toolkit:DataForm.NewItemTemplate>
<DataTemplate>
    </DataTemplate>
</toolkit:DataForm.NewItemTemplate>
```

By using the attached property of `NewItemTemplate`, we are adding that new template to the `DataForm` element. Other templates you may use are `EditTemplate`, which is the template used when the form is in editing mode, and `ReadOnlyTemplate`, which is used when the item that is displayed is set to read-only. Now that we have specified to `DataForm` that we wish to have a new item template, it's time to define it. Add the following code snippet under the `DataTemplate` element:

```
<StackPanel>
<StackPanel Orientation="Horizontal">
    <toolkit:DataField>
        <TextBox Text="{Binding FirstName, Mode=TwoWay}"
MinWidth="200"/>
    </toolkit:DataField>
    <toolkit:DataField>
        <TextBox Text="{Binding LastName, Mode=TwoWay}"
MinWidth="200"/>
    </toolkit:DataField>
    </StackPanel>
    <toolkit:DataField>
        <TextBox Text="{Binding EmailAddress, Mode=TwoWay}" />
    </toolkit:DataField>
</StackPanel>
```

The template is quite simple—we have a root StackPanel element, then we have another StackPanel, which has its Orientation property set to Horizontal. Then, for each field we wish to display in the form, we will use the DataField element and TextBox inside of it.

You're not limited to use only the TextBox control. If you have a property that is better suited for another control, such as a CheckBox, you can use it in the template as well.

> You may notice that unlike other bindings we used so far in this book, the DataForm binding is a bit different. The use of Mode=TwoWay means that the binding goes bidirectional from the entity to TextBox and also from TextBox back to the entity. We will discuss binding and all its modes later in this book.

If you build and run your application now, you will see that the form looks quite different:

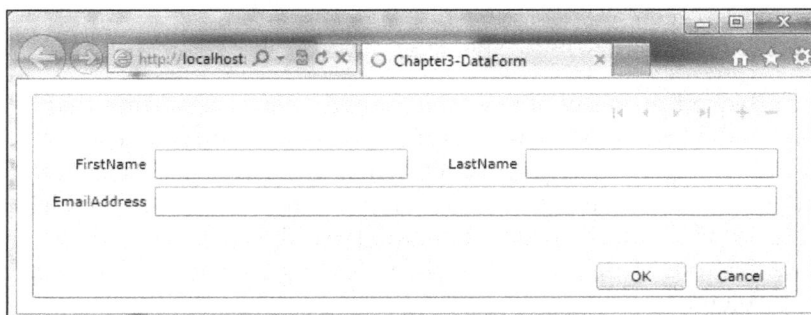

Remember, your template is only as wild as you imagine it, and by using Silverlight, you have the complete freedom of design for it. I would highly recommend you to read Shawn Wildermuth's excellent post on *DataForm Templates* at `http://wildermuth.com/2009/05/25/DataForm_Templates`.

Using UserControl as a data template

A nice trick you can do in Silverlight is to use `UserControl` as your data template. This can be helpful if you are working with designers, who use Microsoft Blend 4 to create their data templates. Using this method, you can work on the code and wire up the control while the designer works on the UI and graphics.

To demonstrate the process, open the **Chapter3-UserControlDataTemplate** project in Visual Studio 2010. The project contains an entity with a single property of the `SolidColorBrush` type, which we will use as the bound property for a rectangle's fill.

Right-click on the Silverlight project, and select **Add** and then **New Item**. Select **Silverlight User Control**, and name it **DataTemplateControl**. Open the `Datatemplatecontrol.xaml` file, and add the following line of code between the opening and closing `Grid` elements:

```
<Rectangle Fill="{Binding Brush}" Height="20" Width="20"/>
```

We defined a 20x20 pixels `Rectangle` element with the `Fill` property bound to the `Brush` property. This property comes from the entity class that we will create later.

Build your application so that Silverlight will recognize your new user control and open up `MainPage.xaml`.

To add a user control to the page, first we have to add its namespace, as we discussed in the previous chapter. Add the following line of code at the top of your `UserControl` element:

```
xmlns:local="clr-namespace:Chapter3_UserControlDataTemplate"
```

Now let's add `ListBox` to this page. Add the following code snippet under the `Grid` element:

```
<ListBox Height="200" Width="200" x:Name="colorsListBox">
<ListBox.ItemTemplate>
   <DataTemplate>

      </DataTemplate>
</ListBox.ItemTemplate>
</ListBox>
```

There's nothing that we haven't seen so far. We've added `ListBox` and defined the schema for the data template. All we need to do now is add the user control to act as our data template!

Add the following line of code between the `DataTemplate` elements:

```
<local:DataTempalteControl/>
```

Build and run your application, and you should get the following result:

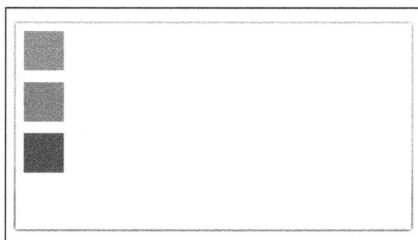

We've just created a `ListBox` control with `UserControl` as its data template. The way it works is pretty straightforward — the `UserControl` contains a rectangle of a specific size that has its `Fill` property bound to a property named `Brush`. When the `UserControl` is added as the data template of the `ListBox`, it receives the `Brush` property from the collection of the `EntityClass` items that the `ListBox` control has set as its data source.

Manipulating visuals

Silverlight, being an RIA platform allows you to manipulate your UI objects in far more ways than simple size or position. You can skew an element, rotate it across its x and y positions, scale it, and even emulate 3D effects by using the perspective transform.

Getting ready

Before we dive into manipulating objects, we need to have an object to manipulate.

Open Visual Studio 2010 and create a new Silverlight 4 project named **Chapter3-ManipulateVisuals**. Once the project is ready, add a `Rectangle` object to `MainPage.xaml` using the following code snippet:

```
<Rectangle Height="100" Width="100" Fill="Red">
</Rectangle>
```

This rectangle will be the base of all our visual manipulations. Build and run your application, and you should get the result, as shown in the following screenshot:

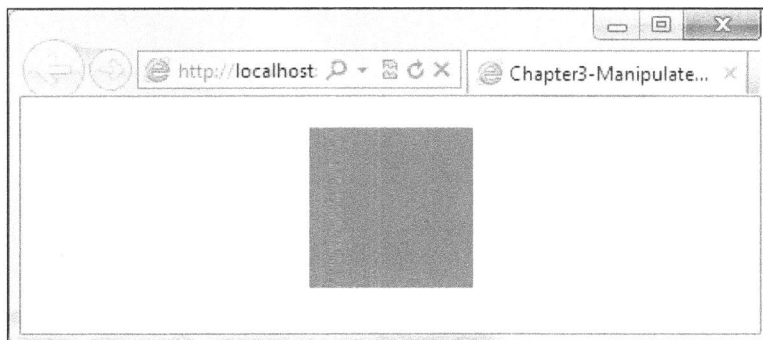

Skew transform

The first transformation we are going to discuss is skew transformation. Skew takes a rectangular element and turns it into a parallelogram by skewing the values of the x or y axis by a specified degree. Let's skew our rectangle 45 degrees on the x axis. Add the following code snippet between the opening and closing Rectangle elements:

```
<Rectangle.RenderTransform>
<SkewTransform AngleX="45"/>
</Rectangle.RenderTransform>
```

By using the RenderTransform attached property, we can define a transform of our choice. In our example, we have used the SkewTransform element, and set its AngleX property to 45 degrees. By using the AngleX property, we have moved the x axis 45 degrees to the right from the top-left corner of the object:

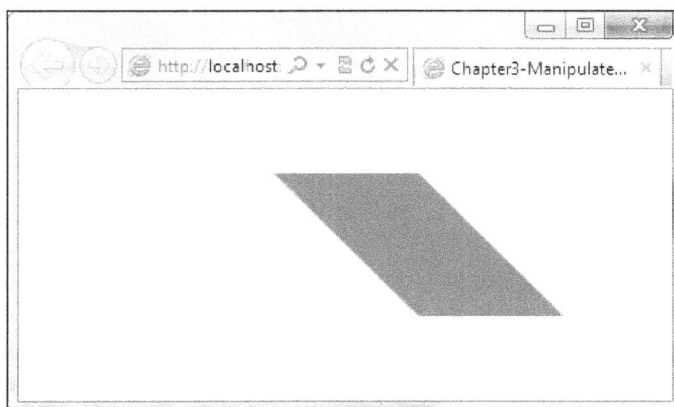

Change the `AngleX` property to `AngleY`, and you'll see that now the y axis moves by 45 degrees as well.

Other properties you could use with the `SkewTransform` element are `CenterX` and `CenterY`, which specify the origin point for the skew transformation.

Rotate transform

Using the rotate transform allows us to rotate an object clockwise around a specific point and by a specified angle. By default, rotations are done around the top-left corner. The `RotateTransform` element exposes three main properties—`Angle`, `CenterX`, and `CenterY`. `Angle` allows us to set the angle by which we wish to rotate our object. `CenterX` and `CenterY` allow us to set the point around which the object should rotate.

To demonstrate the use of rotation, replace the line of code having the `SkewTransform` element in the preceding section with the following line of code:

```
<RotateTransform Angle="-45"/>
```

By setting the `Angle` property to `-45`, we are rotating the rectangle -45 degrees from the top-left corner. Build and run your application, and you should get the result, as shown in the following screenshot:

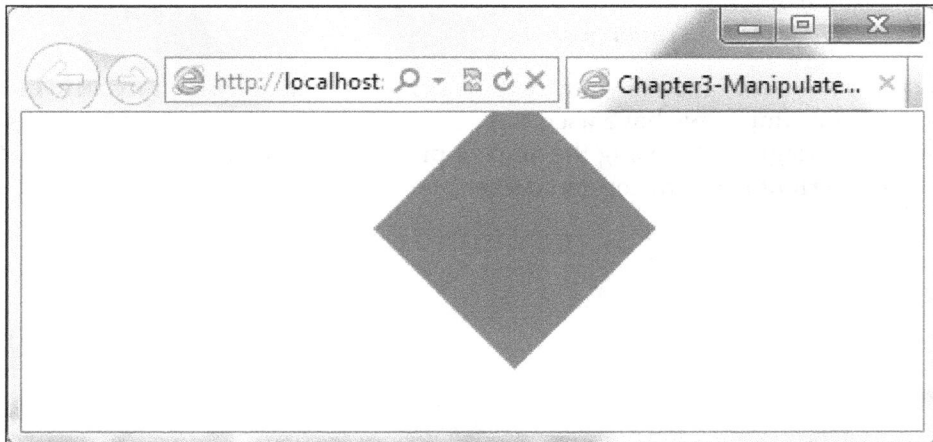

Here's a small quiz. Can you guess what happens if you transform an object 180 degrees? What about 360 degrees?

Scale transform

The scale transform, as its name suggests, allows us to expand or contract an object, an effect similar to zooming in or out from an object.

The ScaleTransform element exposes four main properties — ScaleX, ScaleY, and the two usual properties CenterX and CenterY.

ScaleX and ScaleY represent the amount by which you wish to scale the object. For example, setting both to 1 will show no effect because you multiply the size by 1. Set these properties to 2, and you will get an object twice as big as its original size. Just with the other transformations, the default point of origin is the top-left corner, but this can be changed very easily by setting the CenterX and CenterY properties to the desired point. Replace the line of code having the RotateTransform element in the preceding section with the following line of code:

```
<ScaleTransform  ScaleX="2" ScaleY="2" />
```

If you build and run your application now, you will get the result, as shown in the following screenshot:

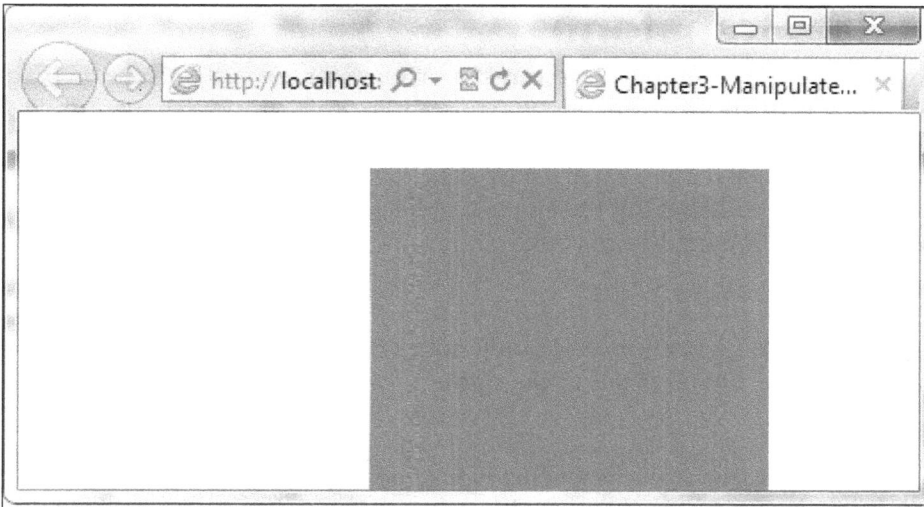

The rectangle is indeed twice as big, but because we haven't set the CenterX and CenterY properties, the sizing took place from the top-left corner. If we wish to position the rectangle at the center again, all we have to do is set these properties as follows:

```
<ScaleTransform  ScaleX="2" ScaleY="2" CenterX="50" CenterY="50" />
```

As the original height and width of our rectangle were 100, to make the scaling from the middle of the object and not the top-left corner, we have to set the center point to the middle of the object, in this case 50, 50:

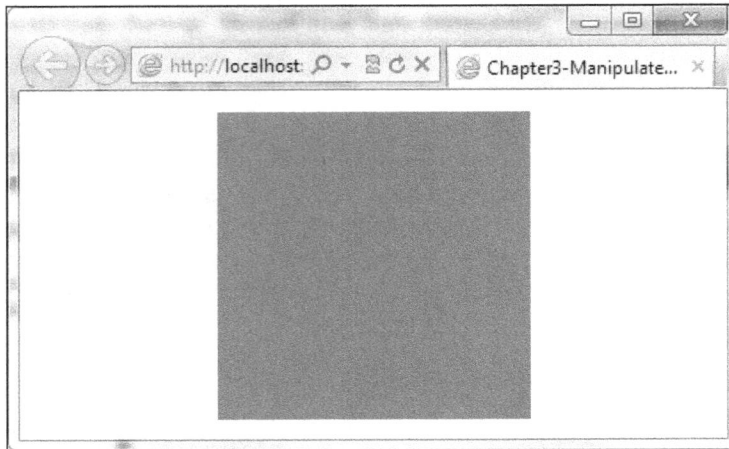

Translate transform

The translate transform allows us to transfer an element to another location based on the x and y properties. The element exposes two main properties—X and Y. Just like any other transformation, the default point of interaction for the translate transform is the top-left corner. Let's move our rectangle 50 pixels to the right. Replace the line of code having the ScaleTransform element in the preceding section with the following line of code:

```
<TranslateTransform X="50"/>
```

Build and run your application, and you'll notice the rectangle is no longer at the center of the screen, but 50 pixels to the right.

> To translate an element to the right or down positions, we use a positive value for the X and Y properties, whereas to translate an element to the left or up positions, we use a negative value for the X and Y properties.

Running your application now will result in the following screenshot:

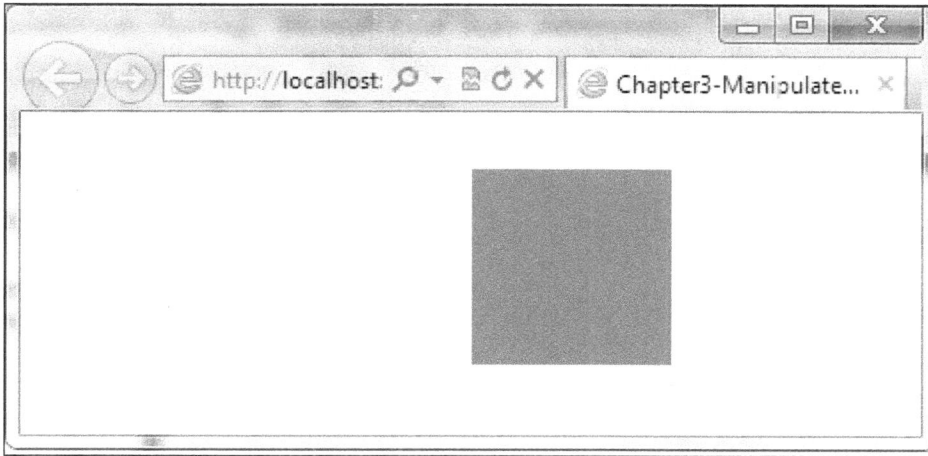

Perspective transforms

The perspective transforms group contains three main elements— PlaneProjection, Matrix3DProjection, and Matrix3D. Matrix3DProjection and Matrix3D are out of the scope for this book, so we will discuss the main member of the perspective transformation group—the PlaneProjection.

PlaneProjection exposes many properties used for 3D simulation. The main ones are as follows:

- RotationX, RotationY, and RotationZ: These properties represent the rotation of the object, in degrees.

- CenterOfRotationX, CenterOfRotationY, and CenterOfRotationZ: All of these properties represent the center of the rotation. The default value for all is 0.5.

The axes are set so that the positive x axis is pointing towards the right, the positive y axis is pointing towards the top, and the positive z axis is closer to you and the negative z axis is further away from you.

Let's demonstrate the projection in action. Remove the `Rectangle.`
`RenderTransform` element, and replace it with the following code snippet:

```
<Rectangle.Projection>
<PlaneProjection RotationY="45"/>
</Rectangle.Projection>
```

By using the `Projection` attached property, we are allowed to use the
`PlaneProjection` element, and in our example we have set its `RotationY`
property to 45. If you run the application, you will get the result, as shown
in the following screenshot:

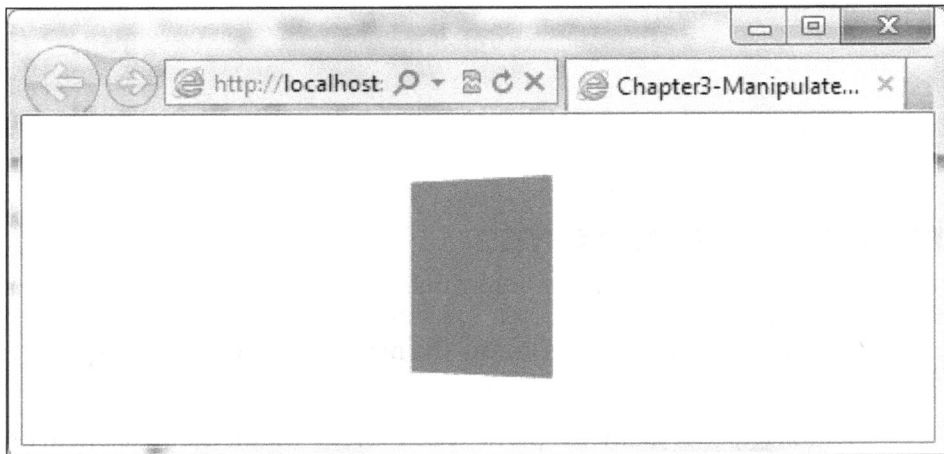

Your rectangle now has a 3D feel to it, doesn't it?

It is strongly encouraged that you check out Jaime Rodriguez's post on
PlaneProjection at `http://blogs.msdn.com/b/jaimer/archive/2009/06/03/`
`silverlight3-planeprojection-primer.aspx` to get a deeper understanding of
this awesome transformation technique, and Switch On The Code's post — *Silverlight
3 Tutorial – PlaneProjection and Perspective 3D* at `http://www.switchonthecode.`
`com/tutorials/silverlight-3-tutorial-planeprojection-and-perspective-`
`3d` for some more hands-on experience.

Grouping transformations together

If you wish to include several transformations together, you can't just write them
one after another under the `RenderTransform` attached property. What you can,
and should, do is group them together under the `TransformGroup` element.
Consider the following code sample:

```
<Rectangle Height="100" Width="100" Fill="Red">
<Rectangle.RenderTransform>
    <TransformGroup>
        <ScaleTransform ScaleX="1.5" ScaleY="1.5" CenterX="50"
        CenterY="50"/>
        <SkewTransform AngleX="20"/>
        <RotateTransform Angle="90"/>
    </TransformGroup>
</Rectangle.RenderTransform>
</Rectangle>
```

Running the preceding code will result in the following screenshot:

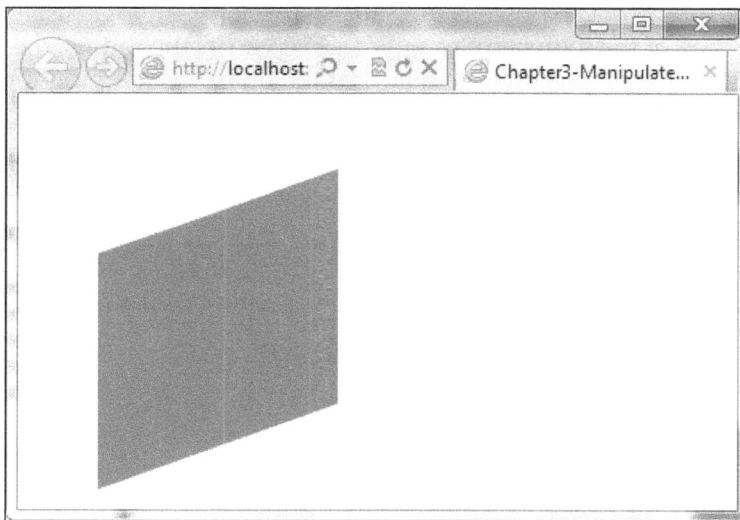

You can clearly see all the transformations being applied to this rectangle.

All of our samples in this topic were performed on a simple Rectangle element, but nothing is stopping you from trying them on other elements such as images, buttons, or even grids, data forms, and stack panels.

Pixel shaders

Silverlight 4 provides us with the ability to use pixel shaders in our applications. Pixel shaders are, in a nutshell, a set of instructions that calculate the color of pixels that are executed on the **graphics processing unit** (**GPU**). Silverlight comes with two prebuilt pixel shaders for blur and drop shadow, but it also gives you the option of building your own.

Building pixel shaders is out of the scope of this book, but if you are interested in the subject, make sure to check Channel 9's *SilverShader – introduction to Silverlight and WPF Pixel Shaders* article at `http://channel9.msdn.com/coding4fun/articles/ SilverShader--Introduction-to-Silverlight-and-WPF-Pixel-Shaders`.

Using these pixel shaders is quite straightforward. Add an `Image` element to your `MainPage.xaml` file, and use the following attached property for `Blur`:

```
<Image.Effect>
<BlurEffect Radius="10"/>
</Image.Effect>
```

If you run your application, you'll notice the image is quite blurred. The only property that `BlurEffect` exposes is the `Radius` property, and it is used to control how large the area of the blur samples will be. The bigger the radius, the blurrier would be the result. It is important to note that the more the computation needed to perform the blur (meaning the larger the radius is), the more likely it is to have a performance hit.

An image with a radius 10 blur effect would look similar to the following screenshot:

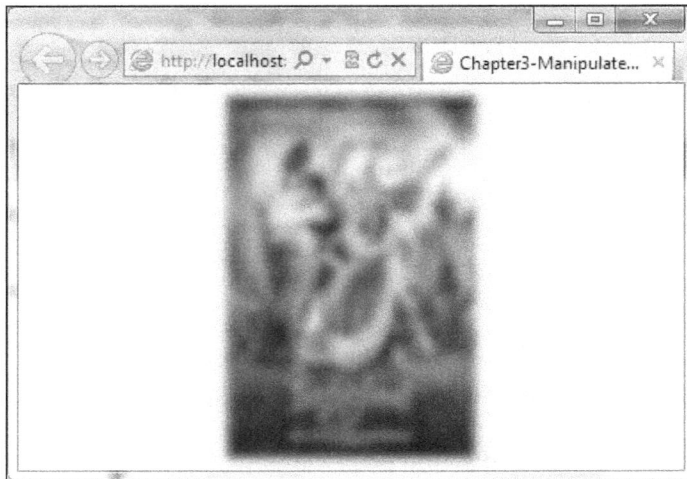

The other effect that Silverlight provides out of the box is the drop shadow effect. Unlike blur, drop shadow exposes five important properties as follows:

- `Color`: This represents the color of the drop shadow.

- `ShadowDepth`: This represents the distance, in pixels, of the shadow relative to the element it's being applied to. If not specified, it defaults to five pixels.

- `Direction`: This represents the angle, in degrees, where the shadow will lie relative to the element it's being applied to. If not specified, it defaults to 315 degrees, which would mean the lower-right corner.

- `BlurRadius`: This represents the blurriness of the shadow. It defaults to 0.5.

- `Opacity`: This specifies how opaque the shadow will be. It expects a double type of value between 1 and 0, but defaults to 1 if not directly specified.

To add a nice subtle shadow to your image, replace the line of code having the `BlurEffect` element with the following line of code:

```
<DropShadowEffect BlurRadius="20" Opacity="0.8"/>
```

Build and run your application, and you should notice a nice subtle blue around your image.

> Effects are not limited to being set using XAML. You could set an effect in the code behind as well as using the following syntax: `<image name>.Effect = new BlurEffect();` for example.

Animating visuals

Animation is a first-class citizen in Silverlight. In LOB type of applications, animations can be used to enhance the user experience. Think about page transitioning in your application. Would users rather have a dull "screen-for-screen" type of transition where the pages just replace one another, or a nice subtle smooth transition where the pages slide, one next to another?

In Silverlight, the animation framework is time based. That means that you set a start and end position, and Silverlight takes care of the interpolation. Animations are best created using Microsoft Expression Blend and not directly with code. Every animation must have a **storyboard**, which is an object that is responsible for organizing and controlling the animation defined within it. Storyboard is the root of all animations, and for this reason, we will begin our discussion on this subject with it.

Creating storyboards

A Storyboard must contain an animation. Silverlight offers three types of animations we can use — `ColorAnimation`, `DoubleAnimation`, and `PointAnimation`. `ColorAnimation` is used when you wish to transition colors (the name does suggest that, doesn't it?). For example, if you want a button to transition from blue to red over a period of one second when a user hovers over it, you would use the `ColorAnimation` object. When you wish to apply an animation for an integer-based or double-based property such as height, width, and so on, you would use the `DoubleAnimation` object. Lastly, for moving things around using the X and Y values, we can use the `PointAnimation` object. Let's create our first animation right now. Create a new Silverlight project in Visual Studio 2010, and name it **Chapter3-Animations**. Once created, add the following code snippet to your `MainPage.xaml` file:

```
<Rectangle Height="200" Width="200" Fill="Red" x:Name="myRect"
MouseEnter="Rectangle_MouseEnter" MouseLeave="myRect_MouseLeave">
</Rectangle>
```

This is just a regular rectangle we are used to seeing from other examples, but it has two events attached to it — `MouseEnter` and `MouseLeave`. Now, it's time to define the animation itself. Add the following code snippet between the `Rectangle` opening and closing elements:

```
<Rectangle.Resources>
<Storyboard x:Name="myColorAnim">
        <ColorAnimation Storyboard.TargetName="myRect"
        Storyboard.TargetProperty="(Fill).(SolidColorBrush.Color)"
            From="Red" To="Green" Duration="0:0:0.5" />
    </Storyboard>
    <Storyboard x:Name="myColorAnimRev">
        <ColorAnimation Storyboard.TargetName="myRect"
        Storyboard.TargetProperty="(Fill).(SolidColorBrush.Color)"
            From="Green" To="Red" Duration="0:0:0.5" />
    </Storyboard>
</Rectangle.Resources>
```

We have defined two storyboards for this rectangle. The first goes from red to green, and the other goes back from green to red. The important things to notice in this code are the `Storyboard.TargetName` and `Storyboard.TargetProperty` properties. The first one defines which element the `ColorAnimation` is aimed at, `myRect Rectangle` in our case. The second property defines what we are animating. We want to animate the color of the fill the rectangle has. We can't simply input `Fill` as the property, because it is not true. We don't want to modify the `Fill` property; we want to modify the color of the `Fill` property, and as the color in our case is a solid color (red), we use the `(Fill).(SolidColorBrush.Color)` value. If you run the application now, you'll notice the color still hasn't changed. The reason for that is because we never told the animation when to start. This is exactly why we have defined the `MouseEnter` and `MouseLeave` events for our `Rectangle`. Switch over to the `MainPage.xaml.cs` file, and add the following event handlers:

```
private void Rectangle_MouseEnter(object sender, MouseEventArgs e)
{
myColorAnim.Begin();
}

private void myRect_MouseLeave(object sender, MouseEventArgs e)
{
myColorAnimRev.Begin();
}
```

All that the event handler is doing is using the `Begin` method of the desired `Storyboard` to start the animation. Build and run your application now, and you should see the rectangle changing its color when you hover over and out of it.

Another option to trigger an animation is to use the `Triggers` attached property of the element we wish to animate. This method supports only the `Loaded` event and as such is perfect to use when you wish to start an animation as soon as an object is loaded.

Let's alter our rectangle to load the animation with `Triggers` instead of event handlers. Change your `Rectangle` code as follows:

```
<Rectangle Height="200" Width="200" Fill="Red" x:Name="myRect">
<Rectangle.Triggers>
        <EventTrigger RoutedEvent="Rectangle.Loaded">
        <BeginStoryboard>
            <Storyboard x:Name="myColorAnim">
            <ColorAnimation Storyboard.TargetName="myRect"
            Storyboard.TargetProperty="(Fill).(SolidColorBrush.Color)"
            From="Red" To="Green" Duration="0:0:0.5" />
            </Storyboard>
        </BeginStoryboard>
        </EventTrigger>
</Rectangle.Triggers>
</Rectangle>
```

By using the `EventTrigger` element, we can specify an event to catch. Currently, only the `Loaded` event is supported so we chose to use it. Right below it, we use the `BeginStoryboard` element, and from there, it's business as usual. You will add a regular `Storyboard` to hold your animation.

Build and run your application now, and you'll see that the rectangle has instantly turned green.

Here's a little challenge for you. Try to switch `ColorAnimation` we defined in `Storyboard` with `DoubleAnimation`, which changes the size of the rectangle from 200 by 200 pixels to 400 by 400 pixels on mouse enter and back to 200 by 200 pixels on mouse leave. The solution will be added to the *Appendix* of this book.

Controlling the storyboard

Controlling your storyboard is as simple as it gets. While you have the usual stop, play, pause, and resume, you can also react when a storyboard ends.

Controlling the storyboard is done via code behind. By using the name of the `Storyboard` object, you can call the `Stop`, `Begin`, `Pause`, and `Resume` methods. We have already seen how to use the `Begin` method in the previous topic where we wanted to start the animation in the event handlers.

If you wish to perform an action when the animation is finished, simply attach the `Completed` event to your `Storyboard` either by code or XAML. To demonstrate the use of the `Completed` event, change your `myColorAnim` element as follows:

```
<Storyboard x:Name="myColorAnim" Completed="myColorAnim_Completed">
```

In your `MainPage.xaml.cs` file, add the following event handler:

```
private void myColorAnim_Completed(object sender, EventArgs e)
{
myColorAnimRev.Begin();
}
```

If you build and run your application now, you'll see that as soon as the first animation has finished playing, the second one (the one that reverses the color back to red) kicks in.

Repeating and reversing storyboards

Having to call an event receiver and fire up another storyboard, just so that we can reverse the animation we've created, looks a little downing. For this exact case, we have a special property called `AutoReverse` for our storyboard. If you set the `AutoReverse` property to `True` on any `Storyboard` element, the animation will automatically play back once done! Change your `Storyboard` element as follows:

```
<Storyboard x:Name="myColorAnim" AutoReverse="True" >
```

Hover over your rectangle now, and you'll see that the animation plays and reverses back to where it started.

Now comes the question of repeating. What if I want to repeat my animation over and over again? This is where the `RepeatBehavior` property comes to your aid. This property allows you to set how many times you wish your animation to repeat (for example, 1, 5, 100 times). If you want it to just keep on going, you can set this property to `Forever`. Again, change your storyboard as follows:

```
<Storyboard x:Name="myColorAnim" AutoReverse="True"
RepeatBehavior="Forever" >
```

Run your application now, and you should see that your animation plays, then reverses, and then repeats itself over and over again until you close the browser window.

Implementing easing functions

As cool as Silverlight animations are, they do seem unnatural at times. The reason for that is the lack of easing. Easing provides a way to make your animation less "flat" and boring. Using the easing functions provides your animation with acceleration and deceleration, or even a bouncy behavior. Easing functions have three modes of use—`EaseIn`, `EaseOut`, and `EaseInOut`. These modes determine how the easing function will be applied to the animation over the course of time. `EaseIn` and `EaseOut` are the exact opposites. While `EaseIn` affects the beginning of the animation, `EaseOut` affects the ending of it. Easing functions are better seen than read about and, thus, I strongly recommend that you visit Silverlight.net's demo application for easing functions over at `http://www.silverlight.net/learn/creating-ui/animation-and-easing/animations-%28silverlight-quickstart%29#easing_functions`.

Applying easing functions to your animation is best done via Microsoft Expression Blend 4, as it provides a graphical environment for creating and editing animations. However, it is perfectly ok to add them directly using XAML as well. Let's add `CubicEase` to our rectangle animation. First, change the animation duration from half a second to a second by replacing the value of the `ColorAnimation Duration` property to `0:0:1`.

Now, inside your `ColorAnimation` element, add the following code snippet:

```
<ColorAnimation.EasingFunction>
<CubicEase EasingMode="EaseInOut"/>
</ColorAnimation.EasingFunction>
```

We used the `EasingMode` property to set the mode to `EaseInOut`. Feel free to change it to `EaseIn` or `EaseOut` if you wish.

Build and run your application, and you should notice the animation looks much more natural. Try to play with the different easing functions to get a feel of the difference they make.

Configuring bitmap caching

Bitmap catching is one of the most requested features of Silverlight. This feature was introduced in Silverlight 3 and continued to exist in Silverlight 4. This feature's main use is for performance enhancement, by allowing visual elements to be cached as bitmaps once they have been rendered for the first time. Just like browser cache, once the visuals are cached, the framework will display them straight from cache instead of going through the entire rendering phase. To use bitmap caching, you have to first enable it on the Silverlight plugin level. We will discuss the plugin in details in the last chapter of the book, but for now you should know that Silverlight is rendered to an HTML page using an `object` tag (`<object>`) and that it is possible to add parameters to it. If you take a look at the last project we worked on, there are two projects in the solution—the Silverlight and the ASP.NET web project. Under the ASP.NET project (**Chapter3-Animations.Web**), open the **Chapter3-AnimationsTestPage.aspx** file and look for the `object` tag. Once found, locate the following line of code:

```
<param name="background" value="white" />
```

This is a parameter added to the plugin that defines the background color of the plugin area.

We will now add the bitmap catching parameter below it:

```
<param name="EnableGPUAcceleration" value="true" />
```

By adding this parameter, we are enabling the GPU acceleration feature of Silverlight and opening the way for the bitmap caching mechanism.

Now all we have to do is specify to Silverlight what we want to cache. To specify this requirement, all we have to do is set a property called `CacheMode` on the object we wish to cache. Let's cache our rectangle. Add the following property to the `Rectangle` element:

```
CacheMode="BitmapCache"
```

That's it. The rectangle is now cached. A few things to remember when using the bitmap caching mechanism are as follows:

- Currently, only the `BitmapCache` cache mode is supported.
- When applying a cache mode to an element, it not only caches the element itself but all its child elements as well.
- Caching is best used when you are using transformations on elements.

Try playing around with caching by adding more elements to the page, and then add and remove the caching mechanism. You'll see how caching affects performance in no time!

Implementing behaviors

Behaviors were introduced in Silverlight 3 and provide a new way of adding interactivity to UI elements without the use of code. **Behaviors** are reusable pieces of code that extend either a specific UI element (for example, `TextBox`) or a whole type of elements (for example, `FrameworkElement`). Behaviors are basically self-contained pieces of functionality that go along with the object they are attached to and react to its environment. Behaviors contain two important elements—`Trigger` and `Action`. `Trigger` elements are used to invoke an action. Take, for example the `PlaySoundAction` behavior that comes bundled with Expression Blend 4. When adding this behavior, you need to set a trigger (when will the sound be played) such as `MouseLeftButtonDown` or `Loaded`, and then set the action itself, which is what sounds to play when the trigger triggers.

One important role of behaviors is controlling storyboard animations. Let's see how we can control animations without the use of code behind!

Triggering storyboards by using behaviors

Adding behaviors using Blend 4 is as simple as it gets. Open a new Silverlight 4 project in Visual Studio 2010, and name it **Chapter3-Behaviors**. Add the following code snippet to your `MainPage.xaml` file:

```
<Rectangle x:Name="rectangle" Margin="32,79,183,92" Stroke="Black"
RenderTransformOrigin="0.5,0.5">
    <Rectangle.Fill>
        <LinearGradientBrush EndPoint="0.5,1" StartPoint="0.5,0">
            <GradientStop Color="Red" Offset="0"/>
            <GradientStop Color="#FFFF841C" Offset="1"/>
        </LinearGradientBrush>
    </Rectangle.Fill>
</Rectangle>
<Button Content="Play" HorizontalAlignment="Left" Height="32"
Margin="32,0,0,35" VerticalAlignment="Bottom" Width="90">
</Button>
```

Directly under the `UserControl` element, add the following storyboard:

```xml
<UserControl.Resources>
    <Storyboard x:Name="Storyboard1">
        <DoubleAnimationUsingKeyFrames
        Storyboard.TargetProperty="(UIElement.RenderTransform).
        (CompositeTransform.TranslateX)"
        Storyboard.TargetName="rectangle">
            <EasingDoubleKeyFrame KeyTime="0" Value="0"/>
            <EasingDoubleKeyFrame KeyTime="0:0:0.6" Value="160"/>
        </DoubleAnimationUsingKeyFrames>
    </Storyboard>
</UserControl.Resources>
```

The storyboard uses keyframes-based animation to move the rectangle to the right-hand side using translations.

Once done, right-click on **MainPage.xaml** and choose **Open in Expression Blend....**

The file will now open in Expression Blend 4. While there is a lot to talk about Expression Blend, this book isn't dedicated to the subject and, thus, I highly recommend you to buy one of the many books that discuss it in detail.

In Expression Blend, mark the button we just created, and then click on **Assets** and choose **Behaviors**, as shown in the following screenshot:

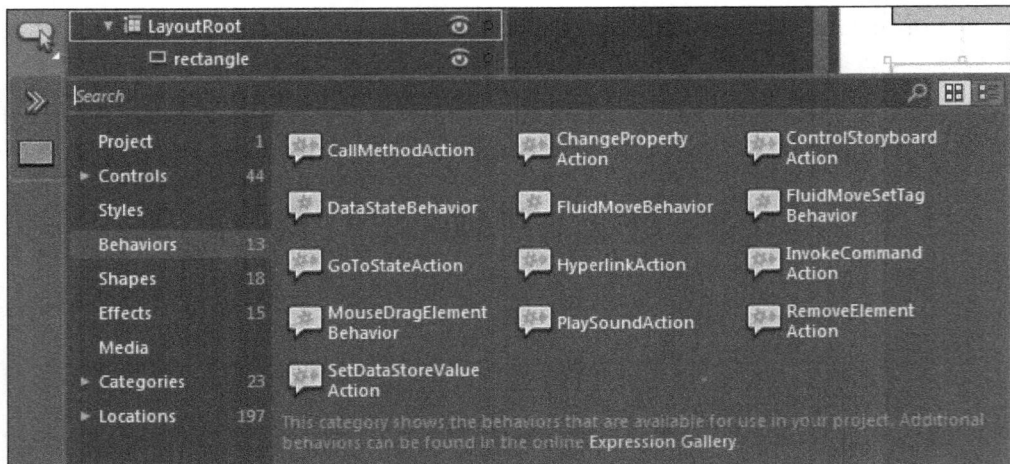

Drag the **ControlStoryboardAction** behavior from the board to the **Play** button.

On the right-hand side, you should notice the following menu:

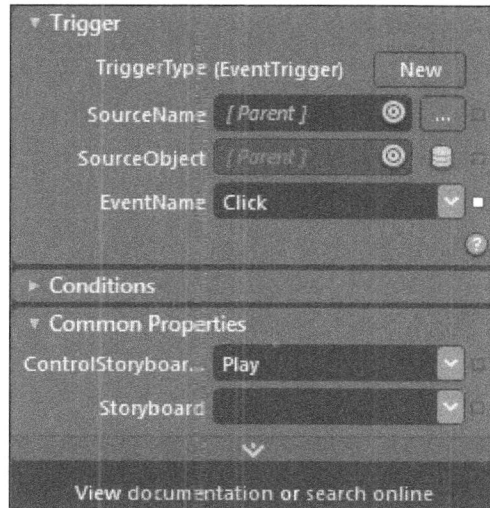

Here you can see the two parameters we discussed earlier—**Trigger** and **Action**.
Under the **Trigger** section, you can select which event will trigger this behavior.
In our example, we are going to leave it on **Click** as we want to react to the button's
`Click` event. Under **Common Properties**, you can select what's going to happen and
on which **Storyboard** element. Leave the **Play** action in place and under **Storyboard**,
select **Storyboard1**.

Build and run your application, and press the play button. You've managed to
trigger the animation using a behavior and not code behind.

But what if you want to have even more control and build your own behavior?
Well, you surely can. Let's create a behavior that will stop and play the animation
from the beginning every time you hover over the associated object.

Creating your own behavior

Before you create your own storyboard-related behavior, you must have something
to control. Create a new Silverlight 4 project in Visual Studio 2010 and name it
Chapter3-NewBehavior. In your project, create a new shape (like a rectangle) and
add animation to it (by creating a storyboard and then using one of the animation
types—`ColorAnimation`, `DoubleAnimation`, or `PointAnimation`). Once done,
right-click on the Silverlight project, select **Add** and then **Class**. Name the class
`ReplayAnimationBehavior`.

Add a reference in your project for `System.Windows.Interactivity.dll`.

In order to create a behavior, the first thing you should do with the class is tell it that it's going to be a behavior. Change your class declaration, so it will inherit from the `Behavior<T>` base class, where `T` stands for generic type. In our case, we are going to use `FrameworkElement`. Change your class declaration as follows:

```
public class ReplayAnimationBehavior : Behavior<FrameworkElement>
```

Each behavior consists of two main activities—`OnAttached` and `OnDetached`—which define what happens to the behavior once it's attached to an object and when it is detached, respectively. We want to react whenever the mouse hovers over the attached object, so in our attached property we are going to attach the `MouseEnter` event. Likewise, we are going to detach the event when the behavior is detached from the object.

Add the following methods to your behavior:

```
protected override void OnAttached()
{
base.OnAttached();
    this.AssociatedObject.MouseEnter += new
    MouseEventHandler(AssociatedObject_MouseEnter);
}

protected override void OnDetaching()
{
base.OnDetaching();
    this.AssociatedObject.MouseEnter -= AssociatedObject_MouseEnter;
}
```

Pay special attention to the object we are attaching the event to. Using `AssociatedObject`, you can get and set all of the properties of the object you are attaching the behavior to!

Now it's time to define the event handler. As this is a simple example, we are going to hardcode the name of the storyboard within the method. This shouldn't be done in a real production environment of course. Add the following event handler to your behavior:

```
void AssociatedObject_MouseEnter(object sender, MouseEventArgs e)
{
  (this.AssociatedObject.FindName("Storyboard1") as Storyboard).Stop();
    (this.AssociatedObject.FindName("Storyboard1") as Storyboard).
Begin();
}
```

The method is quite simple:

1. Find an element using the `FindName` method.
2. Cast it as a `Storyboard` object.
3. Then, stop and play the animation.

We now have a behavior! The last thing we need to do is attach it to an object.

Open `MainPage.xaml` and add the following namespaces, which represent the interactivity between DLL and our behavior:

```
xmlns:local="clr-namespace:Chapter3_NewBehavior"
xmlns:interactivity="clr-namespace:System.Windows.
Interactivity;assembly=System.Windows.Interactivity"
```

Build the application and attach the new behavior to your object using the following code snippet:

```
<interactivity:Interaction.Behaviors>
<local:ReplayAnimationBehavior/>
</interactivity:Interaction.Behaviors>
```

Build and run your application, and you should see your behavior in action every time you hover over the object.

Managing the visual state

Visual states define how a control looks in certain situations. Try to think about the default Silverlight `Button` control. Whenever you hover over it, it changes color. This change is an example of state, hover state in that case. The default look of a control represents its normal state. But in most cases, your control will have more than a single state. To help you manage these states, Silverlight provides you with the `VisualStateManager` element. This element manages the states and the transition between them. A state doesn't have to be a change of color. It can be used to change an object size, border or even to transform it using one of the transformations we discussed earlier.

Each state is identified by its `Name` and `GroupName` properties. `GroupName` defines the group of which the state belongs to. A question that often rises up at this point is why do I need to group states? Can t I just create a big group of states and put them all in there? The answer is "No".

Let's think about the `Button` control for a second. The button has many states—clicked, hover, focused, out of focus, and so on. A button can also be in more than one state at a time. When you click a button, you also have it in focus. The only way a button can be in more than one state at a time is if these states belong to different groups. This is the only way a button can show its clicked and focused states together.

Now, moving from one state straight to another, one would look unnatural and weird. This is why we have transitions. Transitions are represented by storyboards and allow you to 'smooth' things over between the states. Above all those, we have `VisualStateManager` that controls the states and their transitions.

Creating states and their transitions is done in Expression Blend 4. Let's create a new Silverlight 4 project in Visual Studio 2010 and name it **Chapter3-VisualState**. We will use this project now to demonstrate the use of `VisualStateManager`. Once the project is created, right-click on **MainPage.xaml** and select **Edit in Expression Blend...**.

Once in Blend, add a rectangle to the `MainPage.xaml` file and use some fill for its background. We will use a visual state to transition the fill. In Blend's upper-left corner, you can find the **States** tab. Click on it to switch to the state manager:

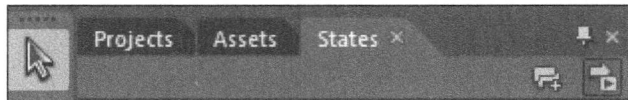

This is the main management area for **States**. Before we can create a state, we need to create a group to hold it. Click on the "add state group" button (pictured in the preceding screenshot at the bottom-right end of the image). Name the new group as **MyNewStateGroup** and change its **Default transition** time to **0.5s**. Your state should look similar to the following screenshot:

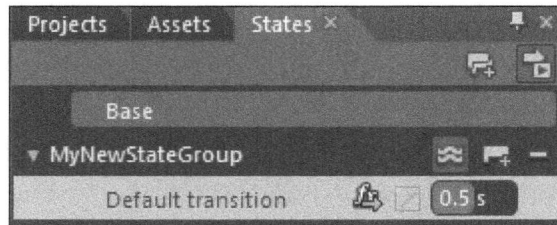

You've now created your first state group. As you noticed, we have given the group a **0.5s** of **Default transition**. That means that every state we have under this group will use this transition time when transited over.

Now let's create the individual states. We are going to have two states — Normal and LeftButton. Click on the "add state" button, located at the right end of the group name area. Name the new state as **Normal**. Now, click on the "add state" button again and name the new state as **LeftButton**. Once you create a new state, you may notice your screen has a red border around it. That means the state is recording your changes. Change the background of your rectangle to any other color. Once done, click on **Base**, located at the top part of the screen. You now have two states. To transition between them, we can use a behavior called GoToState. Just like before, click on the **Assets** button, select **Behaviors**, and drag the **GoToState** behavior to your rectangle. Leave the trigger on **MouseLeftButtonDown** and change the state to **LeftButton**. Your behavior settings area should look as follows:

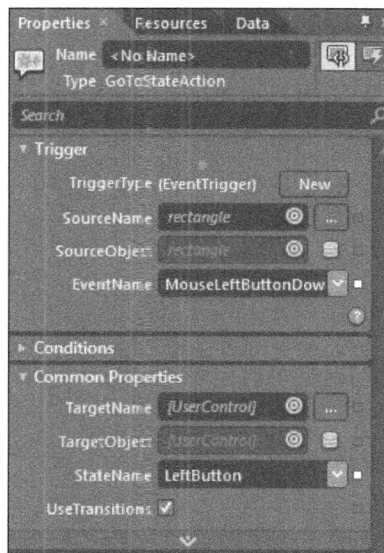

Build and run your application, and you should see how the rectangle changes the states with a **0.5s** transition.

Just like animations, you can use easing for a more natural transition between states. Next to **Default transition settings**, where you set the default transition time, you have the **EasingFunction** button. Click on it to choose an easing function for your transition.

Sometimes, you may need more control over your transitions and for that you can use the `VisualStateManager` object in your code behind. To demonstrate this object, switch back to Visual Studio 2010 and add a button to your `MainPage.xaml` file. Double-click on it to set its `Click` event hander. Add the following line of code to your `Click` event handler:

```
VisualStateManager.GoToState(this, "LeftButton", true);
```

By using the `VisualStateManager` object, we can get an object states group or go to a specific state by using the `GoToState` method as demonstrated previously. Run your application now, and you'll see that clicking the button also changes the state of the rectangle.

Play around with states and their transitioning. This is one of the most fun features Silverlight has to offer.

Test your knowledge

1. You are developing a web application using Silverlight 4. In your application, you have a `Grid` element. On the top of your page, you have the following code:

    ```
    <UserControl.Resources>
    <SolidColorBrush x:Key='GridBackground' Color='Black'/>
    </UserControl.Resources>
    ```

    The `Grid` element looks as follows:

    ```
    <Grid x:Name='LayoutRoot' Background='White'></Grid>
    ```

    What will be the background color of the `Grid`?

    a. Black

    b. White

    c. Impossible to know

    d. Azure

2. You are developing a Silverlight 4 application. Your application contains a custom control with various visual states. You need to change the visual state of the control to a visual state called 'Hover'. Which code should you use?

    a. `<VisualState ChangeTo='Hover'></VisualState>`

    b. `<Storyboard To='Hover'></Storyboard>`

    c. `VisualStateManager.GoToState(this,'Hover',true);`

   d. `<VisualState>`

       `<Storyboard ChangeTo='Hover'></Storyboard>`

       `</VisualState>`

3. You are tasked with creating an implicit style for `ComboBox` that specifies the following settings — `FontFamily = Arial, Foreground = Azure`. Which XAML fragment should you use?

   a. `<Style>`

       `<Setter Property='FontFamily' Value='Arial'/>`

       `<Setter Property='Foreground' Value='Azure'/>`

       `</Style>`

   b. `<Style x:Name='MyComboBox'>`

       `<Setter Property='FontFamily' Value='Arial'/>`

       `<Setter Property='Foreground' Value='Azure'/>`

       `</Style>`

   c. `<Style x:Key='MyCombobox' TargetType='ComboBox'>`

       `<Setter Property='FontFamily' Value='Arial'/>`

       `<Setter Property='Foreground' Value='Azure'/>`

       `</Style>`

   d. `<Style TargetType='Combobox'>`

       `<Setter Property='FontFamily' Value='Arial'/>`

       `<Setter Property='Foreground' Value='Azure'/>`

       `</Style>`

4. You are creating a Silverlight 4 based image gallery application. You need to apply manipulations to your image. Each image manipulation consists of a scale transform and rotation transform. Which of the following codes fulfill the requirement?

   a. `<Image.RenderTransform>`

       `<TransformGroup>`

       `<ScaleTransform ScaleX="0.7" ScaleY="0.7" CenterX="30" CenterY="30"/>`

       `<RotateTransform Angle="90"/>`

       `</TransformGroup>`

       `</Image.RenderTransform>`

b. `<ScaleTransform ScaleX="0.7" ScaleY="0.7" CenterX="30" CenterY="30"/>`

`<RotateTransform Angle="90"/>`

c. `<Image.RenderTransform>`

`<TransformGroup>`

`<ScaleTransform ScaleX="0.7" ScaleY="0.7" CenterX="30" CenterY="30"/>`

`</TransformGroup>`

`</Image.RenderTransform><Image.RenderTransform>`

`<TransformGroup>`

`<RotateTransform Angle="90"/>`

`</TransformGroup>`

`</Image.RenderTransform>`

d. `<Image.RenderTransform>`

`<ScaleTransform ScaleX="0.7" ScaleY="0.7" CenterX="30" CenterY="30"/>`

`<RotateTransform Angle="90"/>`

`</Image.RenderTransform>`

5. You are creating a Silverlight 4 application that relies heavily on visual manipulations. How can you improve the performance of your application?

a. Add the `EnableGPUAcceleration` parameter for the Silverlight object tag.

b. Set the `CacheMode` property of the visual elements to `BitmapCache`.

c. Add both the `EnableGPUAcceleration` and `BitmapCache` parameters to the Silverlight object tag.

d. Only the combination of answers a and b will improve the performance of the application.

Summary

In this chapter we went far beyond the basic UI capabilities of Silverlight. We started with styling our controls on three different levels—element, page, and global. We learned all about the hierarchy they work on and what overrides what. Once we had the firm understanding on styling, we went on to discuss the concept of templates and `TemplateBinding`. Templates are a base concept of Silverlight, and by using them right, you have a full control on how your UI looks. We then extended the templating concept with the use of data templates. Data templates are a concept you will deal a lot with when creating LOB applications. Taking data and visualizing it with templates is one of the most-used concepts Silverlight has to offer. Next in line were the transformations and animations where we discussed how to change an object look and how to animate it. We got to know the `Storyboard` object and all its properties, the different kinds of animation Silverlight offers, and we finished up the subject with our own animation. We summed up the chapter with behaviors and the `VisualStateManager` object. Both are frequently used features that allow you to control the UI without the use of code.

In the next chapter we are going to discuss the logic behind our application. We will work with events, consume services, create dependency properties, interact with attached properties, and finish off with implementing the `ICommand` interface.

4
Implementing Application Logic

So far, we have mainly dealt with the UI layer, but no application can be called an application without some logic. In this chapter, we are going to work mainly on the code behind layer of our application. We will discuss the concept of events, dive deep into dependency properties, interact with attached properties, and finish off with the ICommand interface. With so many exciting topics, we'd better get started right away!

In this chapter, we will cover the following topics:

- Handling events
- Consuming services asynchronously
- Working with background threads
- Working with dependency properties
- Interacting with attached properties
- Implementing ICommand

Handling events

If you have ever worked with events in any .NET-based language, you will feel right at home with Silverlight. Just like other .NET languages, you can select an element in the design area, and generate the event handler automatically using Visual Studio 2010. Of course, you are not limited to adding events only in the designer, you can attach events in the code behind as well.

The Silverlight event model is based upon the concept of bubbling events. This means that a control can raise an event that will be handled by its parent control. For example, if we have a Border control that has a StackPanel with images as its content, we can handle the MouseLeftButtonDown event on the border level, instead of having to handle it for each individual image. Bubbling is a type of routed events and the only one that Silverlight supports. **Bubbling** means going up the control hierarchy and while WPF does support the tunneling type of routed event (going down the hierarchy), Silverlight does not.

> A handful of events in Silverlight are routed events. For a full list of routed events, have a look at the MSDN documentation at http://msdn.microsoft.com/en-us/library/cc189018(v=vs.95).aspx#routed_events.

Silverlight does not support user-created bubbling events. That means that events you create on your own in Silverlight will never bubble.

Let's get the wheels rolling with understanding how to add events in Silverlight.

Adding events

As mentioned previously, we can add events on both the UI (XAML) layer and code behind. Adding events with XAML is as easy as typing the event and specifying its handler. For example, the following line of code demonstrates how to declare a Click handler for a button using XAML:

```
<Button x:Name="myBtn" Content="Click me!" Click="myBtn_Click"/>
```

By specifying the Click method in XAML, Visual Studio creates the event handler (myBtn_Click) in the code behind of the page. If you take a look in the code behind file, you will see the following method:

```
private void myBtn_Click(object sender, RoutedEventArgs e)
{
}
```

The other option of adding an event is purely on the code behind file. To attach an event handler for the Click event of a button, we can use the following line of code:

```
myBtn.Click += new RoutedEventHandler(myBtn_Click);
```

This will also get Visual Studio to create the event handler for us, in this case the event handler will be myBtn_Click, as specified in the declaration code.

Now that we know the basics of adding events in Silverlight, let's go ahead and understand the concept of routed events.

Handling routed events

As we have discussed earlier, when using routed events, the control that raised the event isn't necessarily the one that handles it. This means that the bubbling begins with the control that raised the event and stops when a control, somewhere up the hierarchy handles the event, or when it reaches the top-level control.

Control-specific events, for example the `Click` event for a `Button` control, will never be routed. If you think about that, it's pretty logical too—why make an event bubble up the control hierarchy if it can only be handled by a specific type of control?

To demonstrate routed events, create a new Silverlight project in Visual Studio 2010 and name it **Chapter4-HandleEvents**.

Open `MainPage.xaml` and replace your `LayoutRoot Grid` element with the following code snippet:

```
<Grid x:Name="LayoutRoot" Background="White"
MouseLeftButtonUp="LayoutRoot_MouseLeftButtonUp">
<Border x:Name="myBorder" Background="Aqua" Margin="20"
MouseLeftButtonUp="myBorder_MouseLeftButtonUp">
        <StackPanel Background="Red" x:Name="myStackPanel" Margin="20'
        MouseLeftButtonUp="myStackPanel_MouseLeftButtonUp">
        <Rectangle Margin="20' Height="180" x:Name="myRectangle"
        Fill="DarkSalmon"
        MouseLeftButtonUp="myRectangle_MouseLeftButtonUp"/>
    </StackPanel>
</Border>
</Grid>
```

What we have here is a hierarchy of controls, starting with the top-level `Grid`. Inside `Grid`, we have a `Border` child element, which in turn holds a `StackPanel` child element, which in turn holds a `Rectangle` child element. Each element has a `MouseLeftButtonUp` event attached to it. Before we can run the application, we have to handle these events, so switch over to your `MainPage.xaml.cs` file and add the following code snippet:

```
private void LayoutRoot_MouseLeftButtonUp(object sender,
MouseButtonEventArgs e)
{
results += "LayoutRoot handled the event";
    MessageBox.Show(results);
    results = "";
```

```
}
private void myBorder_MouseLeftButtonUp(object sender,
MouseButtonEventArgs e)
{
results += "myBorder handled the event\n";
}
private void myStackPanel_MouseLeftButtonUp(object sender,
MouseButtonEventArgs e)
{
results += "myStackPanel handled the event\n";
}
private void myRectangle_MouseLeftButtonUp(object sender,
MouseButtonEventArgs e)
{
results += "myRectangle handled the event\n";
}
```

Add the following private variable just above the MainPage constructor declaration:

```
private string results = "";
```

To recap, we have added all the event handlers for the events we declared in the UI layer. Each handler will add its name to the private string variable, and the LayoutRoot event handler will pop up a message box to the user with the content of the results variable.

Go ahead and build your application. Run it and you should get the following result:

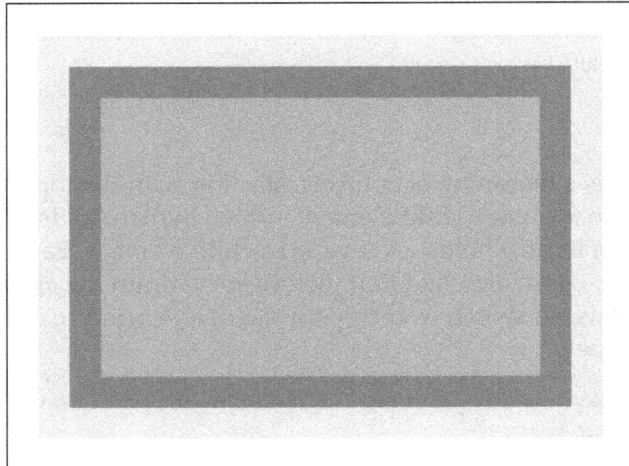

In the preceding diagram, we can see all of our controls. The white area is the top-level `Grid`, below it we have our `Border`, then `StackPanel`, and finally the salmon-colored `Rectangle`. Click on the `Rectangle` element and you should get the result, as shown in the following screenshot:

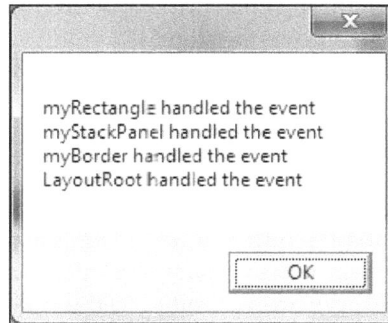

As you can see, the `MouseLeftButtonUp` event has bubbled up all the way to the `LayoutRoot` control, which handled it. We know it was the `LayoutRoot` event handler that finally handled it because it was the only event that popped out a message box for us. Click on any of the other controls and you will see that the event will always bubble up to the top-level control of the hierarchy.

Now you may ask yourself what if we wanted to stop the bubbling at the `Border` control?

The answer to that is very easy — we set the `Handled` property of the desired event handler's `MouseButtonEventArgs` to `true`!

Switch back to your `MainPage.xaml.cs` file and locate the `myBorder_MouseLeftButtonUp` event handler. Add the following line of code at the end of the method:

```
e.Handled = true;
```

Build and run your application, and you should notice that the pop-up message doesn't show up unless you click directly on the `Grid` control area (the white background). By setting the `Handled` property, we have successfully told Silverlight that the event was handled and there is no need for it to keep bubbling up.

The AddHandler method

The `AddHandler` method allows you to add a routed event handler for a specific routed event in the code behind layer. It also provides you with the option to always invoke the specified handler, even if the routed event was already marked as handled by another element along the control hierarchy. To demonstrate the `AddHandler` method, let's remove the `MouseLeftButtonUp` event from the `LayoutRoot` control's XAML declaration. Switch over to your `MainPage.xaml.cs` file and add the following line of code inside the constructor method:

```
this.AddHandler(UIElement.MouseLeftButtonUpEvent, new MouseButtonEvent
Handler(LayoutRoot_MouseLeftButtonUp), true);
```

The preceding line of code will attach the `MouseLeftButtonUp` event to the `this` object, which represents the current active page (`MainPage.xaml` in our example), using the `AddHandler` method. We aren't limited to the use of the `this` object when using the `AddHandler` method, and we could just as easily attach events using the `AddHandler` method to any `UIElement` control in the page (`LayoutRoot` for example).

The `AddHandler` method expects to get the following three arguments:

- The routed event we wish to attach. In our example, we wish to attach the `MouseLeftButtonUp` event.

- A reference to the handler method. As we already had the method in the page from the last example, we just pass its name as an argument.

- A Boolean value that indicates whether or not to handle events that were previously handled by other handlers. As we want to handle the `MouseLeftButtonUp` event within the page level, and we don't care if the event was already handled, we will pass `true` as an argument in our example.

In your code behind, add the following line of code to `myBorder_MouseLeftButtonUp`, `myStackPanel_MouseLeftButtonUp`, and `myRectangle_MouseLeftButtonUp`:

```
e.Handled = true;
```

By setting the `Handled` property of the `EventArgs` object to `true`, we tell the Silverlight framework that this event is handled and shouldn't bubble up the pipe.

Build and run your application. You should see that even though we haven't registered any event on `LayoutRoot` directly, and even though we handled the event on all of the controls, we still get the message box to pop up with the text inside of it.

Try removing the event declarations on all of the controls in your XAML file and see what happens. It should come as no surprise to you that the only event handler that gets called is the one we defined within the `AddHandler` method.

By using the `AddHandler` method on the page level, we basically register that event for any control in the page, so no matter if the control itself declares an event handler for this method or not, the `AddHandler` registered routed event will get called.

Consuming services asynchronously

Services (and most notably web services) are a main ingredient in today's LOB applications. Nowadays, you'll have a hard time finding an application that doesn't require access to data. While Silverlight doesn't offer a native client-side database solution (though you can find some great third-party solutions for that, such as Sterling DB), web services are your main route to access data.

Microsoft made sure that Silverlight is well equipped for the task of accessing data. Silverlight is able to consume services of ASMX, WCF, REST, POX, RSS, and others. Just like any other .NET language, Visual Studio will automatically generate a proxy class in our project when working with an ASMX or WCF service. This proxy class is in charge of making the actual connection to the service, and send and receive data to and from it. The one big difference between Silverlight and other .NET languages is that all communication in Silverlight happens asynchronously. This is a very logical functionality, because it makes sure that Silverlight's UI thread won't be locked down while waiting for a response from a service, which can happen in a synchronous model.

Now that we understand all the background information of the consuming services, let's get down to action and consume our first web service!

Adding your first service reference

Fire up Visual Studio 2010 and open the **Chapter4-ConsumeService** project from the downloadable book files from the Packt website. The project contains a Silverlight application and a WCF service, which reside inside the web project.

> We won't be discussing the details about the WCF service itself, as this is not the focus of our book, but I highly recommend you to pick up *Microsoft Windows Communication Foundation 4.0 Cookbook for Developing SOA* by Packt if you are interested in the subject.

Open the `MainPage.xaml` file and inspect it. You'll notice we have a `DataGrid` control added to the page. Once we hook up the web service to the project, the `DataGrid` control will display its result. To know what we are dealing with, open up the `ContactsService.svc` file in the web project. The service consists of a single method called `GetEmployees` and a class to represent the data we are displaying. Our Silverlight application will call this method and get back an `IEnumerable` control with a list of employees.

To add a service to your Silverlight project, simply right-click on the **Service References** folder under your Silverlight project and choose **Add Service Reference**.

We are now presented with two possible ways to add a service—enter its URL or let Visual Studio discover the service on its own. Visual Studio can only discover services that are added within the solution, and as our service is added under the web project, it fits into this term.

Click on **Discover**. You should get a screen similar to the following screenshot:

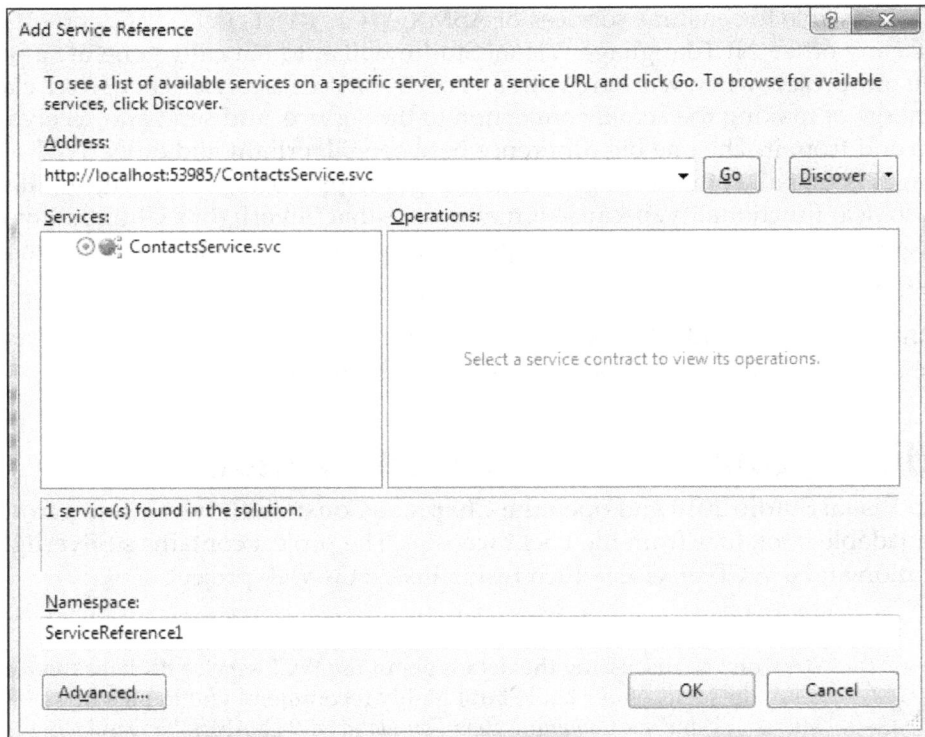

The service details are listed under the **Services** area. If you click on the little arrow to the left-hand side of the service file name, you'll be able to drill down and up until the point you can see all the available methods the service exposes.

Under **Namespace**, you can enter a string value that will represent the service class namespace in the project.

Change the default **ServiceReference**1 namespace to something more meaningful such as **EmployeesService** and click on **OK**.

Now that we have our service added, it's time to use it! Add the following line of code just above the constructor of `MainPage` in the `MainPage.xaml.cs` file:

```
private EmployeesService.ContactsServiceClient proxy = new
EmployeesService.ContactsServiceClient();
```

We can now use our new variable—`proxy`, to communicate with the web service. Silverlight web services only work asynchronously, so we have to declare a completed event handler, for when the method we wish to run finishes. The completed event name will always consist of the name of the method and `Completed` in the end. For example, in our web service we have a method called `GetEmployees`, therefore to attach an event handler for its completed event we will attach the `GetEmployeesCompleted` event handler. Add the following line of code inside the constructor of `MainPage`:

```
proxy.GetEmployeesCompleted += new EventHandler<EmployeesService.GetEm
ployeesCompletedEventArgs>(proxy_GetEmployeesCompleted);
```

We have attached a new event handler called `proxy_GetEmployeesCompleted` to the completed event of our desired method. In our example, there is only one action we wish to perform when the method finishes, and that is to set its result to the lonely `DataGrid` control that we added to `MainPage.xaml`. Add the following code snippet in the `proxy_GetEmployeesCompleted` event hander, so the method will look as follows:

```
void proxy_GetEmployeesCompleted(object sender, EmployeesService.
GetEmployeesCompletedEventArgs e)
{
ContactsGrid.ItemsSource = e.Result;
}
```

As can be seen from the preceding code, we bind the `ItemsSource` property of `DataGrid` to the `Result` property of the `e` object. This `e` object holds many properties in the context of our request. Other than `Result`, you have the `Error` property, which holds details about what went wrong during the asynchronous operation, or the `Canceled` property, which is a Boolean property that indicates whether the operation got canceled.

If we recap what we have done so far, we have added a service, attached an event handler for its completed event, and bound the results of the operation to a `DataGrid` control that was added to the UI layer. There is still one thing missing from our application that prevents it from actually doing something—calling the method on the web service. Calling a method is as simple as the following line of code:

```
proxy.GetEmployeesAsync();
```

Add the preceding line of code just after the event handler declaration and run your application. You should get the result, as shown in the following screenshot:

We have successfully added a service reference and handled its completed event.

Configuring service endpoint

In almost any work environment nowadays, you have a testing and production environment. When you deploy your solution to the testing environment, you will usually reference a service that runs in that environment. But what happens when you move your application to the production environment? You probably guessed it—the services you reference no longer exist. This is exactly the case that service endpoints come to solve. Whenever you add a new service reference via the **Add Service Reference** option in Visual Studio 2010, a new file named `ServiceReferences.ClientConfig` gets created in your Silverlight project. This file contains binding and endpoint configurations for the service you added. If you switch back to Visual Studio and open the `ServiceReferences.CliengConfig` file in the last project we worked on, you will get something similar to the following code snippet:

```
<client>
<endpoint address="http://localhost:53985/ContactsService.svc"
binding="customBinding" bindingConfiguration="CustomBinding_
ContactsService"
contract="EmployeesService.ContactsService" name="CustomBinding_
ContactsService" />
</client>
```

The preceding code snippet shows us the default endpoint that Visual Studio creates for us when we add a service reference, but that doesn't mean we can't interfere with the file a bit by ourselves. We know this endpoint represents our testing environment, so let's add an endpoint for our production environment too! Add the following code snippet just before the closing client element in your file:

```
<endpoint address="http://localhost:53985/ContactsService.svc"
binding="customBinding" bindingConfiguration="CustomBinding_
ContactsService"
contract="EmployeesService.ContactsService" name="ContactsService_
Production" />
```

While in our example the address is exactly the same, in real environments it would be different. Now that we have the new entry in the configuration file, how do we get Silverlight to act on it? Well, do you remember the code we used to initiate our service in the last example?

```
private EmployeesService.ContactsServiceClient proxy = new
EmployeesService.ContactsServiceClient();
```

The constructor for `ContractsServiceClient` is overloaded so it can accept parameters, as well as empty initiation. Change this code in your project to the following code snippet:

```
private EmployeesService.ContactsServiceClient proxy = new
EmployeesService.ContactsServiceClient("ContactsService_Production");
```

Build and run your application, and you'll notice that nothing has changed. Your application works just the same, but this time it uses the production service reference.

In a real project, you'll probably want a better solution than to hardcode these properties in your code. In this case, you can use Visual Studio's Configuration Build Manager to create new profiles but this is out of the scope for this book. If you are interested in the subject, take a look at the MSDN documentation for working with the configuration manager at `http://msdn.microsoft.com/en-us/library/kwybya3w(v=VS.100).aspx`.

Handling timeouts

The default timeout for a service call in Silverlight 4 is 30 seconds. While 30 seconds should be more than enough time for your request to return, sometimes you need a little more. To change the default timeout property, we set the `OperationalTimeOut` property of the web service proxy element's `InnerChannel`. The property accepts a `TimeSpan` value and sets it as the service request timeout. To change our service to a one minute timeout, add the following line of code just above the call to the `GetEmployees` method in your constructor:

```
proxy.InnerChannel.OperationTimeout = new TimeSpan(0, 1, 0);
```

Now your application will wait for a minute before it throws a time-out exception.

Cross-domain networking

Silverlight implements a strict cross-domain policy when accessing assets like web services over the network. In order to appear more secure, Silverlight, just like Adobe Flash, restricts the network connections to only be able to connect to resources on the same domain as the Silverlight application. For example, if our application runs on http://intranet/, it will only be able to consume web services that run on that exact domain.

The one exemption to this rule is services that host what is known as a policy file. This policy file is basically an XML file that defines resources, the services expose to the domains they trust. The `clientaccesspolicy.xml` file defines these policies and has to be placed at the root folder of the hosting domain. The file is only a valid policy file if placed in the root folder. Any other location will be ignored by Silverlight. A simple implementation of this file looks like the following code snippet:

```xml
<?xml version="1.0" encoding="utf-8"?>
<access-policy>
    <cross-domain-access>
        <policy>
            <allow-from http-request-headers="*">
                <domain uri="*"/>
            </allow-from>
            <grant-to>
                <resource path="/" include-subpaths="true"/>
            </grant-to>
        </policy>
    </cross-domain-access>
</access-policy>
```

The preceding code snippet is in an example of a minimum security `clientaccesspolicy.xml` file as it allows access to any resource on the server to any requesting domain. You can adjust the file to fit your security needs quite easily using the provided properties. You can read more about the `clientaccesspolicy.xml` file over at MSDN — `http://msdn.microsoft.com/en-us/library/cc645032(v=vs.95).aspx`.

Working with background threads

Threading is a well-known feature to push time consuming tasks to a separate thread. Silverlight, by default, is running our code in the UI thread, which means that if we have a method that takes time to finish, the UI thread will be blocked and won't allow interaction until the method finishes running. By pushing this time consuming method to a different thread, the method will still take time to complete, but the UI thread won't be blocked, and the user can keep interacting with it while the method computes.

While Silverlight doesn't offer all of the threading options that the full .NET framework offers, it's still powerful enough to drive multithreaded applications. One important aspect you have to remember when working with threads is that your code runs in a whole other environment than your UI, and as such you cannot access any of the elements in the UI thread. Don't fear though; a workaround for this will be shown shortly.

Spawning a background thread to execute code

The `BackgroundWorker` class of Silverlight provides us an easy way to run time-consuming code on a background thread. Moving time consuming calculations to this background thread will free our UI thread from freezing, and give our users the sense of interactivity that they are expecting. The `BackgroundWorker` class provides two important properties for interacting with it as follows:

- `WorkerSupportsCancellation`: A Boolean property indicating whether the background operation can be cancelled or not
- `WorkerReportsProgress`: A Boolean property indicating whether the background operation should report its progress or not

But these properties aren't the reason for which we have gathered here today. The one most important aspect of the `BackgroundWorker` class is, without a doubt, the `DoWork` event handler.

This event handler is where you run your resource hog code on the background thread. If we wish to report progress from the DoWork event handler to the calling process, we call the ReportProgress method, passing it a completion percentage from 0 to 100. Take note though, if we set the WorkerReportProgress property of the BackgroundWorker class to false, the ReportProgress method will throw an exception. To pass data back to the calling process (which is basically the whole point of this event handler), we set the Result property of the DoWorkEventArgs object, which is passed to the event handler. We can read this value when the RunWorkerCompleted event is raised, at the end of the operation. Let's get a first-hand impression on how to use this awesome feature!

Creating your first BackgroundWorker

To get started, fire up Visual Studio 2010, and load the **Chapter4-BackgroundWorker** project from the training files. The project right now is nothing more than a header and a vertical StackPanel consisting of a TextBlock element and a ProgressBar element. We will use the ProgressBar element to show the progress of our background worker in a nice graphical way. Perform the following steps:

1. Switch over to the MainPage.xaml.cs file and add the following using command:

   ```
   using System.ComponentModel;
   ```

2. Next, add the following private variable:

   ```
   private BackgroundWorker _bw;
   ```

   This will be our BackgroundWorker object. We will initiate it under the Loaded event handler.

3. Inside the MainPage constructor, add the following line of code to create an event handler for the Loaded event:

   ```
   this.Loaded += new RoutedEventHandler(MainPage_Loaded);
   ```

4. Now, add the following event handler method:

   ```
   void MainPage_Loaded(object sender, RoutedEventArgs e)
   {
   _bw = new BackgroundWorker();
       _bw.WorkerReportsProgress = true;
       _bw.DoWork += new DoWorkEventHandler(_bw_DoWork);
       _bw.ProgressChanged += new
       ProgressChangedEventHandler(_bw_ProgressChanged);
   ```

```
_bw.RunWorkerCompleted += new
RunWorkerCompletedEventHandler(_bw_RunWorkerCompleted);
        _bw.RunWorkerAsync();
}
```

The preceding code snippet initiates the `BackgroundWorker` object and sets its `WorkerReportProgress` property to `true`. By setting this property to `true`, we enable the background worker to report the progress of its task.

5. Next, we are adding three event handlers:

   ° `DoWork`: This event handler gets called once we call the `RunWorkerAsync` method of `BackgroundWorker`.

   ° `ProgressChanged`: This event handler gets called whenever we call the `ReportProgress` method of `BackgroundWorker`.

   ° `RunWorkerCompleted`: This event handler gets called once the background operation is completed

6. Once everything is set up, we will call the `RunWorkerAsync` method to get the background operation started.

   Let's add the event handler methods now, starting with the `DoWork` handler.

7. Add the following code snippet to your `MainPage.xaml.cs`:

```
void _bw_DoWork(object sender, DoWorkEventArgs e)
{
for (int i = 1; i < 11; i-+)
    {
        System.Threading.Thread.Sleep(1000);
        _bw.ReportProgress(i * 10);
    }
}
```

What we have here is a simple `for` loop, going from 1 to 10, which will suspend the currently used thread for one second at a time. Once it wakes up, the method will call the `ReportProgress` method of the `BackgroundWorker` object passing it the percentage of job completion.

> **Quick quiz**: What do you think would have happened if you ran this exact method on the UI thread? Would everything still run as smoothly as expected?

The two remaining event handlers—`ProgressChanged` and `RunWorkerCompleted`—update the UI with the progress of the background operation.

8. Add the following code snippet to your `MainPage.xaml.cs` file:

```
void _bw_RunWorkerCompleted(object sender,
RunWorkerCompletedEventArgs e)
{
    lblBar.Text = "Loading completed!";
    prgsBar.IsIndeterminate = true;
}


void _bw_ProgressChanged(object sender, ProgressChangedEventArgs
e)
{
    prgsBar.Value = e.ProgressPercentage;
}
```

Nothing particularly interesting is happening in these two methods. The `RunWorkerCompleted` method updates the `TextBlock` and `ProgressBar` elements to indicate that the operation is completed. The `ProgressChanged` method makes use of the `ProgressPercentage` property of `ProgressChangedEventArgs` to set the `ProgressBar` element's value. Remember, we have passed the `ProgressChanged` event handler the value to update using the `ReportProgress` method earlier.

Everything is done! Build and run your application, and you should get the following screenshot:

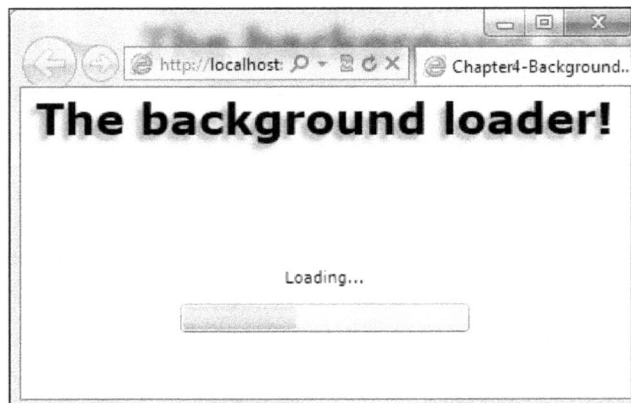

The progress bar will keep filling up, reporting the progress made in the background operation until it gets to 100 percent.

And with this project running, you've finished creating your first `BackgroundWorker` based application.

Using the Dispatcher object

When working with different threads, there may come a time when you have to deal with cross threading. Imagine a case, where your background thread needs to update a control, which is positioned on the UI thread. If you try to update it directly, you'll be greeted with the "Invalid cross-thread access" exception. This happens because a thread in Silverlight cannot access data on another thread directly. So how do you update the UI thread from another thread? You use the `Dispatcher` object.

The `Dispatcher` object exposes the `BeginInvoke` method, which allows us to access the UI thread very easily. Consider the following line of code:

```
Dispatcher.BeginInvoke(UpdateUI);
```

The preceding line of code will call the `UpdateUI` method on the UI thread itself, and not the background thread it was called from.

If you want, you can use lambda expressions to make this code event shorter:

```
Dispatcher.BeginInvoke(() => { prgsBar.Value = 70; });
```

The `Dispatcher` object is a very important concept of Silverlight threading, because without it, we wouldn't be able to interact with the UI thread from any background thread at all. This is the key object that is in charge of the cross threading between the background and UI threads.

Working with the DispatcherTimer object

The `DispatcherTimer` object represents, well, a timer. The difference between the `DispatcherTimer` object and any other timer class you might have encountered before is that the `DispatcherTimer` object is integrated into the `Dispatcher` queue. This means that the timer is processed at a specified interval of time and at a specified priority. The `DispatcherTimer` object exposes the `Interval` property, which accepts a `TimeSpan` object and lets you decide the interval at which the timer will execute. Consider the following code snippet:

```
DispatcherTimer timer = new DispatcherTimer();
timer.Interval = new TimeSpan(0, 0, 20);
timer.Tick += new EventHandler(timer_Tick);
timer.Start();
```

The preceding code snippet initiates a `DispatcherTimer` object called `timer`, and then sets its interval to `20` seconds. The `Tick` handler defines the handler that gets called once the interval has elapsed. To get the timer started, you have to call the `Start` method of the object. If you wish to stop the timer at any point, you just call the `Stop` method. Create a new Silverlight 4 project in Visual Studio and copy the preceding code snippet to your `MainPage.xaml.cs` file. If you put a breakpoint at the beginning of the `timer_Tick` method, you would notice it breaks at that point every 20 seconds. Try to play around with the `TimeSpan` object, and the `Start` and `Stop` methods of the `DispatcherTimer` object to get a better understanding of this mechanism.

Working with dependency properties

If I had to sum up the dependency properties in a single term, I would say that dependency properties are the regular property systems on steroids. The dependency properties really take what you know about properties to a whole new level, but that is also why it is one of the hardest concepts in Silverlight to grasp.

Most properties used on the UI objects in Silverlight use dependency properties. The most common place to write your own dependency properties is when writing your own control. The dependency properties are necessary when you wish to use data binding or styling, so if you think back about the projects we created in this book so far, you've used quite a lot of dependency properties but didn't even know that. Every time you bind a property in XAML, you're actually using a dependency property.

To make my point clearer, let's assume that you are writing a custom control. Other than the regular properties you get from inheriting from control, you wish to let users change the background of the control either by binding to the exposed property or setting its value directly from XAML. The only way this background property is going to be able to achieve these requirements is if it is a dependency property.

The dependency properties obtain their value from different sources. Their real purpose is to compute the value of a property based on values of other inputs such as animations, templates, and so on.

The dependency properties are best explained through example, so without further ado, let's get introduced to our first dependency property!

The structure of dependency properties

As stated in the preceding section, creating a dependency property is a bit more difficult than writing a regular property. The process of writing a dependency property includes registering it with the dependency property system, writing a public wrapper for it, and optionally, writing some actions in the `PropertyChangedCallback` event handler.

A typical property in C# looks as follows:

```
public string CakeColor
{
   get;
   set;
}
```

A dependency property of the same `CakeColor` will looks as follows:

```
public static readonly DependencyProperty CakeColorProperty
= DependencyProperty.Register("CakeColor", typeof(string),
typeof(CakeProperties), new PropertyMetadata(""));
```

But wait, that's not all. This is just the registering code for the property; to actually use it, we need to write a public CLR wrapper for it as well:

```
public string CakeColor
{
get { return (string)GetValue(CakeColorProperty); }
   set { SetValue(CakeColorProperty, value); }
}
```

The wrapper provides an easy way to get and set the value of `CakeColorProperty`, using a getter and a setter, just like any regular property. The major difference here is that instead of returning or setting values directly, you have to call the `GetValue` and `SetValue` methods with the name of the dependency property as their value.

While the wrapper represents how to use the dependency property, to register the property itself, we use the dependency property identifier, which is what `CakeColorProperty` is.

The first part of the identifier is its declaration:

```
public static readonly DependencyProperty CakeColorProperty
```

You declare the `CakeColorProperty` property of the `DependencyProperty` type, which is set to `readonly` and in the majority of cases, `public` and `static`.

The second part of the identifier is its initialization:

```
DependencyProperty.Register("CakeColor", typeof(string),
typeof(CakeProperties), new PropertyMetadata(""));
```

The initialization process is used to register our property in a collection that is not visible and only the Silverlight runtime has access to it. The runtime uses this collection to keep track of all the dependency properties used in the application and manage them.

To register a dependency property, we have to use the `DependencyProperty.Register` method. This method requires a few arguments that help us customize some of the dependency property behaviors.

The first argument we need to supply is the name of the dependency property we wish to register. In our previous example, the name is `CakeColor`. To make things easier down the road, always use the same name you used in the declaration part of the property minus the property part (`CakeColorProperty` - `CakeColor`).

The second argument we supply to the `Register` method is the type of our property. In our case, the cake color will be represented by text, so the type of the property will be `string`.

Next, we need to specify the type of class that the dependency property is part of. This property will vary a lot between projects as you will usually host your dependency properties in different classes. In our example, the dependency property resides in a class called `CakeProperties` and, as such, this is what we supply to the `Register` method.

The last argument defines the metadata that will be used throughout the use of our dependency property. The metadata is managed by the `PropertyMetadata` class and can be used for setting the default value of the dependency property, setting a method to call when the property's value changes, or setting both of them.

Let's create a new dependency property to help sink in all the information we talked about.

Creating your first dependency property

Open the **Chapter4-DP** project from the downloadable book files from the Packt website in Visual Studio 2010.

The project contains a user control called `CircleText`, which resides in the `CircleText.xaml` file. Let's add a few instances of the `CircleText` control to the page. Open the `MainPage.xaml` file, and add the following code snippet under the `LayoutRoot Grid` control:

```
<local:CircleText x:Name="circleText1" Width="120" Height="120"
Margin="12,12,268,168" />
<local:CircleText HorizontalAlignment="Left" Width="80" Height="80"
x:Name="circleText2" VerticalAlignment="Top" Margin="290,122,0,0"
RenderTransformOrigin="0.5,0.5" >
<local:CircleText.RenderTransform>
        <CompositeTransform Rotation="36.135"/>
    </local:CircleText.RenderTransform>
</local:CircleText>
<local:CircleText HorizontalAlignment="Left" Width="100" Height="100"
Margin="83,184,0,0" x:Name="circleText3" VerticalAlignment="Top"
RenderTransformOrigin="0.5,0.5" UseLayoutRounding="False"
d:LayoutRounding="Auto" d:LayoutOverrides="HorizontalAlignment" >
<local:CircleText.RenderTransform>
    <CompositeTransform Rotation="-40.683"/>
    </local:CircleText.RenderTransform>
</local:CircleText>
```

Build and run the application. Now, you should see something similar to the
following screenshot:

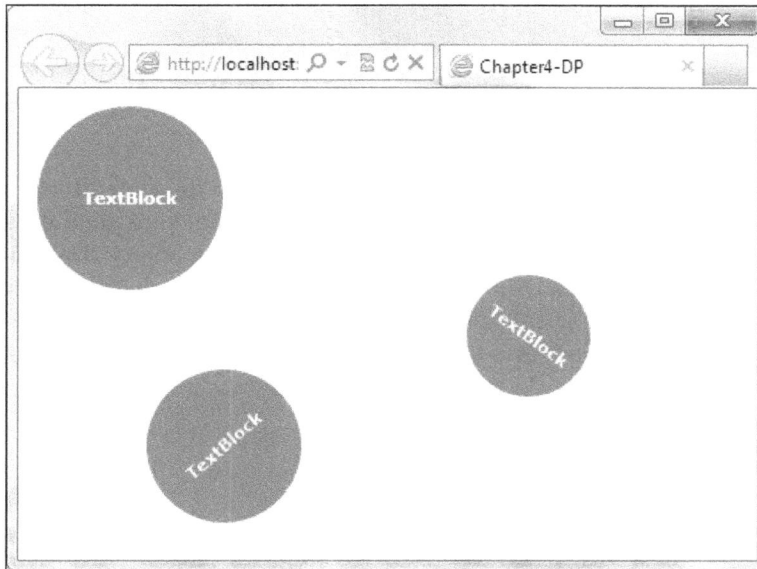

As you can see from the preceding screenshot, all the user controls have the same
text hardcoded in them. As this is hardly what we want from a user control, we are
going to add a dependency property to handle the text inside the circle.

The first thing we have to do is to write the public wrapper of the dependency property. As we mentioned earlier, this will be the **gate** for communicating with the property.

Open the `CircleText.xaml.cs` file, and add the following code snippet below the control's constructor:

```
public string SetTextBox
{
get
    {
        return (string)GetValue(SetTextBoxProperty);
    }
set
    {
        SetValue(SetTextBoxProperty, value);
    }
}
```

Now that we have the wrapper, it's time to register `SetTextBoxProperty` itself. Add the following code snippet right below the preceding code snippet:

```
public static readonly DependencyProperty SetTextBoxProperty
= DependencyProperty.Register("SetTextBox", typeof(string),
typeof(CircleText), new PropertyMetadata(new PropertyChangedCallback(
SetNewText)));
```

We are registering our new property — `SetTextBox`, with the type of `string`. The parent type is `CircleText` because this property resides inside the `CircleText` user control. As we want the text inside the circle to change every time someone sets the property, we need to set a callback method to handle the change. In our case, we are telling the property to call the `SetNewText` method once someone sets the `SetTextBox` property. Let's define the `SetNewText` method now. Add the following code snippet below the dependency property registration code:

```
private static void SetNewText(DependencyObject d,
DependencyPropertyChangedEventArgs e)
{
  (d as CircleText).tbCircle.Text = e.NewValue.ToString();
}
```

There are a few things to notice in this callback method as follows:

- The method must be defined as `static` because the registration code of the dependency property itself is static.

- The method must receive two arguments — DependencyObject and DependencyPropertyChangedEventArgs. The first argument represents the object of the property (CircleText in our case) and the second one refers to the eventargs of the callback.

Once the SetNewText method gets called, it casts DependencyObject to the user control class that runs it and sets its inner tbCircle (the TextBox control) text property to the value that the dependency property was set to.

Build the application. If you run it right now, you won't notice anything different as we haven't set the new dependency property value to anything yet.

Switch back to the MainPage.xaml file, and on any of the CircleText elements you added, set the new SetTextBox property to a value of your choice. An example of such value can be as follows:

```
<local:CircleText x:Name="circleText1" SetTextBox="I'm a red circle!"
Width="120" Height="120" Margin="12,12,268,168" />
```

Build and run your application. You should expect the result, as shown in the following screenshot:

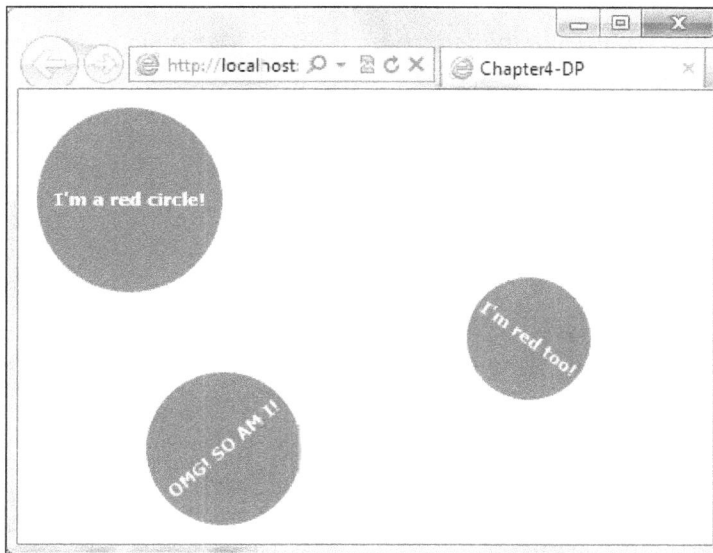

That concludes our exercise on adding the dependency properties. For some extra bragging points, try to create a dependency property for the circle's background color. If you follow the preceding steps, you will notice that only small changes to the code are required!

Interacting with attached properties

The attached properties are a special kind of properties. They are defined on one control but actually affect another control. While this might sound a bit confusing, the truth is we have actually used attached properties all along without knowing what they really are. The attached properties can be recognized quite easily as they have a constant syntax of `PropertyTypeName.AttachedPropertyName`. Think about the `Grid.Row` property for example, or `Grid.Column`. In these cases, `Grid` is the type and the property we are setting for it is either `Row` or `Column`. The element, which we define this property on, `TextBox`, or any other UI Element, doesn't have a `Grid.Row` property. In fact, it doesn't even know if it's placed inside `Grid`, `Canvas`, `StackPanel`, or any other layout control. Instead, the `Grid.Row` property tells the parent `Grid` element in which row to place the calling object. If we take `TextBox`, which resides inside `Grid`, and set its `Grid.Row` property to 3, the element will be placed on the 4th grid row. (Remember, the row collection starts at 0!)

The attached properties aren't limited to the `Grid` element. Examine the following line of code:

```
<Rectangle Fill="#FF14F12C" Height="76" Canvas.Left="25" Canvas.
Top="29" Width="196" RadiusX="5" RadiusY="5"/>
```

Can you recognize the attached properties on the preceding code? (Hint: remember the syntax!).

While the attached properties are mostly used in XAML, you can set and get their value in the code behind as well. Consider the following code snippet:

```
TextBox tb = new TextBox();
LayoutRoot.Children.Add(tb);
Grid.SetRow(tb, 2);
```

We are creating a new `TextBox` control in code, adding it to the `LayoutRoot` Grid control, and finally setting the row property of `Grid` on `TextBox` using the `SetRow` method of `Grid`.

The preceding code is equivalent to the following XAML code:

```
<TextBox Grid.Row="2"/>
```

Reading the row property back in the code behind is just as easy:

```
Grid.GetRow(tb);
```

We are using the `GetRow` method of `Grid` with the instance name of the control, which we wish to read the property from.

The concept of attached properties may be a bit odd at first, but it really becomes like second nature, the more you use it.

I strongly encourage you to read more on the subject of attached properties, in particular, how to create them on the MSDN website located at the following URL: `http://msdn.microsoft.com/en-us/library/cc903943(v=vs.95).aspx`.

Implementing ICommand

The `ICommand` interface is part of the commanding system in Silverlight and is usually recognizable alongside the **Model-View-ViewModel (MVVM)** pattern. The MVVM pattern aids the developer to separate the UI layer (View) from the code layer (Model) using a **connector** in between (ViewModel). The commanding system allows us to wire business logic functionality directly to buttons on the UI layer using XAML. Now, you may be thinking that we can already do that using event handlers and writing code in the code behind file of our XAML, and you would be right. But think about a scenario where you have to use the button logic elsewhere in the application. You will need to write another even handler for the new button, copy the logic over from the old one, and wire the `Click` event of the new button to the new handler. Instead, by using the commanding system, you can bind a command to a button. The command logic is placed in the ViewModel layer, which means that any button on the view can bind to it. In the commanding system, you don't respond to a button's `Click` event anymore; you are binding a command to the button and allowing any button to execute it directly from the UI layer.

The `ICommand` interface is the heart of the commanding system. Every control that inherits from the button base class supports binding to the commands using it. Every command you'll build must inherit from the `ICommand` interface in order to be a bindable command. The `ICommand` interface exposes two methods and one event as follows:

- `CanExecute`: This method returns `true` if the command is allowed to execute
- `Execute`: This defines the method to call when the command is invoked
- `CanExecuteChanged`: This is an event that gets raised when the `CanExecute` property changes

Every command we create that inherits from the `ICommand` interface must implement all of the methods and events of the interface.

Once we have a command, we bind the button's Command property to the name of the command we wish to run, as shown in the following code snippet:

```
<Button x:Name="btnCart" Height="23" Grid.Row="1"
                Width="71"
                Margin="0,5,4,0"
                HorizontalAlignment="Right"
                VerticalAlignment="Top"
                Content="Add to cart"
                Command="{Binding MyCookiesCommand}" />
```

The button has no Click event handler, but instead it has its Command property bound to MycookiesCommand, which is an ICommand inherited class.

Let's see how we will work with the ICommand in an application.

Building your first ICommand

Before we go on building our example project, I would like to say the sample will not be built in MVVM standards in order to keep the simplicity of the example, and help you understand the core concepts of the commanding system. I strongly encourage you to read about the MVVM pattern on the MSDN magazine at http://msdn. microsoft.com/en-us/magazine/dd419663.aspx and check out Laurent Bugnion's *MVVM Light Toolkit* which, in my opinion, is the best MVVM helper toolkit available at http://www.galasoft.ch/mvvm/.

With that being said, let's go ahead and create our first command. Open the **Chapter4-ICommand** project in Visual Studio 2010. You can find the project in the downloadable content over at www.packtpub.com.

The project consists of a datagrid, bound to a collection of the CookieItem items. Each CookieItem contains three properties:

- Name: The name of the cookie
- Milk: A Boolean property that represents whether the cookie goes well with milk or not
- StarFill: A SolidColorBrush property, which sets the background color of a star shape.

Other than the CookieItem class, the project contains another class called CookiesModel.cs. CookiesModel is where we are saving the instance of the selected cookie and initiating our command. Let's start by building and running the application. The following screenshot shows what your result should look like:

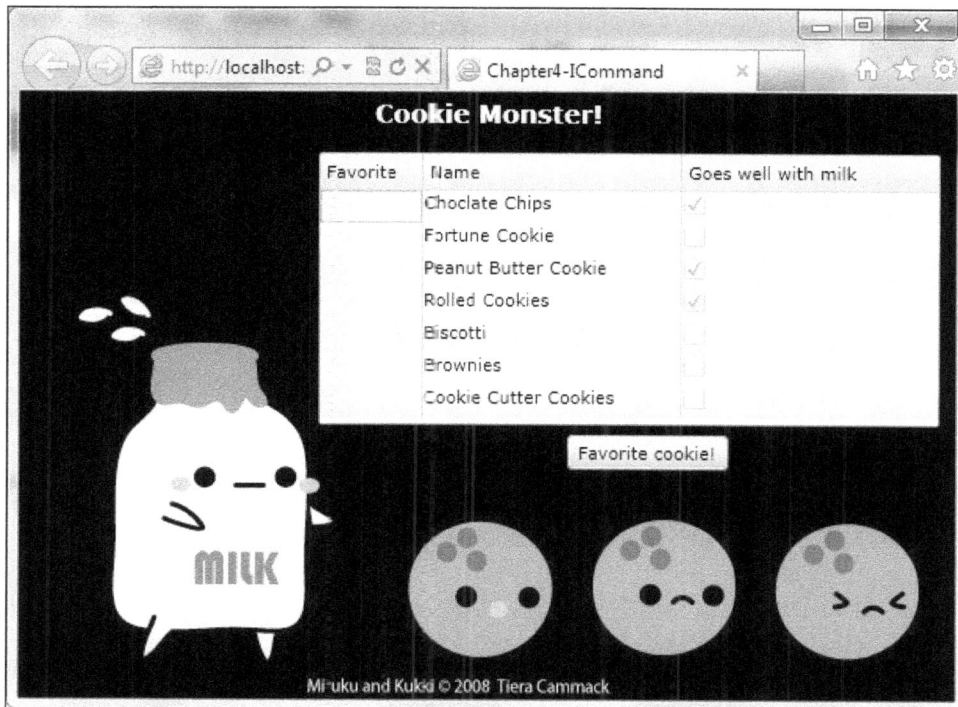

What our command is going to do is to get the button to mark the favorite cookies on the datagrid, as shown in the preceding screenshot. Let's add the new command class. Right-click on **Classes**, and select **Add** and then **Class**. Name your class `CookieCommand.cs`. Make the new class inherit from the `ICommand` interface by changing the class declaration as follows:

```
public class CookieCommand:ICommand
```

Copy the following code snippet inside your new class:

```
public event EventHandler CanExecuteChanged;
public void OnCanExecuteChanged()
{
if   (CanExecuteChanged != null)
        CanExecuteChanged(this, EventArgs.Empty);
}

public bool CanExecute(object parameter)
{
if   (parameter != null)
        return true;
```

```
else
        return false;
}

public void Execute(object parameter)
{
if  (parameter != null)
    {
        (parameter as CookieItem).StarFill = new
        SolidColorBrush(Colors.Yellow);
    }
}
```

Because, our class inherits from the `ICommand` interface, it has to implement its three properties—`Execute`, `CanExecute`, and `CanExecuteChanged`.

We've added an event for the `CanExecuteChanged` property, which the model will call whenever the selected `CookieItem` is changed. We are doing so, because we need to call the `CanExecute` method every time we change an item to check if the command should or should not be executable.

In our example, `CanExecute` performs a very basic check—if the parameter that is passed to it isn't null, then the command should be executable. In the real world, of course, this check should have more meat on its bones.

Our Execute method is also quite simple. Its job is to first check whether the parameter it has got isn't null, and then if it isn't, to cast it to `CookieItem`. This method also sets the `StarFill` property to a yellow fill.

That's all there is to our command. Now, it's time to connect the dots and bind it to the `Button` control in our UI layer.

Open the `CookiesModel.cs` file and add the following property just above the `CookieItem` one:

```
public CookieCommand MyCookieCommand { get; set; }
```

This is the property that will hold our command. Inside the class constructor, add the initialization code for the command:

```
/* init command */
MyCookieCommand = new CookieCommand();
```

All we have to do now is wire the button control to the command.
Open `MainPage.xaml`, and add the following two properties to the
`Button` control:

```
Command="{Binding MyCookieCommand}"
CommandParameter="{Binding SelectedCookie}"
```

In the `Command` property, we are binding the new command we created
(remember, the property name we set to it was `MyCookieCommand`). In the
`CommandParameter` property, we are passing the instance of the currently
selected grid row — `SelectedCookie` (which we defined in our model class).
You can use this property to pass any kind of data you need to your command.
This is the parameter argument that both the `CanExecute` and `Execute` methods
of the command will have.

Everything is done! Build and run your project, and you should get the result,
as shown in the following screenshot:

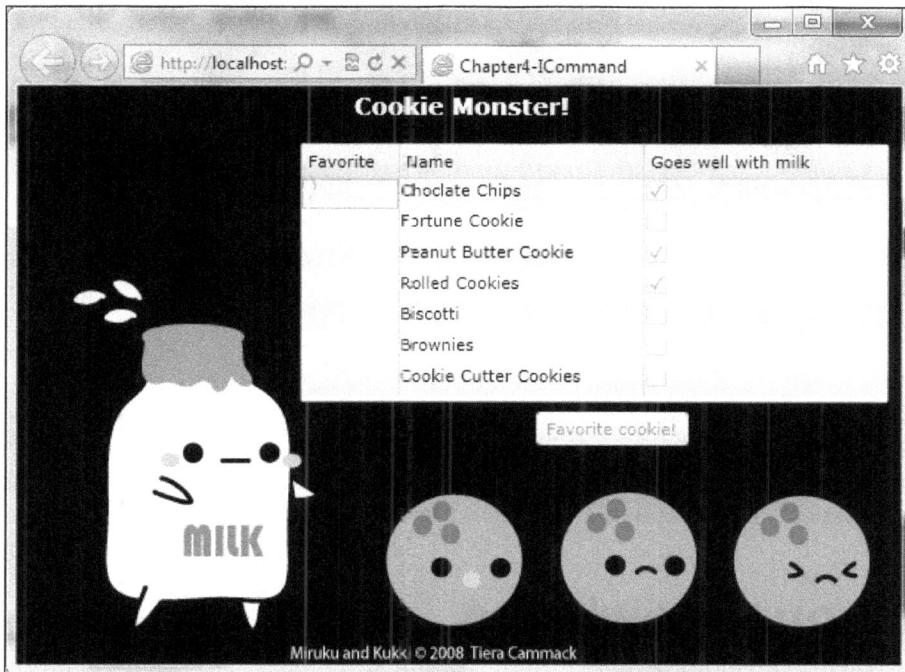

Notice that the button is disabled. Because, we haven't selected any row yet, the
`CanExecute` method of the command will return `false`, which causes the Silverlight
runtime engine to set the command-associated button to the disabled mode.

As soon as a row is selected, the button will be enabled, and clicking it will paint the favorite star in the associated row of the datagrid yellow, as shown in the following screenshot:

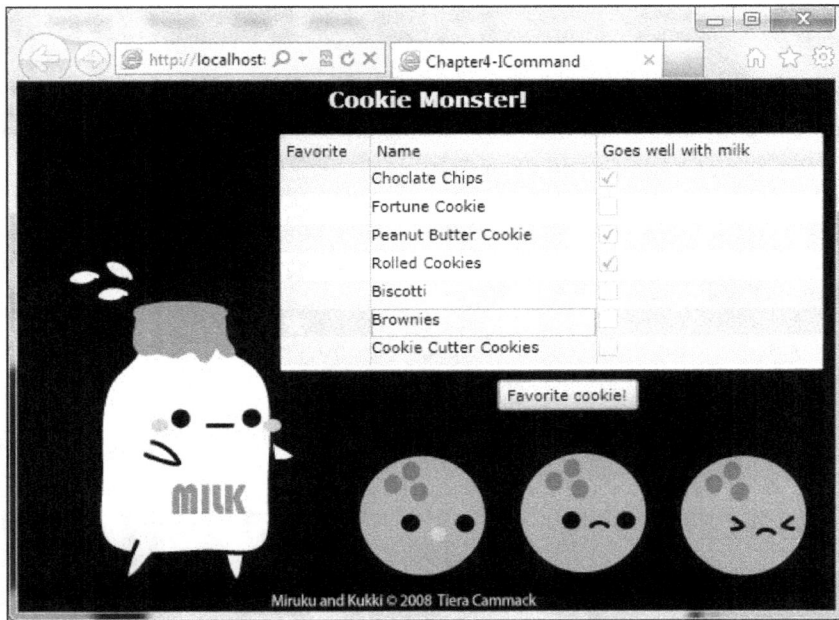

That concludes our `ICommand` implementation. We have created a command that inherits from the `ICommand` interface, binds it to a button using XAML, passes it a parameter, and finally executes it.

While this was quite a simple implementation of the commanding system of Silverlight, the MVVM pattern makes a much heavier use of it. As I stated in the beginning of the topic, I highly suggest you go and learn more about this pattern, as not only is this one of the most popular patterns of Silverlight, it is also the base of clean and neat code that helps you separate your code from your UI.

Test your knowledge

1. You are developing a Silverlight 4 application that uses commands. When a user clicks a button on the page you need to pass it the selected value of a `ComboBox` control named `cbShapes`. What should your button look like?

    a. `<Button Content="Get Shape" Command="{Binding GetShapeCommand}" CommandParameter="{Binding SelectedItem, ElementName=cbShapes}"/>`

b. `<Button Content="Get Shape" Command="{Binding GetShapeCommand}" CommandParameter="{Binding SelectedValue, ElementName=cbShapes}"/>`

c. `<Button Content="Get Shape" Click="{Binding GetShapeCommand}" ClickParameter="{Binding SelectedItem, ElementName=cbShapes}"/>`

d. `<Button Content="Get Shape" Command="{Binding GetShapeCommand}"/>`

2. You are writing a Silverlight 4 application that connects to a **Windows Communication Foundation (WCF)** service. The WCF service is hosted on a domain different from the one running your application. When you run your application, you receive the following error: **Page not found**. What should you do to resolve the issue?

    a. Place a `clientaccesspolicy.xml` file in the root of the Silverlight application.

    b. Place a `clientaccesspolicy.xml` file in the root of the WCF service domain.

    c. Place a `clientaccesspolicy.xml` file in the `ClientBin` folder of the web host that runs Silverlight.

    d. Move the WCF web service to the same domain as Silverlight's.

3. You are writing a Silverlight 4 application that does a heavy calculation job. You decide to move the calculating method to a background thread in order to not have the UI layer freezed while the application calculates. In order to show users the progress of the calculation job, you have added a progress bar to your application — `MainPage.xml`. You implement the `ProgressChanged` event handler to update the progress of the calculation to the progress bar. Users complain that no matter how long they wait, the progress bar never fills up and instead they get an exception error. What can be the reason?

    a. You forgot to set the `WorkerReportsProgress` property of the background worker class to `true`.

    b. Your job finishes too fast for the progress bar to fill up.

    c. You never fired the `DoWork` method of the background thread class.

4. You are writing a Silverlight 4 application with a co-worker. You are tasked with creating a dependency property for your control that will allow users to change the title of the control. Your co-worker wrote the following code:

```
Public class MySweetControl : Control
{
    Public string Title
    {
        Get { return (string)GetValue(TitleProperty);}
        Set { SetValue(TitleProperty, value)}
    }
}
```

Which of the following answers is the correct way to write the dependency property itself?

a. `Public static readonly DependencyProperty TitleProperty = DependencyProperty.Register("Title", typeof(string), typeof(MySweetControl), new PropertyMetadata(""));`

b. `Public static readonly DependencyProperty TitleProperty = DependencyProperty.Register("TitleProperty", typeof(Control), typeof(MySweetControl), new PropertyMetadata(""));`

c. `Public static readonly DependencyProperty TitleProperty = DependencyProperty.Register("Title", typeof(string), typeof(Control), new PropertyMetadata(""));`

d. `Public static readonly DependencyProperty TitleProperty = DependencyProperty.Register("TitleProperty", typeof(string), typeof(MySweetControl), new PropertyMetadata(""));`

5. You are working on a Silverlight 4 application. Your design team has created the UI layer of the application based on the Grid control. You need to dynamically insert a ComboBox control, called cbColors, to the fourth column of the second row of Grid. How will you do that?

a. `Grid.SetRow(cbColors, 4); Grid.SetColumn(cbColors,2)`

b. `Canvas.SetRow(cbColors, 2); Canvas.SetColumn(cbColors,4)`

c. `Grid.SetRow(cbColors, 1); Grid.SetColumn(cbColors,3)`

d. `Grid.SetRow(cbColors, 2); Grid.SetColumn(cbColors,4)`

Summary

In this chapter, we finally got to touch code. While XAML is powerful and fun to work with, sometimes you need to get your hands dirty and write code to get the result you aim for. We started this chapter with learning about events, how to handle them, the different types of event Silverlight offers, and the concept of `AddHandler`.

We then moved on to consuming web services, a key concept in the data driven world of today. We learned how to create service references for the different environments we might work with; we handled asynchronous events, configured service endpoints, and learned how to handle timeouts. We finished the chapter with learning about cross-domain network access and how to build a `clientaccesspolicy.xml` file.

Our next subject was background threads where we built an application that spawned its heavy duty calculation to a background thread, leaving the UI layer free for the user to interact with. Once it was done, we moved on to talk about dependency properties—what they are, and why they are good for us. Once the core concepts were rooted in our minds, we went on and created our first dependency property.

Our next stop in this chapter was the attached properties. We learned what they are and how they work, and saw how we can set these properties on both XAML and code behind.

We finished the chapter off with the introduction of `ICommand` and the Silverlight commanding system.

In the next chapter, we are going to discuss all about data—how to format data, how to implement data binding, how to create converters, and finally, how to perform data validation.

5

Working with Data

Data makes the world go round. I'm sure you have heard this phrase before, and Silverlight is no stranger to that saying. Silverlight offers a rich platform for working with data, and in this chapter, we are going to cover it thoroughly. We will discuss data binding, a major concept for working with data in Silverlight. We will then move on to discussing data formatting and value converters; and finish off with data validation, which is something that no data-driven application is complete without.

In this chapter, we will cover the following topics:

- Implementing data binding
- Formatting data
- Creating and consuming value converters
- Implementing data validation

Implementing data binding

Data binding, at its core, provides a simple way for a Silverlight developer to work with data by separating the display module from the data management module. By establishing a connection between data objects from the backend and the UI layer, you get a mechanism that lets you update UI elements when data changes, or the other way around without the use of code.

The bound data can flow in three distinctive modes as follows:

- OneTime: The target of the bind operation will update with the source only when it's created. For example, if we have a TextBlock element bound to a property, the TextBlock element will only display the value the property had when TextBlock was rendered. TextBlock won't change its value even if the backend property changes later on.

- `OneWay`: The target of the bind operation will update with the source every time the source changes. Using the same example as before, if the `TextBlock` element is bound to a property using the one-way binding mode, it will update its value every time the source property updates as well. This is the default data binding mode in Silverlight.

- `TwoWay`: The bind operation will update both the source and the target when either of them changes. For two-way binding, there is no logic in using a `TextBlock` element, because this mode allows the UI element to update its source property, as well as the other way around. (`TextBlock`, as opposed to `TextBox` only displays text and doesn't allow editing). This mode is used when we wish to get data from the user and a very common use for it is in forms.

In order for the automatic update to occur, the source of the binding must implement an interface known as `INotifyPropertyChanged`. This interface, in a nutshell, contains the `PropertyChanged` event, which is in charge of telling the binding engine that the source has been changed, and it's time to update its bound UI element. We will discuss the `INotifyPropertyChanged` interface in more details in just a bit. To have a better understanding of the whole binding process we have discussed so far, imagine that you need to create a form for adding a new user to your site. The form consists of several text areas the user needs to fill in, including a username field. You want the username field to light up in green if the chosen username is available and red if the username is already taken. By using two-way data binding, the form will update a backend property with the text the user has typed. The property in its turn performs some logic to check for the availability of the username, and then by having a property bound to the border property of the text box, it sets the new color.

At the heart of the binding engine is `DataContext`, and before we go on and dig deeper into binding, let's discuss this important concept.

Setting DataContext

`DataContext`, in a nutshell, allows us to define a common source for all the UI binding in XAML under a certain level. You can set the `DataContext` property at either the page level or an element level depending on your needs. Consider the following code snippet:

```
<toolkit:DataForm HorizontalAlignment="Stretch" Margin="12"
Name="dataForm1" VerticalAlignment="Stretch">
        <toolkit:DataForm.NewItemTemplate>
            <DataTemplate>
                <StackPanel>
```

```
                <StackPanel Orientation="Horizontal">
                    <toolkit:DataField>
                    <TextBox Text="{Binding FirstName,
                    Mode=TwoWay}" MinWidth="200"/>
                    </toolkit:DataField>
                    <toolkit:DataField>
                    <TextBox Text="{Binding LastName,
                    Mode=TwoWay}" MinWidth="200"/>
                    </toolkit:DataField>
                </StackPanel>
                <toolkit:DataField>
                <TextBox Text="{Binding EmailAddress,
                Mode=TwoWay}" />
                </toolkit:DataField>
            </StackPanel>
        </DataTemplate>
    </toolkit:DataForm.NewItemTemplate>
</toolkit:DataForm>
```

The preceding code snippet creates a `DataForm` element with three
fields—**FirstName**, **LastName**, and **EmailAddress**. These fields are bound to
three different properties. How does the `DataForm` control know to bind these
properties? How does the `DataForm` control know where the **EmailAddress**
property is, and how does it update it when the `TextBox` element's text changes?
(Remember, two-way binding can update both the source property and the target
UI element of the bind operation). The answer to these questions is the `DataContext`
object. Open the **Chapter5-DataContext** project in Visual Studio 2010. The project
can be found in the downloadable content of the book and can be downloaded from
`http://www.packtpub.com`.

If I run this code right now, I will get the result, as shown in the
following screenshot:

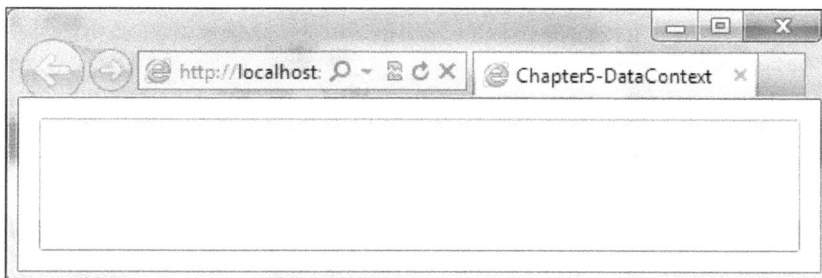

Nothing gets rendered, but the nice default background of the `DataForm` element. The reason for this is that `DataForm` has no context. As stated previously, it has no idea where to take the bound properties from and, thus, doesn't render itself at all.

Let's fix this problem. First, open the `MainPage.xaml.cs` file, and add the following code snippet in the constructor method, below the call to `InitializeComponent`:

```
ObservableCollection<FormEntity> entities = new ObservableCollection<
FormEntity>();
dataForm1.DataContext = entities;
dataForm1.AddNewItem();
```

> The `DataContext` property can also be set directly from XAML. This method requires a bit more work, as it needs a class that holds a collection of items and a resource that references to that class. Have a look at a post by Emil Stoychev at `http://estoychev.wordpress.com/2010/04/24/data-binding-in-silverlight/` for more information on this topic.

The code we added creates a collection of the `FormEntity` class named `entities`. Once the collection is created, it is set as `DataContext` for the `DataForm` control we have in the UI (XAML) layer. Finally, we are telling the `DataForm` control that we wish to add a new item to the collection by using the `AddNewItem` method. If we were to run the application now, we would have got the same result as before — nothing but a nice background. The reason for that is pretty simple; we declared the source of the data that we wish to bind to `DataForm` (If you take a look at the `FormEntity` class in the project files, you will see that it contains the three properties we are binding to — **FirstName**, **LastName**, and **EmailAddress**), but we didn't tell the `DataForm` control itself who is holding its items!

Switch back to the `MainPage.xaml` file, and add the `ItemsSource` property to the opening `DataForm` element, so it will look as follows:

```
<toolkit:DataForm HorizontalAlignment="Stretch" Margin="12"
Name="dataForm1" VerticalAlignment="Stretch" ItemsSource="{Binding}">
```

By setting the `ItemsSource` property to self-binding (you will learn more on that in a moment), `DataForm` now has a source for the binding (the `entities` observable collection), and it knows who holds its items. Run the application now, and you should get the result, as shown in the following screenshot:

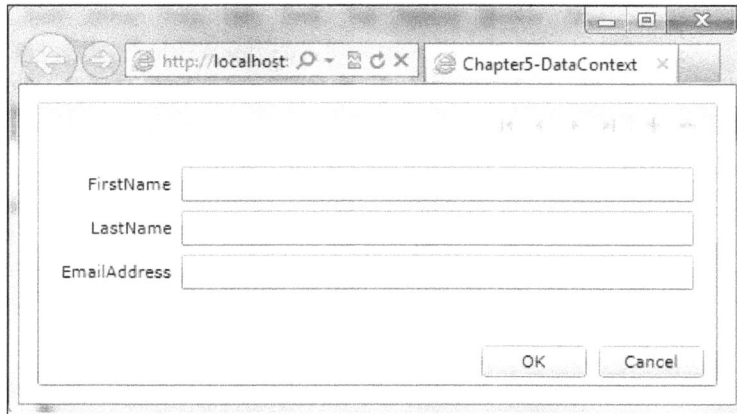

> **Self-binding** refers to a state when an element binds to the
> `DataContext` property of the element above it in the hierarchy.
> In our preceding example, the `ItemsSource` property is
> bound to the `DataContext` object of the element above it in the
> hierarchy, that is, the page itself.

`DataContext` can be bound to any `FrameworkElement` control, and it's not
uncommon to see several different data contexts assigned to several different
controls within a single page or container control. Now that we understand
what the `DataContext` property is and how it works, it's time to move on to
binding data sets to controls.

Binding data sets to controls

Sometimes, you need to bind a collection of items to your control. Think about
a `ListBox` control, or a `ComboBox` control. Both display a collection of items to the
user. For this exact reason, Silverlight binding engine supports the `ItemsSource`
property. Let's see an example of this property. For this example, we will continue
from where we left off in the previous example. Open the `MainPage.xaml` file, and
add the following XAML code snippet below the last `DataField` closing element:

```
<toolkit:DataField Label="Marital status">
<ComboBox ItemsSource="{Binding Statuses}" SelectedItem="{Binding
SelectedStatus,Mode=TwoWay}"/>
</toolkit:DataField>
```

Most of the code is pretty straightforward. We are adding a new `DataField` element to the `DataForm` control with a `ComboBox` control as its input control. The less trivial part here is the binding. We are basically binding two properties— `ItemsSource` and `SelectedItem`.

The `ItemsSource` property is what the `ComboBox` control is going to show to the user. This is the data set of items that the `ComboBox` control uses as its source. In the following code snippet, `Statuses` is the name of the property that holds the collection of items. Add `Statuses` to the `FormEntity` class in your project as follows:

```
private List<string> statuses = new List<string>() { "Single",
"Married", "Divorced" };
public List<string> Statuses
{
get { return statuses; }
    set { statuses = value; }
}
```

We first create a hardcoded list of strings called `statuses`. Then, we create the `Statuses` property, which will set and return the `statuses` variable.

The `SelectedItem` property is the value of the item the user chose from `ComboBox`. As we are binding a list of `string` items as the `ComboBox` control's items source, the selected item will also be a `string`. In addition, as `SelectedStatus` is a property that the user sets from the UI layer, we set its binding mode to TwoWay. Let's add the `SelectedStatus` property to the `FormEntity` class now. Add the following code snippet to the `Statuses` property:

```
private string selectedStatus;
public string SelectedStatus
{
get { return selectedStatus; }
    set { selectedStatus = value; }
}
```

That's it! Build and run your application, and you should get the result, as shown in the following screenshot:

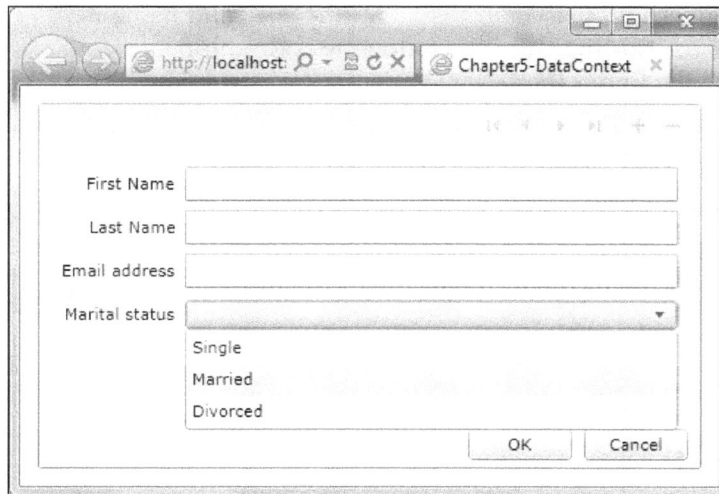

> **Setting ItemsSource in code behind**
>
> Setting the `ItemsSource` property from code behind is as simple as it gets. If we were to set `ItemsSource` to `dataForm1` in the code behind, all we would have done is use the `ItemsSource` property as follows:
>
> `dataForm1.ItemsSource = entities`

Binding elements to other elements

While building **line of business (LOB)** applications in Silverlight, there may come a time when you wish to bind a property of a control to another control. Think about a page with a slider control and a rectangle. The value of the slider control determines the size of the rectangle. The more to the right the slider is, the bigger the rectangle is. While this can be done using code behind, with events, it is much easier to do so in the XAML layer. Let's create this example now to have a better understanding of elements to elements binding.

Create a new Silverlight project in Visual Studio 2010 and name it **Chapter5-ElementBinding**. Add the following code snippet to your `MainPage.xaml` file under the `LayoutRoot Grid` control:

```
<Rectangle HorizontalAlignment="Center" Margin="0,15,0,0"
Name="rectangle1" Stroke="#FFFF9800" StrokeThickness="1"
VerticalAlignment="Top" Width="{Binding ElementName=slider1,P
ath=Value}" Height="{Binding ElementName=slider1,Path=Value}"
Fill="#FFFFD200" />
<Slider Height="23" HorizontalAlignment="Center" Name="slider1"
VerticalAlignment="Center" Width="100" Minimum="100" Maximum="150"
Value="100" />
```

Can you spot the bindings in the preceding code example?

Elements binding have a constant syntax; we first declare the `Binding` keyword, then we use the `ElementName` property to set the source element for the binding, and finally we set the `Path` property, which is the value of the source element we wish to bind. In our example, we are binding the `Value` property of the `slider1` control as both the width and height of our rectangle. Build and run your application, and you should get the result, as shown in the following screenshot:

Move the slider to the right, and you should see that the rectangle grows. Move the slider to the left and the rectangle shrinks:

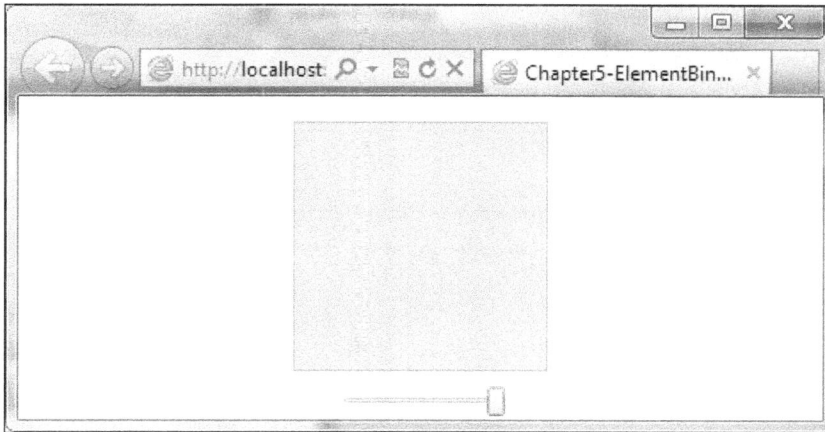

The INotifyPropertyChanged interface

We've already mentioned the INotifyPropertyChanged interface earlier when we talked about binding modes. When we are binding a UI element to a source property using either a OneWay or TwoWay binding mode, the binding engine needs to know that the source property has changed so it can in turn update the UI element the source is bound to.

The only way the engine can know that it is time to perform the update is if the source of the binding implements the INotifyPropertyChanged interface. When implementing the interface, a new event will get added to the class named PropertyChanged. This is the event the binding engine listens to in order to know when to update. When the event is raised, Silverlight will update the bound UI element with the new value of the source.

Let's implement the INotifyPropertyChanged interface in our project. Just like before, we are going to use the **Chapter5-DataContext** project and add the interface to its properties class. Open the FormEntity.cs file, and change the class declaration as follows:

```
public class FormEntity:INotifyPropertyChanged
```

To implement the interface, mark **INotifyPropertyChanged**, then click on **Implement interface 'INotifyPropertyChanged'**, as shown in the following screenshot:

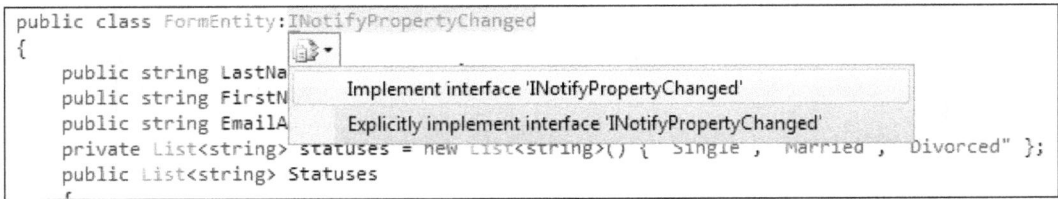

```
public class FormEntity:INotifyPropertyChanged
{
    public string LastNa
    public string FirstN        Implement interface 'INotifyPropertyChanged'
    public string EmailA
    private List<string> statuses = new List<string>() { "Single", "Married", "Divorced" };
    public List<string> Statuses
```

The interface adds a single event to the class called `PropertyChanged`:

```
public event PropertyChangedEventHandler PropertyChanged;
```

To actually raise the event, we add the `OnPropertyChanged` method to the class. Add the following code snippet below the `PropertyChanged` event declaration:

```
public void OnPropertyChanged(string propertyName)
{
var handler = PropertyChanged;
    if (handler != null)
    {
        handler(this, new PropertyChangedEventArgs(propertyName));
    }
}
```

Now, whenever a property wishes to raise the `PropertyChanged` event to let the binding engine know it's time to update its bounded UI element, all it has to do is call the `OnPropertyChanged` event and pass its name as an argument to it. Change the `SelectedStatus` property so that it uses the `OnPropertyChanged` method as follows:

```
public string SelectedStatus
{
get { return selectedStatus; }
    set
    {
        selectedStatus = value;
        OnPropertyChanged("SelectedStatus");
    }
}
```

To actually see it in action, add the following `DataField` control to your `DataForm` control on `MainPage.xaml`:

```
<toolkit:DataField Label="Selected status:">
<TextBlock Text="{Binding SelectedStatus}"/>
</toolkit:DataField>
```

Build and run your application, and you should get the result, as shown in the following screenshot:

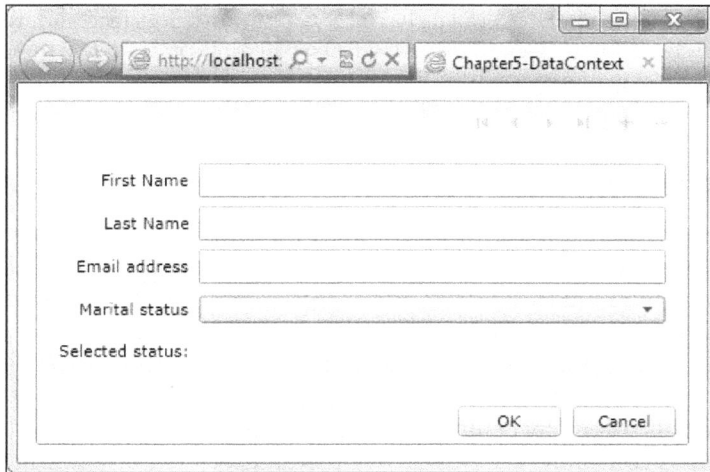

Change the **Marital status** combobox, and you should notice that whenever the value in the combobox changes, the newly added **Selected status** field is updated with the new value, as shown in the following screenshot:

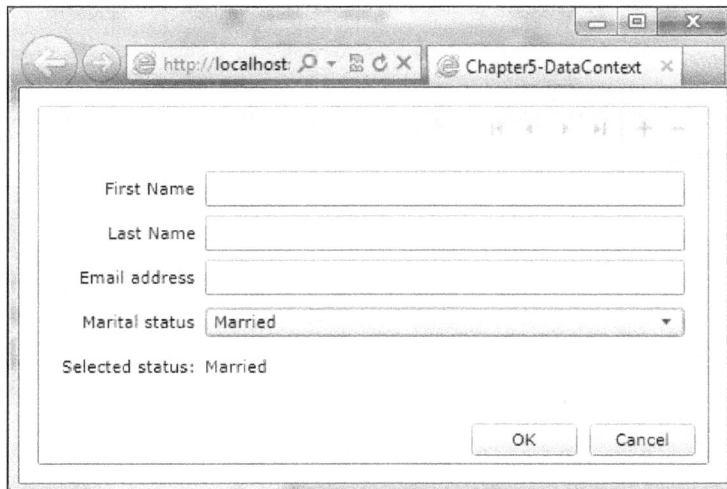

Try to remove the call to the `OnPropertyChanged` method from the `FormEntity.cs` class, and you'll see that the **Selected status** field no longer gets updated.

> If you are binding to a collection of items, and you want the UI to stay in sync with the source, you should use the `ObservableCollection` collection type. This collection already implements the `INotifyPropertyChanged` interface and, thus, whenever an item in `ObservableCollection` updates, the binding engine updates the UI as well.

Setting a fallback value

So far, we've dealt with binding and showing the result of that bind operation to the user. What happens if your binding fails? In such a case, you would probably want to present some kind of message to the user. This message is exactly what the fallback value is all about. This is the value that gets displayed to the user when a binding fails or has no value. Setting the fallback value is done using the `TargetNullValue` property. In the last example we created, you might have noticed that when the application starts for the first time, nothing is shown for the **Selected status** field. This is completely logical as we haven't selected any marital status yet. If we change the binding of the field and add the `TargetNullValue` property to it, we can show a nice friendly message to the user specifying that he/she hasn't selected a **Marital status** yet. Change the `TextBlock` for the **Selected Status** field as follows:

```
<TextBlock Text="{Binding SelectedStatus, TargetNullValue='No status
selected!'}"/>
```

The `TargetNullValue` property is set to a string, which acts as the fallback value for this binding. Run the application now and you should get the result, as shown in the following screenshot:

Another property that we have for fallback values is the `FallBackValue` property. Not surprisingly, this property can also be used to set a default fallback value for our binding.

Formatting data

New to Silverlight 4 is the ability to format bound data using the `StringFormat` property that we all know and love from .NET. Using the `StringFormat` property when doing data binding is perfect for when you wish to format the value that returns from the bind in a specific way, such as currency or any numerical format. Using `StringFormat` is pretty straightforward; just add the `StringFormat` property after the binding declaration, just like you did with the mode earlier:

```
<TextBlock Text="{Binding Price, StringFormat=c}"/>
```

The preceding line of code will format the `Price` property to a currency, which on my machine translates to 5.00$. But why did it choose the dollar symbol and not any other currency symbol? The reason for that is that formatting picks up on the default culture of the system. As my default culture is en-US, I get the dollar symbol. If I had my culture set as he-IL, I would have got the **New Israeli Shekel** (**NIS**) symbol.

Currency is just one example of use for StringFormat, of course. Another example for this feature can be formatting strings. Let's say we wish to have a dynamic label, for example, "Your teacher expects to receive *X* apples today!", where *X* is a random number between 1-10. Instead of using three separate TextBlock elements (one for the text until the random number, the second for binding the random number, and the last one for the rest of the phrase), we can use a single TextBlock element as follows:

```
<TextBlock Text="{Binding RandomNumber, StringFormat='Your teacher
expects to receive \{0\} apples today!'}"/>
```

There are many usages for StringFormat and when building an LOB application using Silverlight, you will find yourself using this feature for a fair amount of time.

For a list of options and usages of StringFormat, visit Matthias Shapiro's great post in his blog at http://www.designersilverlight.com/2010/05/28/silverlight-4-binding-and-stringformat-in-xaml/.

Creating and consuming value converters

A **value converter** allows you to dynamically convert values during the process of data binding before the bound value is actually used. A value converter at heart, is a custom class that inherits from the IValueConverter interface. This interface contains two methods—Convert and ConvertBack—which we have to implement. Once the value converter is created, we can use it directly in our XAML.

Converters let us define custom logic for the different properties we have in our application. It is not uncommon to see a converter that converts one type of value to a completely different type, for example, a converter that converts a number value to a color value. Another example would be a conversation of text to Boolean values so a checkbox can be checked based on certain words.

Let's go ahead and create our first converter and see with firsthand experience why this feature is so powerful.

Creating your first converter

Open the **Chapter5-Converters** project from the downloadable content of this book in Visual Studio 2010. Build and run the application and you should get the result, as shown in the following screenshot:

This application allows you to change the color of the rectangle by using the **Choose your color** drop-down menu above it. The thing is that if you try to change the color using that drop-down menu now, nothing happens. If you think about it for a minute, you'll realize we now have two completely different types of values, which we are going to work with in order to change the color of the rectangle's fill — the combobox color names (strings) and the actual color for the rectangle fill (SolidColorBrush). This is where value converters come into play. We are going to use a string value on the Fill attribute of the rectangle, and by using a value converter, we'll convert it into something the Fill attribute can understand — SolidColorBrush.

Under the Classes folder in the project, create a new class called ColorConverter.cs.

Change the class declaration so that it will inherit from the IValueConverter interface and implement the interface. Your class should look as follows:

```
public class ColorConverter:IValueConverter
{
public object Convert(object value, Type targetType, object parameter,
System.Globalization.CultureInfo culture)
    {
        throw new NotImplementedException();
    }


public object ConvertBack(object value, Type targetType, object
```

```
parameter, System.Globalization.CultureInfo culture)
    {
        throw new NotImplementedException();
    }
}
```

The interface requires us to implement two methods — `Convert` and `ConvertBack`. The `Convert` method is used when the data is moving from the source to the target; in our example that would be when the `Fill` property of the rectangle receives its string binding. `ConvertBack` is the exact opposite; it is used when the data moves from the target back to the source. We won't be using the `ConvertBack` method in our example, so you can leave it as not implemented. Now it's time to implement the `Convert` method. We know we are getting a string as input, and based on that string, we will output a `SolidColorBrush` object. Replace the content of the `Convert` method with the following code snippet:

```
string ChosenColor = value!=null ?  (value as ComboBoxItem).Content.
ToString() : null;
switch (ChosenColor)
{
    case "Red":
        return new SolidColorBrush(Colors.Red);
    case "Blue":
        return new SolidColorBrush(Colors.Blue);
    case "Black":
        return new SolidColorBrush(Colors.Black);
}
return null;
```

Here, there's nothing that we haven't seen before. We first check if the value that we receive from the binding expression is not null. If it isn't, we are casting the value as `ComboBoxItem`, because this is the item that we receive from the binding (check the `ColorEntity` class, and you'll see that the `TheColor` property is defined as `ComboBoxItem` type), and then use the `ToString` method on its content to get the name of the color the user chose from the drop-down menu.

Once we have the color name, we will use a simple `switch`/`case` statement to return the correct `SolidColorBrush` based on the chosen color.

Our converter is now complete, so it's time to use it in our binding expression by using the `Converter` object of the `Binding` class. In order to be able to use our new converter in XAML, we first have to add it as a resource. We will discuss resources in detail in *Chapter 7, Structuring Applications*, but for now it's enough to know that a resource is a piece of code or style that you can reference in your XAML. **Resources**, like styling, which we discussed earlier, can be defined on various levels from element to page. In this case, we are going to add the element to the page level, so open the `App.xaml` file and add the namespace for the `Classes` folder of our project as `local`:

```
xmlns:local="clr-namespace:Chapter5_Converters.Classes"
```

Next, we need to add the converter itself as a resource. Resources are accessed in XAML by their `Key` property, so make sure you use that property when setting your resource. Add the following line of code between the opening and closing of the `Application.Resources` elements:

```
<local:ColorConverter x:Key="ColorConverter"/>
```

That's it. We can now access our converter in XAML by using its `Key` value—`ColorConverter`.

Open the `MainPage.xaml` file and change the rectangle's `Fill` property as follows:

```
Fill="{Binding TheColor,Converter={StaticResource ColorConverter}}"
```

The syntax here is as follows; we first tell the `Fill` property that it is bound to the `TheColor` property. We then use the `Converter` object and bind it to the `ColorConverter` resource we defined earlier using the `StaticResource` keyword. Can you tell the reason why the fill will change every time the drop-down value changes? (Hint: it's got to do with an interface).

Build and run your application, and you will see that every time you change the value of the combobox, the rectangle's fill changes accordingly:

Passing parameters to the value converter

There may be times when you wish to pass parameters to your value converter. Passing parameters is easily done by using the `ConverterParameter` object exposed by the `Binding` class. Let's assume we want to pass the value of `'true'` to the converter in the previous example. All we have to do is change the `Fill` property's binding expression as follows:

```
Fill="{Binding TheColor,Converter={StaticResource ColorConverter},Conv
erterParameter='true'}"
```

As parameter is an object you can practically pass on to it just about anything you want. This can be useful if you need to pass more than just a single parameter to your converter. Once set, you can read this parameter back in your converter class using the parameter argument.

While binding is most commonly done in the XAML layer, sometimes you may need to create dynamic binding in code behind. The following code snippet is a representation of the preceding binding expression in the code behind layer of the application:

```
Binding binding = new Binding("TheColor");
binding.Source = entity;
binding.Converter = new ColorConverter();
binding.ConverterParameter = true;
rect.SetBinding(Rectangle.FillProperty, binding);
```

We first initiate a new instance of the `Binding` class and pass it the name of the property we are binding to. Next, we set the source of the binding, the converter if needed, a converter parameter. Finally, we use the `SetBinding` method on `FrameworkElement` we wish to use (in our case, `rect` is the rectangle we used so far), and specify the name of the property we wish to bind and the binding instance.

Implementing data validation

In a perfect world, every user that uses our forms would enter the exact right data at the right places. In such a world, data validation would be useless. We aren't living in such world, and so data validation is a concept no form can go without. Whenever you are interacting with the user, you want to make sure that he inputs what you expect him to input and nothing else. Silverlight 4 introduced two new interfaces for validation— `IDataErrorInfo` and `INotifyDataErrorInfo`. These two interfaces join the other approach of data validation in Silverlight known as the **data binding exception approach**, which includes the `NotifyOnValidationError`, `ValidatesOnExceptions`, `ValidatesOnDataErrors`, and `ValidatesOnNotifyDataErrors` objects.

Throughout this topic, we are going to work with a sole project—**Chapter5-DataValidation**. The project contains a simple grid with a few text boxes that we will validate using the various data validation approaches in Silverlight. If you build and run the application right now, it will look, as shown in the following screenshot:

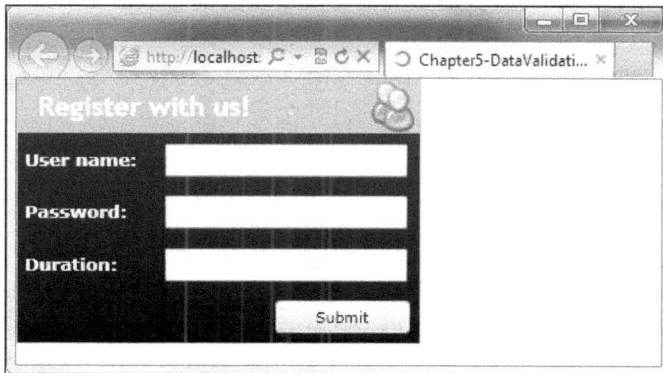

Using exception-based validation

The main player in exception-based validation is the `ValidatesOnExceptions` object of the `Binding` class. Setting this object to `true` will inform the binding system to report any binding exception to the object that used that binding expression. This is also the simplest way to add validation to an element. Let's add this form of validation to the **Duration** textbox. Change the binding expression of the **Duration** textbox as follows:

```
{Binding NumDays,Mode=TwoWay,ValidatesOnExceptions=True}
```

Now, the `Binding` class knows it needs to notify the user about exceptions. But where do exceptions come from? If your guess was the `numDays` property's `Setter` method, you were correct. If we throw an exception in a property's `Setter` method, and the same property is bound to an element, and has `ValidatesOnException` set as `true`; whatever we throw in the exception will be shown to the user. We have already set `ValidatesOnException` to `true` in the `NumDays` binding expression, so let's throw an exception now if the data the user enters isn't a number. Open the `FormEntity.cs` file and change the `numDays` property as follows:

```
public string NumDays
{
get { return numDays; }
    set
    {
        try
```

```
    {
        int number = Convert.ToInt32(value);
        numDays = number.ToString();
        OnPropertyChanged("NumDays");
    }
    catch
    {
        throw new Exception("Only numbers are allowed!");
    }
    }
}
```

In the preceding code snippet, we are trying to convert the value that the user inputs to the Int32 type. If the conversation succeeds, then we will set the internal numDays property to the value. If it fails, we will throw an exception to the UI letting the user know that something went wrong. Run the application now and enter letters in the **Duration** textbox. You will see the result, as shown in the following screenshot:

Using this method, we are not limited to just one exception. If we want to add another exception where the user inputs **0** as the duration length, all we had to do is to change the property as follows:

```
public string NumDays
{
get { return numDays; }
    set
    {
        try
        {
            int number = Convert.ToInt32(value);
            if (number==0)
```

```
        throw new Exception("Invalid duration!");

    numDays = number.ToString();
    OnPropertyChanged("NumDays");
    }
    catch
    {
        throw new Exception("Only numbers are allowed!");
    }
    }
}
```

Now, when the user inputs **0**, another exception will raise, as shown in the following screenshot:

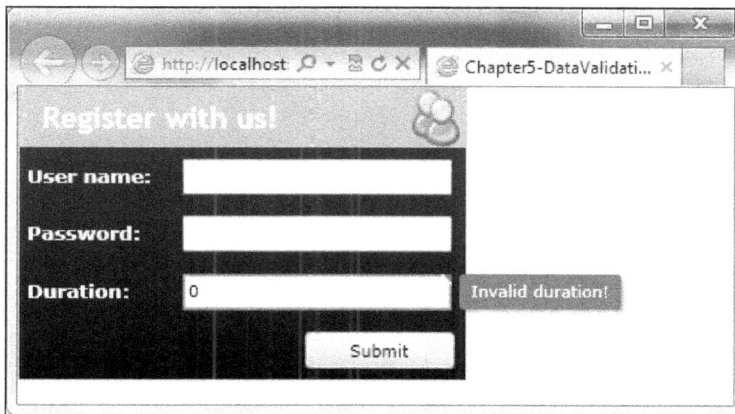

Implementing the IDataErrorInfo interface

With Silverlight 4, the `IDataErrorInfo` and `INotifyDataErrorInfo` interfaces were introduced. These interfaces offer a much more flexible alternative to handle exceptions regardless of whether or not the setter of the property was called. The `IDataErrorInfo` interface contains two properties as follows:

- **Error**: This allows you to set a single error message that applies to the entire project
- **Item**: This is a collection of error messages that are indexed by the property name, which allows you to set individual error messages to specific fields

In order for our XAML to respond to the `IDataErrorInfo` inherited class, we must add the `ValidatesOnDataErrors` object of the `Binding` class to our binding expression and set its value to `true`. This object tells the binding engine that instead of responding to exception-based errors, it needs to watch the `IDataErrorInfo` inherited class for any error reporting.

Add the `ValidatesOnDataErrors` property to the binding of the **Password** field, so its `Password` property looks as follows:

```
Password="{Binding Password,Mode=TwoWay,ValidatesOnDataErrors=True}"
```

Now, it's time to change the `FormEntity` class so that it inherits from `IDataErrorInfo` as well as `INotifyPropertyChanged`. Change the class declaration as follows:

```
public class FormEntity:INotifyPropertyChanged,IDataErrorInfo
```

Implement the new interface, and you should see two new properties added to your class:

```
public string Error
{
get { throw new NotImplementedException(); }
}

public string this[string columnName]
{
get { throw new NotImplementedException(); }
}
```

These are the two properties we mentioned earlier. `Error` is the class-level error message property, and the second property is the `Item` property, which is based on a column name returning an error message. As `Error` is referring to the object itself, we have no use for it for now, and we will deal with the `Item` property now.

The validation we wish to implement for the **Password** field is that the minimum length for a password must be five characters. Let's change the `Item` property of the `IDataErrorInfo` interface to implicate our logic:

```
public string this[string columnName]
{
    get
    {
        string errorMessage = string.Empty;
        switch (columnName)
        {
            case "Password":
```

```
        if (Password.Length < 5)
            errorMessage = "Minimum password length is 5
charecters";
        break;
    }
    return errorMessage;
  }
}
```

By using a `switch/case` method on the `columnName` argument, we can set the logic for any object in our application that has the `ValidatesOnDataErrors` object set to `true` in its binding expression. Once we find the column that raised the property, we will just set the error message we wish and return it to the object. Running the application now will result in the following screenshot:

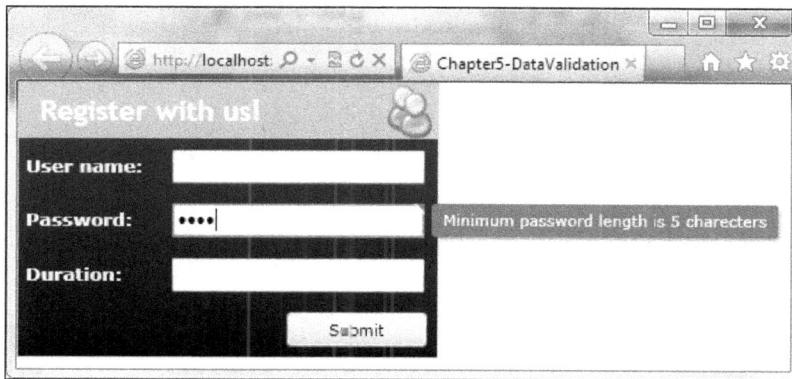

Implementing the INotifyDataErrorInfo interface

While `IDataErrorInfo` works synchronously and doesn't support multiple errors for the same property, the `INotifyDataErrorInfo` interface works asynchronously and supports multiple errors on the same property. And why do we need asynchronous data validation, you will ask. Well that's easy. In our form, we have a **UserName** field. If we want to check whether or not a specific username is already taken without blocking the UI layer, we have to check it asynchronously. The `INotifyDataErrorInfo` interface contains three members as follows:

- `GetErrors`: This is a method that returns a collection (of the `IEnumerable` type) of validation errors for a specific field. As the method returns a collection, we can return more than one error per field.

- `HasErrors`: This is a simple Boolean property that returns `true` if the object contains any errors, or `false` if it doesn't.

- `ErrorsChanged`: This is an event similar to the `PropertyChanged` event in the `INotifyPropertyChanged` interface, which must be raised when you either add, remove, or change errors to notify the binding system that a change has occurred.

It's important to note that Silverlight will call the `GetErrors` method on each `public` member of the class, even if you didn't specifically set it up. If you implement the `INotifyDataErrorInfo` interface, you must take care of the `GetErrors` method.

First, let's add an event handler just like we did with the `INotifyPropertyChanged` interface so that the properties can raise the `ErrorsChanged` event. Add the following code snippet to your `FormEntity.cs` file:

```
private void NotifyErrorsChanged(string propertyName)
{
var handler = ErrorsChanged;
    if (handler != null)
        handler(this, new DataErrorsChangedEventArgs(propertyName));
}
```

Next, we need to add a `Dictionary` object that uses the property name as key and a list of strings for the error messages for that property. Add the following `private` dictionary to your `FormEntity.cs` file:

```
private Dictionary<string, List<string>> errors;
```

To read data from the `errors` dictionary, add the following property:

```
public Dictionary<string,List<string>> Errors
{
get
    {
        if (errors == null)
        {
            errors = new Dictionary<string, List<string>>();
        }
        return errors;
    }
}
```

When we call the `Errors` property for the first time, it will initiate the dictionary. The next time, it will just return it.

Next, let's implement the `HasErrors` property. This is going to be a very easy implementation as the `HasErrors` property's job is just to return `true` if there are any errors we stored or not. Change the `HasErrors` property as follows:

```
public bool HasErrors
{
get { return Errors.Values.Count > 0; }
}
```

The last method of the `INotifyDataErrorInfo` interface members we need to implement is the `GetErrors` method. Just like the `IDataErrorInfo` interface's `Item` property, the `GetErrors` method gets a property name as argument and outputs a list of errors for that specific property name. Change the `GetErrors` method as follows:

```
public System.Collections.IEnumerable GetErrors(string propertyName)
{
if (!Errors.ContainsKey(propertyName))
    {
        Errors.Add(propertyName, new List<string>());
    }
    return Errors[propertyName];
}
```

Within our web project we have a WCF service. The service is called `UsernameService.svc` and it contains a single method, `CheckUsername`, which gets a username as an argument and checks if it's one of the three predefined occupied usernames. If the supplied username is already taken, the method will return `false`; if it's free, it will return `true`.

To add a reference to the web service in the Silverlight project, right-click on **References**, add service reference, and click on **Discover**. Use `UsernameService` as the namespace.

Once we have the entire infrastructure ready, let's add a call to the method to actually check if the username is taken or not. In the `FormEntity.cs` file, change the `Login` property setter as follows:

```
set
{
login = value;
    OnPropertyChanged("Login");
    CheckForUsername();
}
```

Now, we must add the `CheckForUsername` method. Add the following code snippet to the `FormEntity.cs` file:

```
public void CheckForUsername()
{
UsernameService.UsernameServiceClient proxyClass = new
UsernameService.UsernameServiceClient();
    proxyClass.CheckUsernameCompleted += new
    EventHandler<UsernameService.CheckUsernameCompletedEventArgs>
    (proxy_CheckUsernameCompleted);
    proxyClass.CheckUsernameAsync(Login);
}
```

Just like we did in the previous chapter, we will add a proxy class for the `Username` service, attach a complete event handler, and call the `CheckUsername` method asynchronously, passing to it the currently typed login name.

The implementation of the completed event handler of the `Checkusername` method is as follows:

```
void proxy_CheckUsernameCompleted(object sender, UsernameService.
CheckUsernameCompletedEventArgs e)
{
if (e.Error == null)
    {
        bool result = e.Result;
        if (result == false)
        {
            CreateErrorInDictionary("Login");
            Errors["Login"].Add("Username taken!");
            NotifyErrorsChanged("Login");
        }
    }
}
```

First, we cast the result of the method as Boolean, as we know it can return either `true` or `false`. If the result is false, that means the username is not available, and we should notify the user. To do that, we call the `CreateErrorInDictionary` method, which checks if the property already has a key in the dictionary and if not, it creates a key. The implementation of `CreateErrorInDictionary` is as follows:

```
private void CreateErrorInDictionary(string property)
{
if (!Errors.ContainsKey(property))
    {
        Errors.Add(property, new List<string>());
    }
}
```

Once we know for sure that the `Errors` dictionary contains a key for our property, we will add an error message and use the `NotifyErrorChanged` method we created earlier to let the binding engine know an error was raised.

That's it! You've created a working implementation of the `INotifyDataErrorInfo`! Run your application, and try to enter one of the following usernames—Silverlight, SL4, or Packt. Your screen will be similar to the following screenshot:

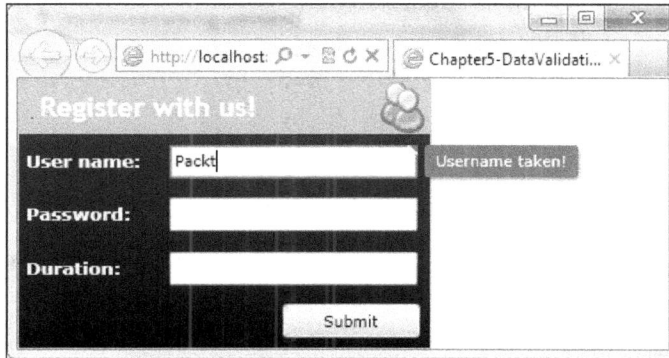

In a real-world scenario, the web service will probably perform a check against a database or something similar to check if a username is taken. An action like this can be time consuming and, thus, performing this activity asynchronously makes a lot of sense. We want the user to keep on going with the form, and once we get back a result from the web service, we should update him.

That concludes our discussion on data validation in Silverlight. I hope you'll take what you learned here and use it to create a better, safer, and interactive experience for the user while interacting with him/her through your application.

Test your knowledge

1. You are writing a Silverlight 4 application. The application contains a class that has a Boolean property named `ToShow`. You wish to have a field that will only be shown to the user if the bound `ToShow` property returns `true`. Which code segment should you use?

    a. Only implement the `Convert` method with the following code snippet:

```
if (value != null)
    {
        bool result = (Boolean)value;
        return result == true ? Visibility.Visible :
```

```
        Visibility.Collapsed;
    }
    return Visibility.Collapsed;
```

b. Only implement the `ConvertBack` method with the following code snippet:

```
if (value != null)
    {
        bool result = (Boolean)value;
        return result == true ? Visibility.Visible :
        Visibility.Collapsed;
    }
    return Visibility.Collapsed;
```

c. Only implement the `Convert` method with the following code snippet:

```
if (value != null)
    {
        bool result = (Boolean)value;
        return result;
    }
    return Visibility.Collapsed;
```

d. Only implement the `ConvertBack` method with the following code snippet:

```
if (value != null)
    {
        bool result = (Boolean)value;
        return result;
    }
    return Visibility.Collapsed;
```

2. You are developing a Silverlight 4 based form. The form contains a `TextBox` control that is data bound to a property in a class that implements the `INotifyPropertyChanged` interface. When an invalid value is entered to the `TextBox`, the property throws an exception. You need to display the error message the property throws to the user. Which code segment should you use?

a. `<TextBox Text="{Binding ZipCode,Mode=TwoWay,ValidatesOnDa taErrors=True}"/>`

b. `<TextBox Text="{Binding ZipCode,Mode=OneWay,ValidatesOnDa taErrors=True}"/>`

c. `<TextBox Text="{Binding ZipCode,Mode=TwoWay,ValidatesOnEx ceptions=True}"/>`

d. `<TextBox Text="{Binding ZipCode,Mode=TwoWay,NotifyOnValid ationError=True}"/>`

3. You are developing a Silverlight 4 based application. The application contains a `TextBlock` control that is bound to a property called `FirstName`. The `TextBlock` control needs to display the string "Welcome back" before the value of `FirstName`. Which code segment should you use?

a. `<TextBlock Text="{Binding FirstName,StringFormat='Welcome back {FirstName}'}'"/>`

b. `<TextBlock Text="{Binding FirstName,StringFormat='Welcome back {0}'}"/>`

c. `<TextBlock Text="Welcome back {Binding FirstName}"/>`

d. `<TextBlock Text="{Binding FirstName,ConverterParameter='W elcome back {0}'}"/>`

4. You are developing a Silverlight 4 based application that contains a slider control. The slider is named `Degrees` and its values are between 1 and 360. You need to display the value of the control in a `TextBlock` control. Which code segment should you use?

a. `<TextBlock Text="{Binding Path=Value, ElementName=Degrees}"/>`

b. `<TextBlock Text="{Binding Path=Value, Converter=Degrees}"/>`

c. `<TextBlock DataContext="Degrees" Text="{Binding Path=Value}"/>`

d. `<TextBlock Text="{Binding Path=Degree, ElementName=Degrees}"/>`

5. You are developing a Silverlight 4 application that contains a field that is bound to a property called `TotalPrice`. The field must be read-only, and it should not update the backend property. When a user updates other fields in the application, `TotalPrice` changes and needs to update the UI layer. Which binding mode should you use?

a. TwoWay

b. OneTime

c. None

c. OneWay

Summary

In this chapter, we got to work with one of the more commonly used aspects of Silverlight, which is data handling. We discussed data bindings in details, learned about the different modes and options it offers, understood how to bind elements to other elements and how to validate the data we are binding. In addition, we learned how to format the data we get back from the binding and we got to use the all-important concept of converters.

In the next chapter, we are going to discuss how to work with the host platform. We will discuss printing directly from Silverlight using the new printing API. Then, we will move on to discuss out-of-browser applications and interacting with different variables of the host-like network connectivity or the clipboard. We will also discuss how to work against the COM Interop and updating our out-of-browser application remotely.

We will then move on to discuss interacting with the HTML DOM and finish off discussing how to handle alternative input methods such as the mouse's right-click or wheel.

6

Interacting with the Host Platform

Up until now we have only dealt with Silverlight itself. Now it's time to take things to a higher scope and deal with the environment of Silverlight. Not every piece of your application can be part of your Silverlight solution. Sometimes you may want to store data on the user's computer, interact with a JavaScript function, or even create an application that runs on the user's computer directly without the need for a browser. In this chapter we are going to deal with all of these things. We are going to discuss all the ways Silverlight can interact with its host platform.

In this chapter we will cover the following topics:

- Implementing the printing API
- Creating out-of-browser applications
- Accessing the isolated storage
- Interacting with the HTML DOM
- Accessing the clipboard
- Reading from and writing to the host filesystem
- Handling alternative input methods

Implementing the printing API

You've just created the perfect LOB application. Everything works great and users are happy. After a while, a few of them come to you with a request that seems quite trivial — they need to print forms and pages off your application. As trivial as this request sounds, up until Silverlight 3 this would have been impossible. Silverlight 3 introduced the `WriteableBitmap` class, which allows you to save any element in your application as a bitmap and then print it. Silverlight 4, however, was the first Silverlight release to introduce a real solution to the printing problem, known as the **printing API**.

The entire printing process in Silverlight relies on an object called `PrintDocument`. This object contains three events that cover the entire lifespan of the printing process — `BeginPrint`, `PrintPage`, and `EndPrint`.

The `BeginPrint` event is raised as soon as the `Print` method gets called on the `PrintDocument` object. Then, for each page that needs to be printed, `PrintDocument` raises the `PrintPage` event. This is the most important handler, as it enables you to build and design the printing area and set if there are any more pages to be printed.

Once Silverlight lays out the content to be printed, a bitmap is rasterized and sent to the printer driver. A note to be taken here is that as Silverlight sends a bitmap to the printer driver, its size might be bigger than expected.

Once the page is sent to the printer driver, Silverlight checks if there are any more pages to be printed. If there are, the `PrintPage` event gets raised again. If not, the `EndPrint` event is raised.

Other than these three events, the `PrintDocument` object exposes a property called `DocumentName`, which defines the name of the print job, and `HasMorePages`, which is a Boolean type property that can inform whether or not there are more pages to print.

Let's go ahead and print some pages!

Creating your first print job

To get started, open the **Chapter6-PrintingAPI** project in Visual Studio 2010 from the downloadable content of the book. The project's UI consists of a simple layout of text and an image and a print button.

To get started with the printing API, we first have to initialize the PrintDocument object. Switch to MainPage.xaml.cs and add the following line of code above the MainPage constructor:

```
private PrintDocument _pd = new PrintDocument();
```

As discussed earlier, the most important event of the PrintDocument object is the PrintPage event. The handler of this event enables us to set what is going to get printed. Let's add the event handler right now. Add the following line of code inside the MainPage constructor:

```
_pd.PrintPage += new EventHandler<PrintPageEventArgs>(_pd_PrintPage);
```

Inside the _pd.PrintPage handler, we can access the event arguments of the event. The arguments enable us to specify what we want to print (using the PageVisual property), get the size and margin of the currently printing page (using the PrintableArea and PageMargins properties), and set if we have anything else to print (using the HasMorePages Boolean property). As we have a single element that we wish to print—the LayoutRoot Grid element—let's set the event handler as follows:

```
void _pd_PrintPage(object sender, PrintPageEventArgs e)
{
    e.PageVisual = LayoutRoot;
    e.HasMorePages = false;
}
```

Now that we have set the visual to print, and told the framework it's the only page we wish to print, all that's left to do is call the Print method of the PrintDocument object to actually print the page. Add the following code snippet in your MainPage.xaml.cs file:

```
private void btnPrint_Click(object sender, RoutedEventArgs e)
{
    _pd.Print("Sample Silverlight Document");
}
```

Build and run the application, and you should get the result, as shown in the following screenshot:

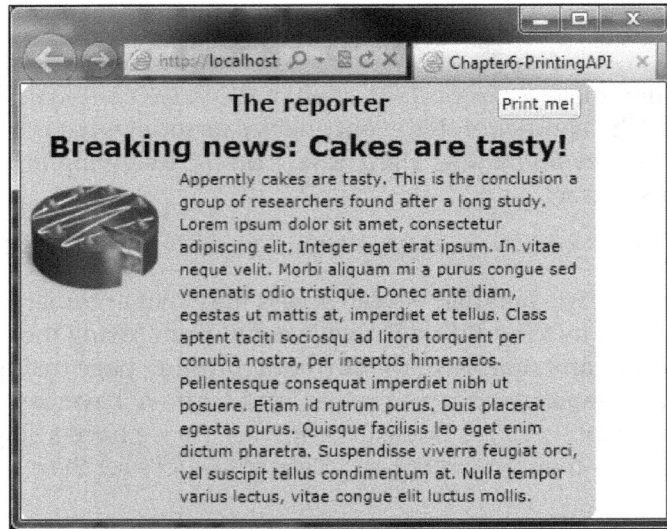

Click the **Print me!** button, and you should be greeted with the familiar print dialog box.

If you print the page, you will get the exact same visual as your application:

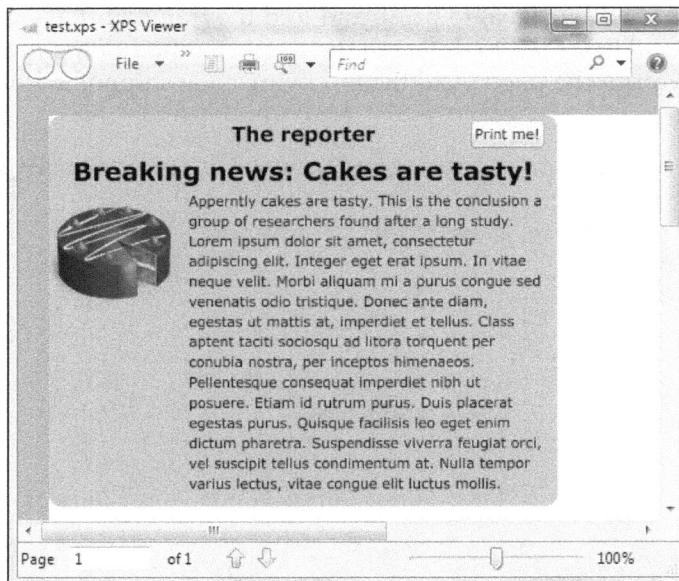

Now, this **Print me!** button has no place in the printed material. What if we want to hide it from the printed version of our page?

This is where the `BeginPrint` and `EndPrint` events come into play. As mentioned earlier, `BeginPrint` happens just before the `PrintPage` event is called, and `EndPrint` is called as soon as the page is sent to the printer. If we wish to hide the **Print me!** button from the printed page, all we have to do is hide it in the `BeginPrint` handler and show it again on the `EndPrint` handler.

Add the following handlers to your code, just below the `PrintPage` handler:

```
_pd.BeginPrint += new EventHandler<BeginPrintEventArgs>(_pd_
BeginPrint);
_pd.EndPrint += new EventHandler<EndPrintEventArgs>(_pd_EndPrint);
```

Add the actual handler methods to your code:

```
void _pd_BeginPrint(object sender, BeginPrintEventArgs e)
{
    btnPrint.Visibility = Visibility.Collapsed;
}
void _pd_EndPrint(object sender, EndPrintEventArgs e)
{
    btnPrint.Visibility = Visibility.Visible;
}
```

Build and run your application again. Print the page, and you should get the result, as shown in the following screenshot:

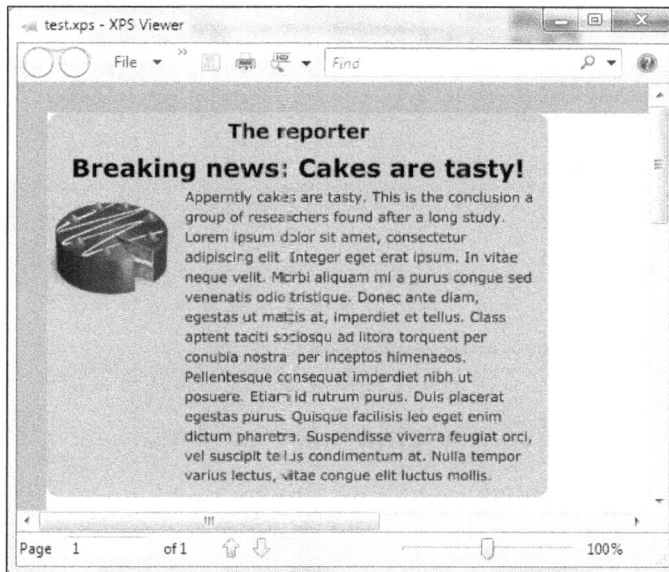

Printing multiple pages with page numbers

To demonstrate how to handle multiple pages with Silverlights printing API, open the **Chapter6-MutliPrinting** project in Visual Studio 2010.

We are going to focus on the printing part, so the UI and corresponding code have already been written for us. The application is a simple agenda viewer based on a `ViewBox` control and binding to an entity.

The application contains the following two entities that the UI binds to:

- `AgendaEntity`: This is the main entity of the application. It contains the attendee's name, the currently viewed page number, the width of the printing area, and a collection of the `MeetingEntity` entities, each of which represent a meeting.

- `MeetingEntity`: This is an entity that represents a meeting. It contains the meeting title, abstract, and time.

In addition, the application contains a user control named `PrintPage.xaml`. This control will be used as the visual for our printing needs.

To better understand what we are going to print, build and run the application now. You should get the result, as shown in the following screenshot:

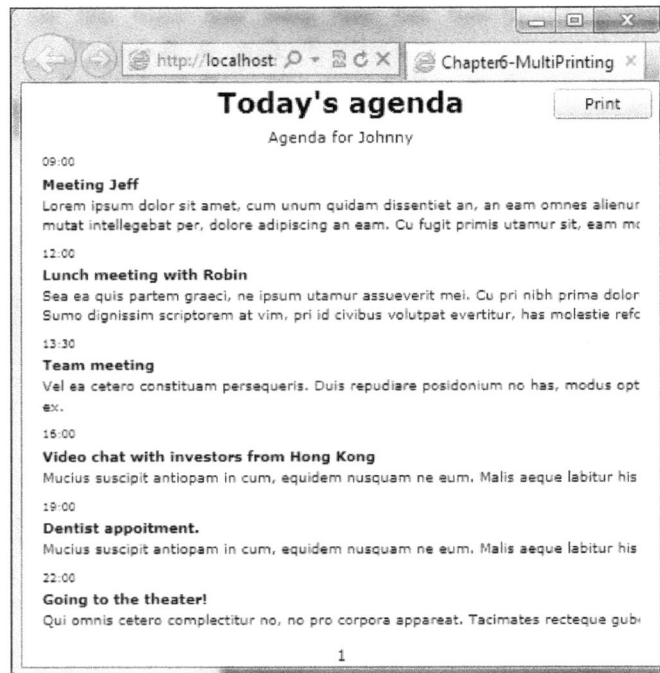

By binding the meetings `ObservableCollection` to `ViewBox` and setting its `DataTemplate`, we get a nicely charted list of meetings. While this entire agenda can be printed on one page, for the sake of the example, we will assume only three meetings can fit into a single page. As this is the case, we need to handle multipage printing and set the right page number for the printed page.

First, we call the `Print` method of the `PrintDocument` object when the user clicks on the `Print` button. Add the following line of code to the `printBtn_Click` event handler in the `MainPage.xaml.cs` file:

```
_pd.Print("My Agenda");
```

Next, we need to handle the `PrintPage` event. Change the `_pd_PrintPage` event handler as follows:

```
void _pd_PrintPage(object sender, PrintPageEventArgs e)
{
PrintPage pp = new PrintPage();
    ObservableCollection<MeetingEntity> meetings = new
    ObservableCollection<MeetingEntity>();
    while (_rowCounter < _entity.Meetings.Count)
    {
        meetings.Add(_entity.Meetings[_rowCounter]);
        _rowCounter++;
        if (_rowCounter % 3 == 0)
        {
            if (_rowCounter == _entity.Meetings.Count)
            break;
            else
            {
                e.HasMorePages = true;
                break;
            }
        }
    }
    AgendaEntity entity = new AgendaEntity();
    entity.Meetings = meetings;
    entity.AttendeeName = _entity.AttendeeName;
    entity.PageNumber = _entity.PageNumber;
    entity.PrintWidth = e.PrintableArea.Width;
    pp.DataContext = entity;
    e.PageVisual = pp;
    _entity.PageNumber++;
}
```

Even though it seems like a lot of code, the logic is pretty simple.

We first create an instance of `PrintPage`, which is the user control we have mentioned earlier. The user control contains the same UI as `MainPage.xaml` minus the print button. We then create a new `ObservableCollection` of the `MeetingEntity` items to hold the meetings we wish to print on a particular page. Next, we have a `while` loop that checks whether or not the `_rowCounter` parameter is less than the total sum of meetings the main entity holds, and if it is less, it adds the meeting to the `meetings` collection, increments the `_rowCounter` parameter by 1, and checks if it can be divided by 3 without a remainder. If it can, that means we have added three items to the new collection. Then, we check if the counter equals the number of meetings the agenda has. If it does, that means we've finished and we should just break the loop and continue with the rest of the method. If it doesn't, that means we have more to print and, thus, we set the `HasMorePages` Boolean property of the event to `true`. That will cause the `PrintPage` method to run again for the new page that needs to be printed. Finally, we create a new `AgendaEntity` instance and set its different properties, such as the collection of items (meetings), attendee name, page number, and the width of the printing area. It is important to note that we progress the page number counter by 1 at the end of the method, so that we can get the correct number for the currently printed page.

Finally, we have to deal with the `EndPrint` handler. This handler contains a single line of code that simply resets the `PageNumber` property to `1`, as the UI shows all the meetings on one page, no matter how many meetings are shown. Add the following line of code to the `_pd_EndPrint` handler:

```
_entity.PageNumber = 1;
```

That's it. Handling multiple pages in the printing API can be a bit tricky at first so it's highly recommended you go over the code again, just to make sure you understand what's going under the hood there.

Build and run the application, and click on the **Print** button. If printed to an XPS, you should get the result, as shown in the following screenshot:

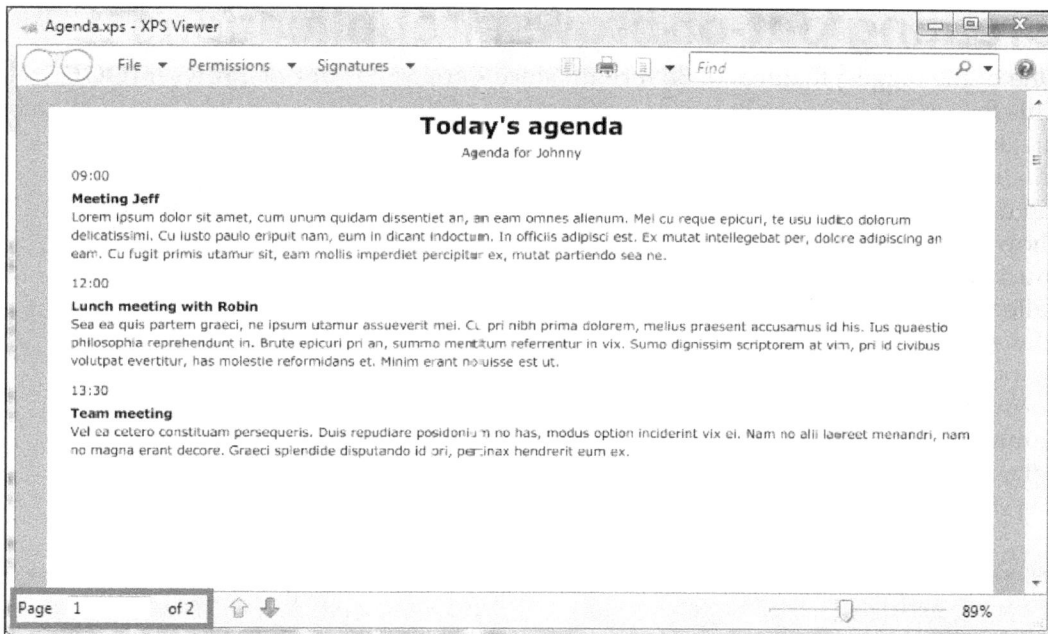

There are a total of two pages, each with three meetings.

> You don't have to add the entire `LayoutRoot` as the `PageVisual` to be printed. You can also specify specific elements, both on and off the screen. For example, if we only want to print a `ViewBox` control named vb, all we have to do is set the `PageVisual` property of the `PrintPageEventArgs` argument of the `PrintPage` handler to the name of the `ViewBox` control. In other words, e.`PageVisual` = vb.

Creating out-of-browser applications

One of the biggest features of Silverlight since Version 3 is **out-of-browser** (**OOB**). This feature allows us to create an application in Silverlight that will be installed on the user's local machine. Once installed on the user's local machine, our application can interact with the desktop capabilities of the user's machine in various ways. Among the different integrations we get, we can read the machine's network state, show toast notifications, display web content, run applications on full screen, and much more. Silverlight 4 introduced a new powerful mode for OOB applications called **elevated trust**. Running our application in this mode, we can read local files and resources, show fewer confirmation prompts to the user, and use COM automation to communicate with other applications (such as Microsoft Office) or software APIs such as the speech API of the OS or drivers, which allows COM communication. An OOB application looks, and behaves, like any other regular software you know. The following screenshot, which is taken from `http://www.seesmic.com` shows an OOB Silverlight 4 application called **Seesmic Desktop 2**:

To get started with OOB applications, let's build our first OOB application. We will start with understanding how to install and uninstall applications and extend the application as we progress through the chapter.

Creating your first out-of-browser application

The major difference between an out-of-browser application and a regular Silverlight application is, well, that it runs out-of-browser. To get a better understanding on how this mechanism works, we will build a super simple Silverlight application that allows you to install it on the desktop and shows you its current status (installed or not installed).

Create a new Silverlight 4 application in Visual Studio and name it **Chapter6-SimpleOOB**. Open the `MainPage.xaml` file and add the following XAML code:

```
<Button x:Name="instBtn" Content="I'm in browser. click me!"
Click="instBtn_Click"/>
```

There is nothing special here, just a button with an event handler for the `Click` event, which we will handle soon. In order to make an application installable, we need to set it in its properties. Right-click on the project name in the solution explorer and click on **Properties**. One of the properties we can set is the **Enable running application out of the browser** option, as shown in the following screenshot:

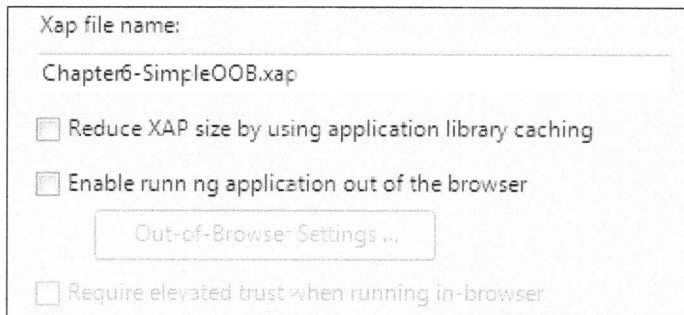

Select the **Enable running application out of the browser** checkbox and click on the **Out-of-Browser Settings** button. The following screen will appear:

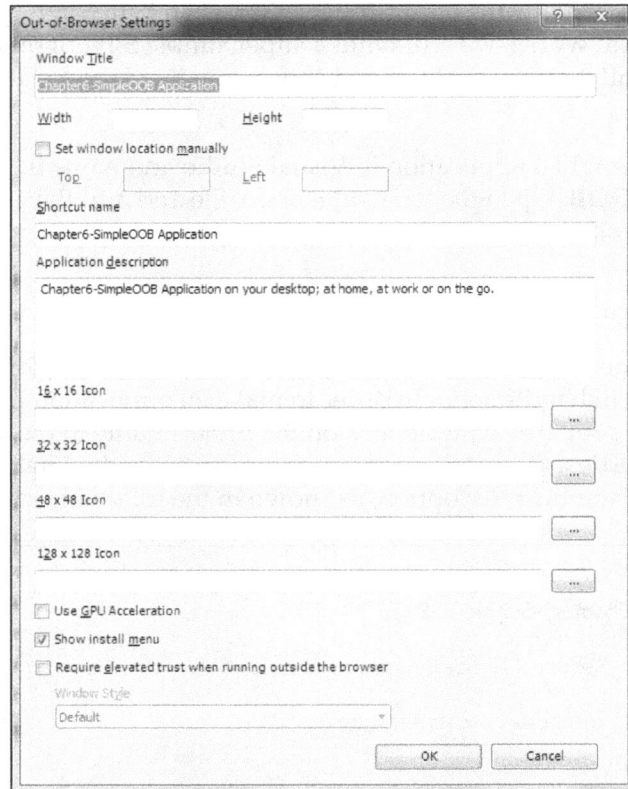

All of the OOB application settings can be set in this dialog box. Most of the settings, such as **Window Title**, or **Width** and **Height**, are self-explanatory. If you select the **Set window location manually** checkbox, you can specify how far from the top and left-hand sides of the user's monitor you wish to initially show the application. Another set of settings you should set are the different icon sizes. Each application has a different size of icons for different purposes in that application. The last three checkboxes are what we should focus on. They are as follows:

- **Use GPU Acceleration**: Checking this box will enable our application to use GPU acceleration. This can benefit a GFX-heavy application by allowing it to use the GPU for its graphic needs.

- **Show install menu**: This should stay checked, as it shows the user the installation menu of the application.

- **Require elevated trust when running outside the browser**: To enable our application to run as an elevated trust application, we have to check this box. Checking this box will give our application many more abilities such as accessing local files, creating cross-domain calls, and interacting with the COM API.

> If we check the elevated trust checkbox, we get to set a new property — **Window Style**. This property sets how the window hosting the application will look. The different options you have for this property are **Default, No Border, Single Border**, and the most exciting option of them all — **Borderless Round Corners**. These modes (and the **No Border** mode) are also referred to as **chromeless**, as they remove any chrome from the application window. A chromeless application window offers designers much better control over how it will look, and it's one of the more popular choices when creating an OOB application.

Leave all of the default options intact, but check the elevated trust checkbox and click on **OK**. Save your project and switch over to the `MainPage.xaml.cs` file.

Our main point of interest when it comes to dealing with OOB is the `Application` object. In conjunction with the `Current` object, we can get a reference to the current active application and check different properties of the application state. For example, we can check whether or not the application is installed on the user's computer. Other properties we can check include the installation state of the application, available updates, and so on. In addition, the object exposes different events we can register to, such as `InstallStateChanged`, which handles changes in the installation states (installation, uninstallation, and so on) or `NetworkAddressChanged`, which reports on the user's network state.

The first task of our application is to check whether or not the application is currently installed on the user's computer; and if it does, change the content of the button. First, register to the `Loaded` event by adding the following line of code to the `MainPage.xaml.cs` file's `MainPage` constructor:

```
this.Loaded += new RoutedEventHandler(MainPage_Loaded);
```

Next, add the `MainPage_Loaded` method as follows:

```
void MainPage_Loaded(object sender, RoutedEventArgs e)
{
    if (Application.Current.InstallState == InstallState.Installed)
    {
        ChangeUI();
    }
}
```

The code first checks the current installation state of the application. If it's already installed on the user's computer, the method will call another method — ChangeUI, which changes the button content and disables it. The content of ChangeUI is as follows:

```
private void ChangeUI()
{
    instBtn.Content = "Application is out of browser!";
    instBtn.IsEnabled = false;

}
```

If we leave the code as it is, the change to the UI will occur only after the next time the users try to access our application. This is not good practice, as we wish the button's content and state to change as soon as we install the application. For that we can register to the InstallStateChanged event of the Application.Current object. This event fires every time the installation state changes and, thus, it is perfect for our current needs. Add the call to event handler in your constructor method, just below the call to the Loaded event, as follows:

```
Application.Current.InstallStateChanged += new EventHandler
(Current_InstallStateChanged);
```

Also, add the event handler as follows:

```
void Current_InstallStateChanged(object sender, EventArgs e)
{
    ChangeUI();
}
```

The last remaining task is to actually call the Install method and install the application.

Add the instBtn_Click method as follows:

```
private void instBtn_Click(object sender, RoutedEventArgs e)
{
    Application.Current.Install();
}
```

All it takes to install the application is to call the Install method of the Application.Current object.

Build your application but instead of running it the usual way, right-click on the **Chapter6-SimpleOOBTestPage.aspx** file in the web project, and click on **View** in browser.

You'll be greeted with the following screen:

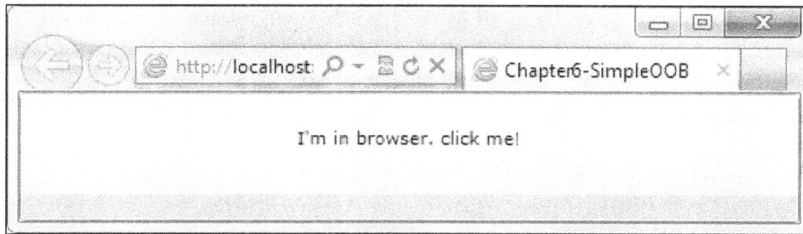

Click on the button. The default installation screen of Silverlight pops up allowing you to select which shortcuts you wish to create and whether you want to allow the installation of the application. If you have uploaded icons in the OOB settings window beforehand, it will be shown in this installation menu as well. Click on **Install**. Immediately the button's content will change as follows:

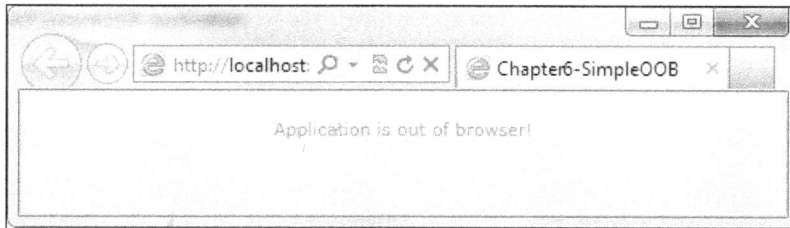

On your desktop (if you selected to have a shortcut there), you shall now see a shortcut to the application as well!

Click on the shortcut, and the application will run outside the browser:

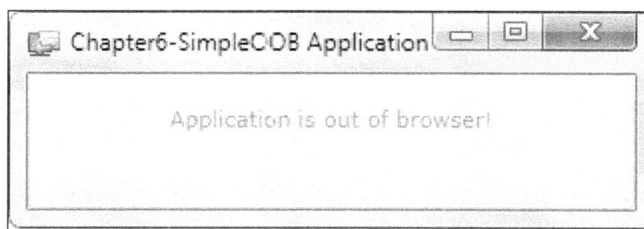

Uninstalling the application is a simple matter. Just run the application from the shortcut, right-click on it, and choose **Remove this application**.

We now have a basic OOB application up and running.

Checking network connectivity

In many scenarios of using OOB applications, your application will need to know whether or not it is connected to a network or needs to detect network changes. Silverlight allows us to check for both of those conditions using the `System.Net.NetworkInformation` namespace.

By using the `GetIsNetworkAvaliable` method of the `System.Net.NetworkInformation` namespace, we can tell if there is any sort of a network connection on the user's computer. It is important to note that having a network connection doesn't guarantee that the computer is connected to the Internet or can access the resources you are asking for. A good practice to fully detect connection to your resource is first check whether a network connection is available, and if so, call a service on the server you're trying to reach. If the call succeeds, you will be connected.

To detect network changes, the `NetworkInformation` namespace exposes the `NetworkAddressChanged` event. This event fires every time the network state of the user's computer changes. Let's see both of these concepts in action. Open the application that we have previously created in Visual Studio 2010, and then open the `MainPage.xaml` file.

We will now add a simple UI element to tell us whether we have a network connection or not. Add the following code snippet just below the `Button` element in `LayoutRoot`:

```
<StackPanel Height="30" Orientation="Horizontal"
VerticalAlignment="Bottom">
    <Ellipse Width="20" Height="20" Margin="20,0,0,0"
    x:Name="elNetwork"/>
    <TextBlock TextWrapping="Wrap"  x:Name="tbNetwork"
    VerticalAlignment="Center" Margin="10,0,0,0"/>
</StackPanel>
```

Now that we have the UI, let's add the login information. Open the `MainPage.xaml.cs` file, and add the following code snippet inside the constructor method:

```
System.Net.NetworkInformation.NetworkChange.NetworkAddressChanged +=
new System.Net.NetworkInformation.NetworkAddressChangedEventHandler
(NetworkChange_NetworkAddressChanged);
```

By using the preceding code snippet, we are registering to the
NetworkAddressChanged event and, thus, can change the UI
based on the network change.

Next, add the ChangeNetworkUI method, and call it from the
NetworkChange_NetworkAddressChanged handler:

```
private void ChangeNetworkUI()
{
    if (System.Net.NetworkInformation.NetworkInterface.
    GetIsNetworkAvailable())
    {
        elNetwork.Fill = new SolidColorBrush(Colors.Green);
        tbNetwork.Text = "Network is available!";
    }
    else
    {
        elNetwork.Fill = new SolidColorBrush(Colors.Red);
        tbNetwork.Text = "No network detected...";
    }
}
```

Lastly, we need to call the ChangeNetworkUI method from the Loaded event so
that it will show the initial state of the user's network. Change the MainPage_Loaded
method as follows:

```
if (Application.Current.InstallState == InstallState.Installed)
{
    ChangeUI();
    ChangeNetworkUI();
}
```

Build and run the application. If your computer isn't connected to any kind
of network, you will get the result, as shown in the following screenshot:

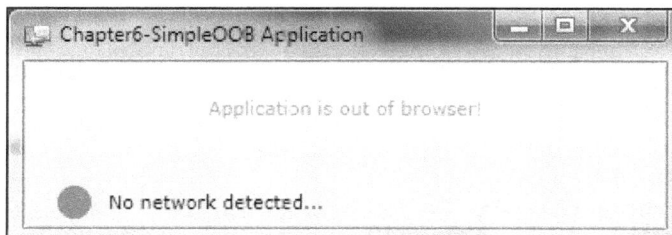

As soon as I connect my computer to a network, the UI will change as follows:

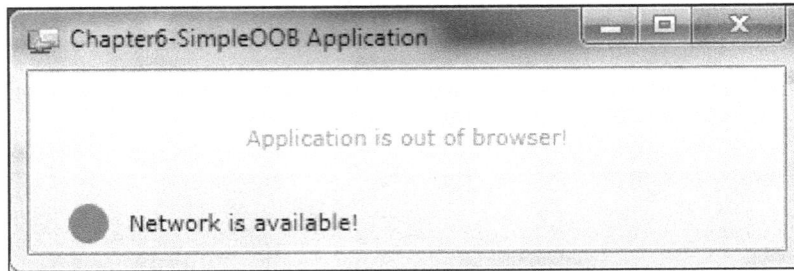

Displaying toast notifications

A cool feature that got added to Silverlight 4 OOB applications is toast notifications. Even if you are unfamiliar with the term "toast notification", I'm pretty sure you've seen your share of it. Do you know how Outlook pops out a little window on the bottom-right corner of your monitor when a new e-mail arrives? That's toast notification. These notifications can be used for anything—from alerting the user that a new update has been applied to your application (which we will do in the next topic) to showing a preview of an e-mail or a new tweet that someone tweeted on Twitter. In Silverlight, handling notifications is done using the NotificationWindow class. This class exposes different properties, such as Height, Width, and Content, for specifying the look of the window. Content defines the content of the window and can contain any kind of framework element or even a user control. To actually show the notification window, we will call the Show method while providing it with the number of milliseconds, we wish to show the window for.

Let's add a simple notification window to our application that will notify the user about changes in his/her network state.

Add the following method to your MainPage.xaml.cs file:

```
private void ShowNotification()
{
    NotificationWindow nw = new NotificationWindow();
    nw.Height = 80;
    nw.Width = 200;
    TextBlock tb = new TextBlock() { Text = "Your network state has
    changed!" };
    nw.Content = tb;
    nw.Show(5000);
}
```

Find the `ChangeNetworkUI` method and add a call to the `ShowNotification` method at the bottom of it. Build and run the application, and you'll notice that every time the network state changes, a little notification pops up at the bottom-right corner of your screen, as shown in the following screenshot:

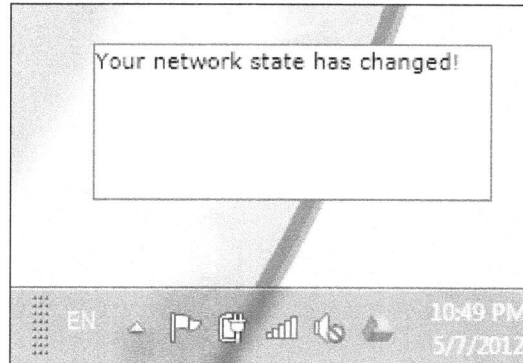

To show a nicer looking notification window, add a new user control to the project and name it `ToastWin`. Change its XAML code as follows:

```
<Grid x:Name="LayoutRoot" Background="White">
    <Grid.RowDefinitions>
        <RowDefinition Height="15"/>
        <RowDefinition Height="*"/>
    </Grid.RowDefinitions>
    <Border Background="Blue"/>
    <StackPanel Grid.Row="1">
        <TextBlock Text="Network status" HorizontalAlignment="Center"
        FontWeight="Bold"/>
        <TextBlock Text="The network status has changed. please check
        your computer settings for more information."
        TextWrapping="Wrap"/>
    </StackPanel>
</Grid>
```

Now change the value of the notification window's `Content` property as follows:

```
nw.Content = new ToastWin();
```

Build and run the application, and once your network state changes,
the new notification window pops up, as shown in the following screenshot:

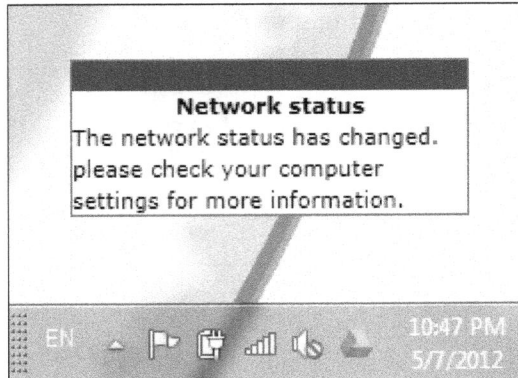

When working with notification windows, keep in mind the following limitations:

- Only one notification window can be active at a time. Double notification is impossible.

- There is no such thing as notification queuing. You cannot create a queue of notification windows and display them one after another.

- Notification is limited in time. You cannot create a notification without setting its duration.

- A notification window cannot exceed 400 pixels of width and 100 pixels of height.

Checking and updating application versions

When developing a regular Silverlight application, you have the benefit of being able to update your application from one central place and have all the users use the latest version of it. While OOB applications also support updates, their mechanism is a bit different. The Application object, which we mentioned earlier, exposes a method called CheckAndDownloadUpdateAsync. This method checks whether or not the XAP file on the server is newer than the XAP file of the user, and if so, downloads and updates the application. Once the download is completed, the CheckAndDownloadUpdateCompleted event fires. This event's argument object (e) contains a Boolean property called UpdateAvaliable, whose value will be true if an update is found and downloaded. This is how we can notify the user that his application has just been updated. The code for this process is quite straightforward. Let's add the ability to check and update the application version of our sample application. Perform the following steps:

1. First, add the event handler for `CheckAndDownloadUpdateCompleted` inside the constructor method of `MainPage.xaml.cs`:

```
Application.Current.CheckAndDownloadUpdateCompleted +=
new CheckAndDownloadUpdateCompletedEventHandler(Current_
CheckAndDownloadUpdateCompleted);
```

2. Next, add the `Current_CheckAndDownloadUpdatecompleted` method:

```
void Current_CheckAndDownloadUpdateCompleted(object sender,
CheckAndDownloadUpdateCompletedEventArgs e)
{
    if (e.UpdateAvailable)
    {
        MessageBox.Show("The application was updated!");
    }
}
```

If an update is available, a message box will pop up, informing the user about the update.

3. The last step left for this section is to add the call to actually check for the update. Change the `MainPage_Loaded` handler as follows:

```
void MainPage_Loaded(object sender, RoutedEventArgs e)
{
    if (Application.Current.InstallState ==
    InstallState.Installed)
    {
        ChangeUI();
        ChangeNetworkUI();
        Application.Current.CheckAndDownloadUpdateAsync();
    }
}
```

That's it. If an update is available to the application, it will be downloaded in the background. Once it finishes, the message box will pop up informing the user of the recent change.

Displaying HTML content in an OOB application

Silverlight 4 introduced the ability to display HTML content in OOB applications. Using the `WebBrowser` control, it is now possible to render HTML pages and JavaScript in any OOB application. It's important to note here that only OOB applications support the `WebBrowser` control, and if you try to use it in an in-browser application, it will not display anything.

To demonstrate the use of the WebBrowser control, we will create a browser-like OOB application. Open the **Chapter6-OOBHtml** project in Visual Studio 2010. The UI here is pretty simple—a TextBox control for entering an address for a website and a Button control.

There are three ways to load content into a WebBrowser control:

- Set its Source property in XAML
- Use the Navigate method
- Use the NavigateToString method

Setting the Source property is an XAML-friendly option to use the WebBrowser control. Add the following code snippet to the project's MainPage.xaml file just below the closing element of StackPanel:

```
<WebBrowser x:Name="wbControl" Source="http://www.packtpub.com" Grid.
Row="1"/>
```

If you run the application now, you should get the result, as shown in the following screenshot:

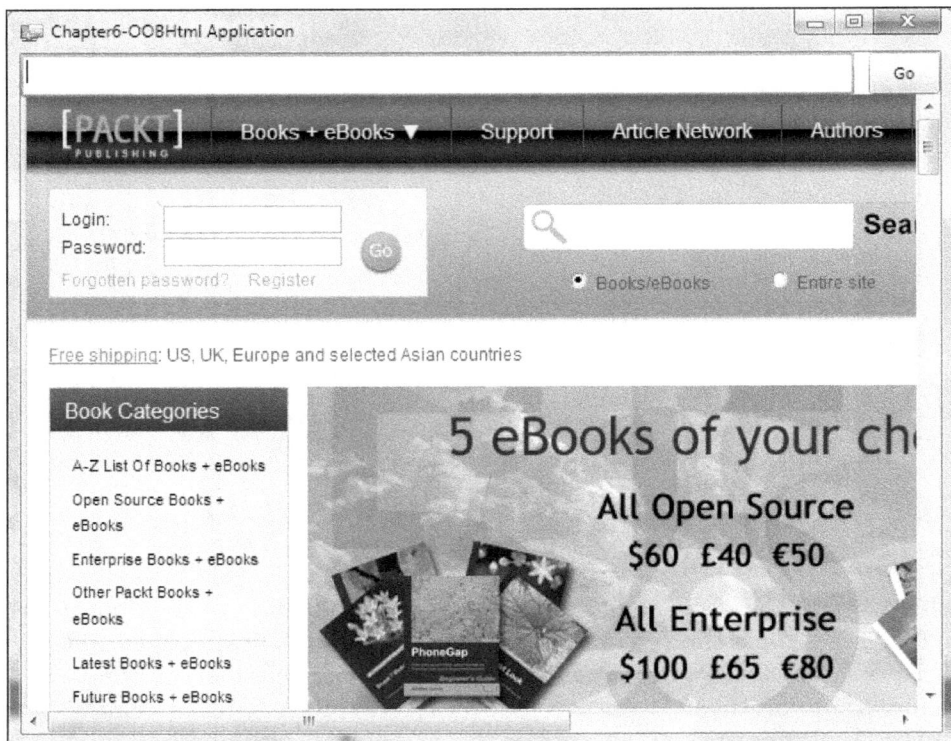

The live Packt website can now be seen inside your OOB application. As cool as that might be, our application currently offers no interactivity, as the user cannot change the displayed website. Let's change this now. Switch over to the `MainPage.xaml.cs` file, and add the following code snippet inside the `btnGo_Click` method:

```
if (tbAddress.Text != "")
    wbControl.Navigate(new Uri(tbAddress.Text, UriKind.Absolute));
else
    MessageBox.Show("Please enter a valid url");
```

The preceding code snippet uses the `Navigate` method of the `WebBrowser` control to change its source. The `Navigate` method requires a single argument of the `Uri` type. Build and run your application, and change the address in the `TextBox` control at the top. Enter any address you wish into the textbox (in my example, I used `http://www.yahoo.com`), and click on the **Go** button. Your desired website will now be shown in your application.

The last method of loading content to the `WebBrowser` control is the `NavigateToString` method. Using this method, you can 'feed' the `WebBrowser` control your own HTML code.

Let's change the logic of the button's `Click` event to check if we have entered a URL address (starting with `http`) or direct HTML code (starting with `<html>`). If we have typed an address, then we should continue using the `Navigate` method; if not, we will use the `NavigateToString` method. Change your `btnGo_Click` method as follows:

```
private void btnGo_Click(object sender, RoutedEventArgs e)
{
    if (tbAddress.Text != "")
    {
        if(tbAddress.Text.IndexOf("http")==0)
            wbControl.Navigate(new Uri(tbAddress.Text,
            UriKind.Absolute));
        else if (tbAddress.Text.IndexOf("<html>") == 0)
        {
            wbControl.NavigateToString(tbAddress.Text);
        }
        else
            MessageBox.Show("Please enter a valid url or HTML code.");
    }
    else
        MessageBox.Show("Please enter a url or HTML code.");
}
```

The code looks quite similar to the previous code snippet we wrote. The only difference here is that we check whether or not we have entered a URL of a website. If not, we will use the `NavigateToString` method and pass it the HTML code we wrote in the textbox. The result of typing `<html><body><div style='background-color:blue;color:white'>I'm a div</div></body></html>` will be as follows:

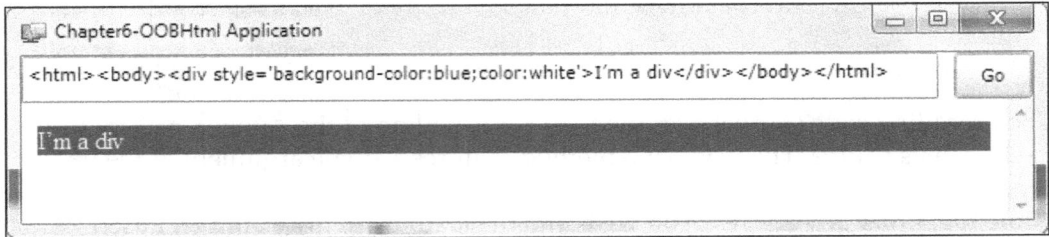

This chapter should get you started working with out-of-browser applications. OOB applications offer a lot of freedom while creating your applications. A feature we haven't covered in this chapter is working with COM Interop. While this feature is out of the scope of this book, I strongly recommend reading Justin Angel's post on COM located at `http://justinangel.net/CuttingEdgeSilverlight4ComFeatures`.

> COM Interop is only available on Windows. You cannot do COM calls on Mac, as there are no Coms on Mac.

Accessing the isolated storage

The isolated storage is a storage mechanism of Silverlight. Just like the HTML cookies, the isolated storage allows developers to store the data while their application is running, and restore it later when needed. The isolated storage is both user-specific and application-specific, meaning that for a single application, each user will have its own isolated storage, even if two users are running the application on the same computer. Isolated storage is also persistent, which means that even if you clean your browser's cache and temporary files, the data in the isolated storage will stay intact.

The default size of the isolated storage is 1 MB per application. If needed, the size can be increased through a dialog to the user, asking his permission to increase the size. We will discuss how to increase the size of the isolated storage soon.

To demonstrate the use of isolated storage, we will build a simple application that stores and retrieves notes written by the user from the isolated storage. To get started, open the **Chapter6-IsolatedStorage** solution in Visual Studio 2010.

The project contains a simple UI to save and show notes saved by the user. First, let's add the logic to save a note to the isolated storage. We will begin by getting an instance of the user's isolated storage area by using the GetUserStoreForApplication method of the IsolatedStorageFile class. Add the following code snippet to the btnSave_Click method, which resides in MainPage.xaml.cs:

```
IsolatedStorageFile isf = IsolatedStorageFile.
GetUserStoreForApplication();
```

Now that we have a representation of the user's isolated storage, we need to create a file that will hold the notes (that is, notes.txt) and just use the WriteLine method of the StreamWriter class to actually save it. Add the following code snippet just below the initialization of the IsolatedStorageFile class in the btnSave_Click method:

```
using (IsolatedStorageFileStream isfs = isf.OpenFile("notes.txt",
FileMode.Append))
{
    using (StreamWriter writer = new StreamWriter(isfs))
    {
        writer.WriteLine(tbNote.Text);
    }
}
tbNote.Text = string.Empty;
```

The preceding code snippet first tries to open a file named notes.txt from the isolated storage using the IsolatedStorageFile object's OpenFile method with a file mode of Append. Append will first check whether the specified file exists. If it does, Append will search for the end of that file in order to add new data; if it doesn't, it will create the file. From there we are using the good old StreamWriter object and just writing the notes the user has written in the textbox to the file.

Now that we have a way of writing the notes, let's add the method that randomly reads a note and displays it. The process of reading data from the isolated storage is quite similar to the writing process. Instead of using the Append mode for the OpenFile method, we will use the Open mode. Instead of using the StreamWriter object, we will use the StreamReader object (it does make sense after all; we want to read and not write). Add the following code snippet to the btnRnd_Click method:

```
IsolatedStorageFile isf = IsolatedStorageFile.
GetUserStoreForApplication();
List<string> notes = new List<string>();
```

```
if (isf.FileExists("notes.txt"))
{
    using (IsolatedStorageFileStream isfs = isf.OpenFile("notes.txt",
    FileMode.Open))
    {
        using (StreamReader reader = new StreamReader(isfs))
        {
            while (!reader.EndOfStream)
            {
                notes.Add(reader.ReadLine());
            }
        }
    }
    Random rnd = new Random();
    int rndNote = rnd.Next(0, notes.Count);
    noteText.Text = notes[rndNote];
}
else
    MessageBox.Show("no notes for you!");
```

The preceding code snippet first gets an instance of the user isolated storage and creates a new list of strings to represent the notes. Next, we will perform a check to see if there are any notes saved for this user at all. From there we will use the StreamReader object to read the file, save its content to a list, and then generate a note with a random number to read and display it for the user.

Build and run the application. Save some notes and try to read them back using the **Random** button. You should get something similar to the following screenshot:

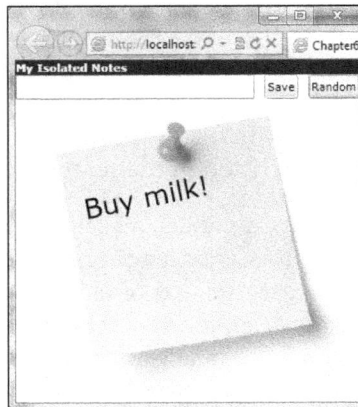

As you can see, working with the isolated storage is easy and straightforward.

Increasing the isolated storage size

While our little note application may never need more then 1 MB of storage, some other applications you develop might need it. Increasing the storage size is a simple matter of calling the `IncreaseQuotaTo` method of the `IsolatedStorageFile` object while supplying it with the new size (represented by a long) in bytes. For example to increase the quota to 2 MB, we will pass `2097152` to the method. An example for such a call would be as follows:

```
IsolatedStorageFile isf = IsolatedStorageFile.
GetUserStoreForApplication();
isf.IncreaseQuotaTo(2097152);
```

As soon as we call the `IncreaseQuotaTo` method, a dialog box pops up asking the user to confirm that he wishes to increase the quota size, as shown in the following screenshot:

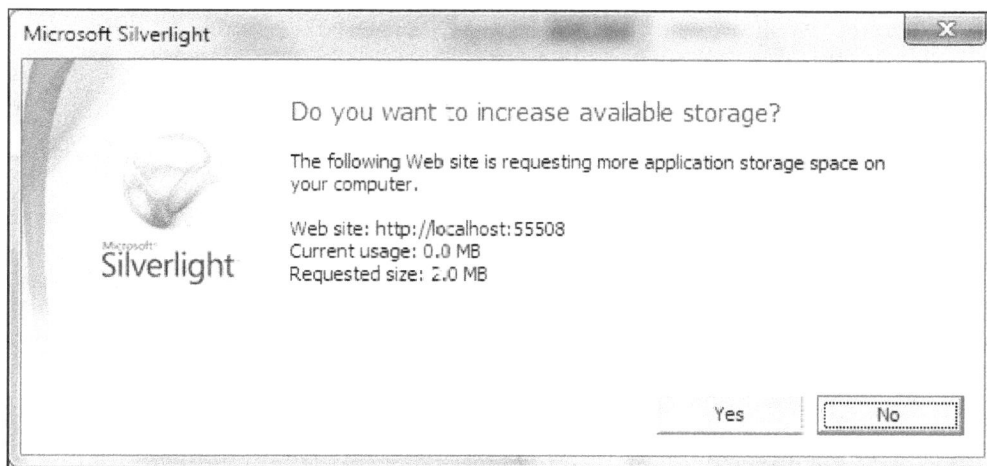

As soon as the user clicks on **Yes**, the quota increases.

Another useful property of the `IsolatedStorageFile` class is `UsedSize`. This property will return the amount of space the application is already using. This property is most commonly used when you wish to calculate the amount of available space you have left in the isolated storage, or when you wish to request more space and need to know how much is already in use.

You can find a sample of implementing the `IncreaseQuotaTo` method in the final version of this project within the downloadable content of this book.

Interacting with the DOM

When hosted in a browser, Silverlight is a part of the page, the same as any other HTML object in it, so it's only fair that Silverlight will be able to interact with the different elements on the page. Meet the `System.Window.Browser` namespace. It will be your starting point for communicating with the HTML DOM. The namespace exposes different methods for accessing cookies and query strings, calling the JavaScript functions, and even manipulating the DOM elements.

Accessing cookies and query strings

We all know (and some of us love) HTML cookies, which are those little text nuggets that the browser saves on the user's computer and are mostly used for authentication, session tracking, and so on. Well, the good news is that you can access and save cookies using Silverlight as well.

Saving a cookie is a simple matter of calling the `SetProperty` method of the `HtmlPage` class's `Document` object with a string in the following format:

```
Key=Value;expires=ExpireDate
```

The following code snippet can be used to save a cookie on the user's computer:

```
public void SaveCookie(string key, string value, DateTime expireDate)
{
    string newCookie = string.Format("{0}={1};expires={2}", key,
value,
    expireDate.ToString("R"));
    HtmlPage.Document.SetProperty("cookie", newCookie);
}
```

The `newCookie` object will hold a formatted string, as explained in the preceding code snippet. It is important to note that the `DateTime` object must be passed using the R parameter of its `ToString` method, which will output the date as follows:

```
Sun, 25 Jan 2012 22:45:07 GMT
```

Once we have the string for the cookie we wish to save, all that's left to do is to call the `SetProperty` method of the `Document` object. The `SetProperty` method requires two properties. First, is the property name we wish to set (in our case cookie) and second, is the value of that property (in our case the cookie string).

Retrieving a cookie can be done using the following code snippet:

```
public string GetCookie(string key)
{
    string[] cookiesCollection = HtmlPage.Document.Cookies.Split(';');
```

```
    foreach (string cookie in cookiesCollection)
    {
        string[] keyValue = ccokie.Split('=');
        if (keyValue.Length == 2)
        {
            if (keyValue[0] == key)
            return keyValue[1];
        }
    }
    return null;
}
```

First, we get all the cookies the browser stores using the Cookies properties of the Document object. Once we have all the cookies, we will just iterate through them one by one using the foreach loop and once we find a cookie whose key is the same as the one we are looking for, we will return its value.

Getting the query string values is just as easy. By using the QueryString object of the Document object, we can pass in a key and get the value. For example, say my Silverlight application is hosted on a page whose URL is http://localhost:1080/Page/Silverlightapp.aspx?ID=5. Here, the query string I wish to read is ID, so in the Silverlight application we will use the following line of code:

```
string id = HtmlPage.Document.QueryString["ID"];
```

If you wish to first check whether the URL contains the key that you are after, simply use the ContainsKey method as follows:

```
string id;
if(HtmlPage.Document.QueryString.ContainsKey("ID"))
id = HtmlPage.Document.QueryString["ID"];
```

Working with cookies and a query string is a common scenario when working with Silverlight. Luckily, it's not an overly complicated process, and you would probably get used to it quickly.

Communication between JavaScript and Silverlight

When working with Silverlight as an in-browser application, there may come times when you wish to get additional data from the hosting context by using JavaScript. Silverlight allows us to do a two-way communication with JavaScript—a JavaScript method can call a Silverlight object's methods, and Silverlight can call JavaScript methods and get back data from them.

Calling a JavaScript function from Silverlight is done using the `Invoke` method of the `HtmlPage` class's `Window` object. Let's assume we have a JavaScript function in the host page of our Silverlight application called `GetData`, which accepts no arguments and returns a string value. The following line of code will be used to call it from Silverlight:

```
string dataFromJS = HtmlPage.Window.Invoke("GetData");
```

Another variation of communicating with JavaScript can be passing data to a JavaScript function from Silverlight. For example, let's assume we have the following JavaScript function:

```
function ShowName(name) {
alert("Hello, " + name);
}
```

The `ShowName` function must get a string argument from the calling party. The `Invoke` method allows us to specify an optional array of parameters to pass to the JavaScript function we are calling. In the `ShowName` function's case, the calling code will look as follows:

```
HtmlPage.Window.Invoke("ShowName","Johnny");
```

Calling a Silverlight method from JavaScript is quite a simple process as well. The first step is to declare either the entire class as scriptable using the `ScriptableType` attribute or declare specific methods as scriptable using the `ScriptableMember` attribute. For example, if I wish to expose all the `public` methods on my `MainPage.xaml.cs` file to JavaScript, it will use `ScriptableType` as follows:

```
[ScriptableType]
public partial class MainPage : UserControl
{
    ...
}
```

To expose specific methods and not the entire class to JavaScript, we will use the `ScriptableMember` attribute as follows:

```
[ScriptableMember]
public void ExposedMethod()
{
    ...
}
```

Once we declare what we wish to expose, we need to create a so-called bridge to JavaScript so that it will be able to access the scriptable member. The bridge itself is nothing more than an alias that can be used in the JavaScript function to gain access to the Silverlight content. Creating the bridge is a simple matter of calling the `RegisterScriptableObject` method of the `HtmlPage` class. Let's assume we have declared the entire `MainPage.xaml.cs` class as `ScriptableType` and we wish to create an alias for it. The following code snippet will get the job done:

```
public MainPage()
{
    InitializeComponent();
        HtmlPage.RegisterScriptableObject("myScriptableClass", this);
}
```

Our Silverlight code is now ready for some JavaScript communication!

The Silverlight plug-in exposes an object called content which exposes to the world (or in this case JavaScript) the content of the plug-in. When we register an object using the RegisterScriptableObject method, the alias we chose for it will be appended to that content property. The last steps of accessing the Silverlight method using JavaScript is retrieving the plugin instance (using `document.getElementById` for example) and then refering the scriptable method using the content property. Assuming that our Silverlight object has the ID of `MySilverlightControl` and our Silverlight control has a method called `ExposedMethod`, which is scriptable and was registerd using the `RegisterScriptableObject` with the alias of `myScriptableClass`, we will be able to access it from JavaScript using the following code snippet:

```
function GetDataFromSilverlight() {
var slCtrl = document.getElementById("MySilverlightControl");
slCtrl.content.myScriptableClass.ExposedMethod();
}
```

Manipulating the HTML DOM

Silverlight's interaction with its host doesn't end at JavaScript. Silverlight is also powerful enough to manipulate the **HTML Document Object Model (DOM)** as well.

The main entry point for working with the HTML DOM in Silverlight is the `Document` object of the `HtmlPage` class. Once you have a reference to the `Document` object, you can get any HTML element using the `GetElementById` method and set any property that you wish on it. Let's assume our host ASPX page has a `div` tag with `id` of `messageText`:

```
<div id="messageText">
</div>
```

We wish to have a button on the hosted Silverlight application which, when clicked, will change the content of messageText div (using the InnerHTML property) to a predefined value. Examine the following code snippet:

```
private void btnHtmlMessage(object sender, RoutedEventArgs e)
{
    HtmlDocument hDoc = HtmlPage.Document;
        HtmlElement divElement = hDoc.GetElementById("messageText");
        divElement.SetProperty("innerHTML", "Hello from
Silverlight!!!");
}
```

The preceding code snippet will first get an instance of the Document object of the HTML DOM using the HtmlPage class's Document object. Once we have the HtmlDocument object declared, we will find the element we wish to alter using the GetElementById method (an other alternative would be using the GetElementsByTagName method, which gets all the elements of a specific tag, such as div or span) and set its property using the SetProperty method.

The SetProperty method isn't limited to just the innerHTML property. Any valid HTML property (for example, Background or Width) can be used within SetProperty.

Silverlight to Silverlight communication

Silverlight 3 introduced the concept of local messaging. Local messaging allows us to communicate multiple Silverlight controls hosted on the same page, across browser tabs or even across browsers! The following screenshot shows how a message from a Silverlight application running in one instance of Internet Explorer is shown in a Silverlight application running in a completely different instance of Internet Explorer:

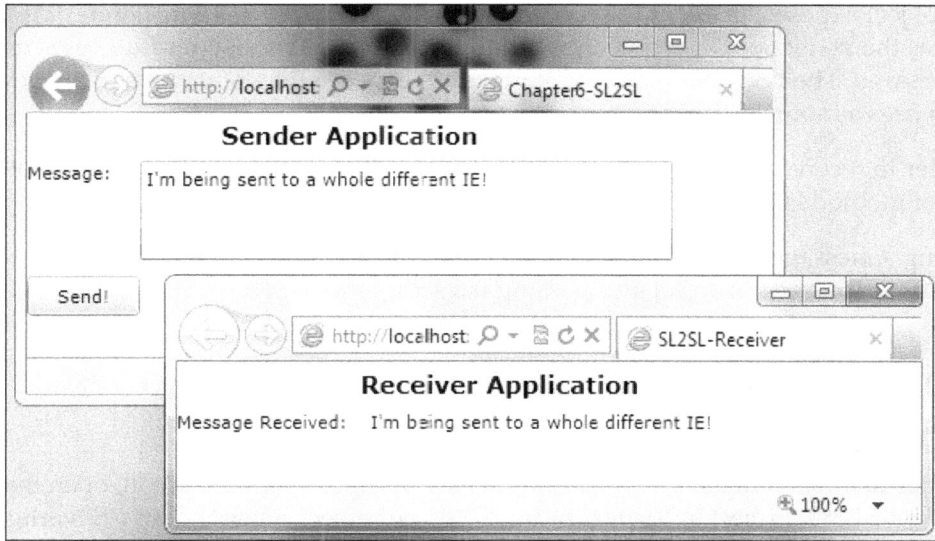

The `System.Windows.Messaging` namespace contains two objects that allow us to create the communication. The `LocalMessageSender` class represents the sending end of the local messaging channel and the `LocalMessageReceiver` class represents the receiving end of that same channel. A basic configuration of local messaging is given ahead.

On the sender application, we will have the following object initialized:

```
LocalMessageSender messageSender = new LocalMessageSender("localChann
el");
```

The argument passed to the constructor represents a name for the channel communication. In order for the receiver to be able to receive communication from the sender, it must specify the same channel communication name. By default, the name supplied will be scoped to the domain level, but by specifying a second parameter of the `ReceiverNameScope` type, you can scope it to global level as well.

In order to receive communication from the preceding sender, the receiving application will have the following object initialized:

```
LocalMessageReceiver messageReceiver = new LocalMessageReceiver("loca
lChannel");
```

Each object exposes an event to serve its purpose. The `LocalMessageSender` class exposes the `SendCompleted` event, which fires as soon as the sender finishes sending the message. The `LocalMessageReceiver` class exposes the `MessageReceived` event, which fires as soon as the receiver receives a message from a sender.

In order to receive a message, the receiver has run the `Listen` method. Once the `Listen` method is run, the receiver configuration cannot be changed.

Sending a message is a simple matter of calling the `SendAsync` method of the `LocalMessageSender` object and passing it a string message.

Creating a local communication demo application

To better demonstrate the use of Silverlight to Silverlight communication, open the **Chapter6-SL2SL** project in Visual Studio 2010. The project consists of two Silverlight projects and a web project. Each Silverlight project represents one end of the solution. The first project will act as the sender, meaning we will send text messages from it to the other project, which will act as the receiver.

Both Silverlight projects have a simple UI that consist of a `Grid` control, and a few `TextBox` and `TextBlock` controls. The sender application's `TextBox` is named `tbMessage` and the receiver's `TextBlock` is named `tbMsgReceived`.

To get started, open the `MainPage.xaml.cs` file of the **Chapter6-SL2SL** sender project. The first thing we need to do is to define the `private` variable to hold an instance of `LocalMessageSender`. `LocalMessageSender` is a class, which represents the sending end of the local messaging channel between the Silverlight applications.

Add the following line of code just above the `MainPage` constructor:

```
private LocalMessageSender _sender;
```

Next, we need to initiate the new variable using the `LocalMessageSender` constructor. The constructor of `LocalMessageSender` requires one argument—the name of the receiver that will receive messages from it. Inside the `MainPage_Loaded` method, add the following line of code:

```
_sender = new LocalMessageSender("msgReceiver");
```

We now have a sender object ready for use! The last task we have for this application is to actually send the message when the **Send** button is clicked. Sending a message is a simple matter of using the `SendAsync` method of the `LocalMessageSender` method, with the message we wish to send as the argument. Because this is an asynchronous method, we can also handle the `SendCompleted` event, which fires as soon as the message is sent. For this simple demo application though, we won't use it. Add the following line of code inside the `btnSend_Click` method:

```
_sender.SendAsync(tbMessage.Text);
```

Now that we are done with the sending end of our application, it's time to handle the receiving end. To get started, open the `MainPage.xaml.cs` file of the **Chapter6-SL2SL** receiver project. In order to handle incoming messages, we first need to create an instance of the `LocalMessageReceiver` class and attach a handler to its `MessageReceived` event. Add the following code snippet to the `MainPage_Loaded` method:

```
LocalMessageReceiver rec = new LocalMessageReceiver("msgReceiver");
            rec.MessageReceived += new EventHandler
            <MessageReceivedEventArgs>(rec_MessageReceived);
```

The preceding code snippet creates a new instance of the `LocalMessageReceiver` class, passing the same receiver name to the constructor as we did in the `LocalMessageSender` class. In addition to the preceding code snippet, register a handler to the `MessageReceived` event, which fires as soon as a message is sent to the specific receiver (named `msgReceiver`).

In order for `LocalMessageReceiver` to be in a state that it awaits incoming messages, we have to use the `Listen` method of the class. Add the following line of code in the `MainPage_Loaded` method:

```
rec.Listen();
```

The last thing we need to deal with for this application is what happens when the receiver receives a message. For that we need to handle the `rec_MessageReceived` method. Add the following code snippet to the `MainPage.xaml.cs` file:

```
void rec_MessageReceived(object sender, MessageReceivedEventArgs e)
{
    tbMsgReceived.Text = e.Message;
}
```

Build and run the application. A browser will be opened with the **Chapter6-SL2SLTestPage.aspx** page open. Copy the URL and open a second browser. Paste the URL to the address bar and change the page from **Chapter6-SL2SLTestPage.aspx** to **SL2SL-ReceiverTestPage.aspx**. Try to enter a message in the sender application and click on **Send**. If all goes well, you will see the same message in the receiver application!

A screenshot of the application can be seen at the beginning of this topic.

If you wish to learn more about local communication, please refer to the MSDN documentation located at `http://msdn.microsoft.com/en-us/library/dd833063(v=vs.95).aspx`.

Accessing the clipboard

Silverlight 4 introduced a new API for working with text via the clipboard. Currently Silverlight's clipboard API is limited only to text, but it is still a great way for your application to interact with not only its host page, but the entire host OS. Working with the clipboard is all about using the new `Clipboard` static class. The `Clipboard` class exposes three methods for working with text as follows:

- `ContainsText`: This queries the `Clipboard` object to check whether or not it includes any text
- `GetText`: This retrieves any saved text in the `Clipboard` object
- `SetText`: This sets the text you wish to save in the `Clipboard` object

Setting and getting text from the clipboard is as trivial as it gets. To get data from the clipboard, we will use the following line of code:

```
string textFromClipboard = Clipboard.GetText();
```

To set the clipboard's text, we will use the following line of code:

```
Clipboard.SetText("Some sample text.");
```

When trying to use the `Clipboard` class in a non-elevated application, the user will be shown the following dialog box:

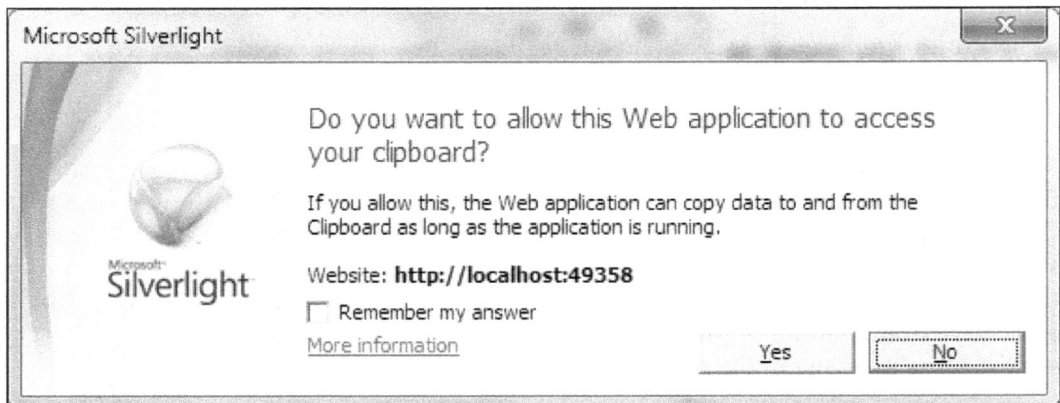

This dialog box helps to protect the user from potentially harmful applications that might try to either steal data from the clipboard or fill the clipboard with spam.

To handle a situation where the user might not allow our application to access his clipboard, we will wrap the call to the clipboard with the following `try-catch` expression:

```
try
{
    Clipboard.SetText("Text");
}
catch (SecurityException se)
{
    MessageBox.Show("Clipboard access failed.\n"+se.Message);
}
```

If the user declines the application from accessing the clipboard, a security exception will be raised. This exception is just what our `catch` expression catches.

Reading from and writing to the host filesystem

The new I/O dialog boxes in Silverlight allow our application to store and read files from outside of the isolated storage area, which we have discussed earlier.

To open a file in Silverlight, we use the `OpenFileDialog` class, which enables us to ask the user for one or more files from his system and load the data from these files to the memory. The `OpenFileDialog` class exposes the following three properties for customizing the selections presented to the user when the dialog box is launched:

- `Filter`: This enables us to filter which type or types of files the user can select from this dialog box.
- `FilterIndex`: If you allow the user to select from multiple file formats, setting this property will determine which filter is the default one.
- `MultiSelect`: This is a Boolean property, which specifies whether the user can select a single file or multiple files. If not set, the default behavior of the dialog box is to allow the user to select a single file.

As opposed to the `OpenFileDialog` class, the `SaveFileDialog` class is used to save a file on the user's computer. Just like its opening file sibling, the `SaveFileDialog` class exposes the `Filter` and `FilterIndex` properties, but instead of the `MultiSelect` property, the `SaveFileDialog` class exposes the `DefaultExt` property, which enables us to specify a default file extension, if the user types a filename without one.

To demonstrate the use of both classes, open the sample project—**Chapter6-IO** from the downloadable content in Visual Studio 2010.

The project contains a simple UI of two buttons that are used for loading and saving files and a `TextBox` control.

First, let's wire up the `Load` button's `Click` event, so it will let us load a `.txt` file from the user's computer and display its content in the `TextBox` control. Open the `MainPage.xaml.cs` file and add the following code snippet to the `btnLoad_Click` method:

```
OpenFileDialog ofd = new OpenFileDialog();
ofd.Filter = "Text Files (*.txt)|*.txt";
if (ofd.ShowDialog() == true)
{
    StreamReader fileStream =  ofd.File.OpenText();
        tbText.Text = fileStream.ReadToEnd();
}
```

The first thing the above code does is create a new instance of the OpenFileDialog class. Once declared we set the OpenFileDialog's Filter property to allow the users to only load text files with the file extension of txt. The next line is where the magic happens. The ShowDialog method fires up the load file dialog and returns true if the user selected a file or false if he/she clicked cancel.

If the user did select a file we use the `OpenText` method of the File object of the `OpenFileDialog` to get a `StreamReader` object and use its `ReadToEnd` method to read the content of the file to the `TextBox` control. Build and run the application and load a text file of your choice. You will see its content in Silverlight as soon as the file loads.

Now that we have the load part working, let's wire up the save part. Add the following code to the `btnSave_Click` method:

```
SaveFileDialog sfd = new SaveFileDialog();
sfd.DefaultExt = "txt";
sfd.Filter = "Text Files (*.txt)|*.txt";
if (sfd.ShowDialog() == true)
{
```

```
Stream stream = sfd.OpenFile();
    StreamWriter sw = new StreamWriter(stream);
    sw.WriteLine(tbText.Text);
    sw.Flush();
    sw.Close();
}
```

We start off with initializing a new `SaveFileDialog` object. Once done, we set a default extension for the saved file and set a filter so only text files will be shown in the dialog. Once we fire up the `ShowDialog` method, the dialog for saving a file pops up. If the user typed a filename and clicked save we start the writing process.

We first get the Stream object of the selected file by using the `OpenFile` method of the `SaveFileDialog` object. Then, we create a new `StreamWriter` object, passing it to the file stream we declared earlier. We finish off the process by calling the `WriteLine` method to write the text the user wrote in the `TextBox` and then flush and close the `StreamWriter` object.

Go ahead and build the application. Run it and write some stuff in the `TextBox`. When done, click the save button and the new file should be created just where you set it with your text inside of it.

Handling alternative input methods

Apart from support for the good old left mouse button, Silverlight 4 has added support for the right mouse click and mouse wheel as well. Up until Silverlight 4, whenever you tried to right-click on an application, you were getting the Silverlight options menu. With the introduction of Silverlight 4, however, we can now override this default behavior and implement our own logic. In RIA applications, you would usually want to display a contextual menu.

Just like its left button sibling, handling the right mouse button can be done by handling the events of `MouseRightButtonDown` and `MouseRightButtonUp`. In order to prevent the default Silverlight options menu from showing up, you have to handle the `MouseRightButtonDown` event, and set the `Handled` property of the `MouseButtonEventArgs` object to `true`.

Open the **Chapter6-RightClick** project from the downloadable content. The project contains a simple `Border` control. Handlers were added on the `Border` control for both the `MouseRightButtonDown` and `MouseRightButtonUp` controls. Switch over to the `MainPage.xaml.cs` file. As stated in the preceding paragraph, we first have to prevent the default Silverlight menu to show up. Add the following line of code to the `rightBrd_MouseRightButtonDown` method:

```
e.Handled = true;
```

The ContextMenu class represents a context menu, just like Silverlight's default. Menu items are represented by the MenuItem class. In order to create such a contextual menu, we have to first create an object from the ContextMenu class, then create a few MenuItem instances, and finally add them to the ContextMenu object we have created previously. Add the following code snippet to the rightBrd_MouseRightButtonUp method:

```
_menu = new ContextMenu();
MenuItem item = new MenuItem();
item.Header = "Test item 1";
_menu.Items.Add(item);

MenuItem item2 = new MenuItem();
item2.Header = "Test item 2";
_menu.Items.Add(item2);
MenuItem item3 = new MenuItem();
item3.Header = "Test item 3";
_menu.Items.Add(item3);

_menu.HorizontalOffset = e.GetPosition(this).X;
_menu.VerticalOffset = e.GetPosition(this).Y;
_menu.IsOpen = true;
```

Notice how both the HorizontalOffset and VerticalOffset properties of the ContextMenu object have to be defined, otherwise the Silverlight rendering engine won't know where to position the contextual menu. Using the GetPosition method of the MouseButtonEventArgs object enables us to get the current position of the mouse on both the x and y coordinates.

That's it! Build and run the application, and you should get the following result after right-clicking on the Border control:

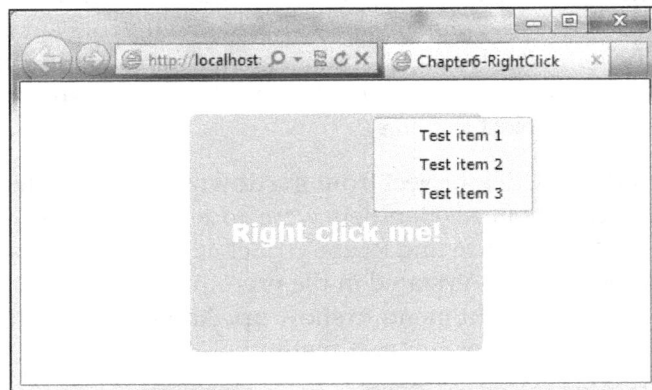

Handling the mouse wheel

Just like the mouse buttons, Silverlight allows us to react to the mouse wheel as well. In order to handle the mouse wheel, you have to handle the `MouseWheel` event of a control. For example, to handle the `MouseWheel` event of the `rightBrd` control in the previous example, you can add the following line of code in the constructor method of `MainPage`:

```
rightBrd.MouseWheel+=new MouseWheelEventHandler(rightBrd_MouseWheel);
```

Inside the `rightBrd_MouseWheel` method, you can access the `Delta` property of the `MouseWheelEventArgs` object, which is a double type of object representing the "amount" of scroll by which the user has scrolled.

I encourage you to check Laurent Duveau's great blog post on handling the mouse wheel event located at `http://weblogs.asp.net/lduveau/archive/2009/11/20/silverlight-4-mouse-wheel-support.aspx`.

Test your knowledge

1. You are developing a Silverlight 4 application that uses the isolated storage. The application you just created is a module of a bigger application already running. Your newly created application will need 6 MB of free space in the isolated storage. You need to ensure that the minimum amount of space needed to save those 6 MB is requested. Which code snippet should you use?

   a. `Using(IsolatedStorageFile isf = IsolatedStorageFile.GetUserStoreForApplication()) { isf.IncreaseQuotaTo(6291456) });`

   b. `Using(IsolatedStorageFile isf = IsolatedStorageFile.GetUserStoreForApplication()) { isf.IncreaseQuotaTo(isf.UsedSize+6291456) });`

   c. `Using(IsolatedStorageFile isf = IsolatedStorageFile.GetUserStoreForApplication()) { isf.IncreaseQuota(6291456) });`

   d. `Using(IsolatedStorageFile isf = IsolatedStorageFile.GetUserStoreForApplication()) { isf.IncreaseQuotaTo(isf.AvaliableSpace+6291456) });`

2. You are developing an image gallery application using Silverlight 4. Your application is running in browser. You need to provide a user with a way to upload images from his computer to the application. Which action should you perform?

    a. Use the `SaveFileDialog` class.

    b. Call a JavaScript function from the application that will handle the image uploading logic.

    c. Use the `OpenFileDialog` class.

    d. Use the `Environment.GetFolderPath` method of the `CreateFileDialog` class.

3. You are developing a Silverlight 4 application. The application contains a `Grid` element. You wish to create a contextual menu on the grid headers that will appear when a user right-clicks on them. You handle the `RightMouseButtonDown` event of the `Grid` element to create the `ContextMenu` object and its items. When you test the application, you discover that when the right mouse button is released, the standard Silverlight options menu appears. What should you do to prevent the standard menu from appearing?

    a. Set the `MouseButtonEventArgs.Handled` property to `true`.

    b. Handle the `RightMouseButtonUp` event.

    c. Set the `Grid` control's element — `IsHitTestVisible` property to `false`.

    d. Set the `MouseButtonEventArgs.Handled` property to `false`.

4. You are developing an out-of-browser Silverlight application. The application will be used both offline and online. You need to display a toast notification to the user when the network connection goes offline. You handle the event of `NetworkAddressChanged`. Which code snippet should you use inside of the handler to raise the notification when the network is offline?

    a.
```
If(!NetworkInterface.GetIsNetworkAvailable())
{ NotificationWindow nw = new NotificationWindow();
nw.Height = 80; nw.Width = 200; TextBlock tb = new
TextBlock() { Text = "You are now offline" };
nw.Content = tb;
nw.Show(5000)
};
```

b. ```
    If (NetworkInterface.GetIsNetworkAvailable())
    { NotificationWindow nw = new NotificationWindow();
    nw.Height = 80; nw.Width = 200; TextBlock tb = new
    TextBlock() { Text = "You are now offline" };
    nw.Content = tb;
    nw.Show(5000)
    };
    ```

c.  ```
    If (!NetworkInterface.GetIsNetworkAvailable())
    { NotificationWindow nw = new NotificationWindow();
    nw.Height = 80; nw.Width = 200; TextBlock tb = new
    TextBlock() { Text = "You are now offline" };
    nw.Show(5000)
    };
    ```

d. ```
    If (NetworkInterface.GetIsNetworkAvailable())
    { NotificationWindow nw = new NotificationWindow();
    nw.Height = 80; nw.Width = 200; TextBlock tb = new
    TextBlock() { Text = "You are now offline" };
    nw.Content = tb;
    };
    ```

5.  You have a Silverlight 4 application hosted in an ASPX page that has a JavaScript function called `ShowMyName`. The function expects a single parameter called `Name`. The Silverlight application has a `TextBox` element called `tbName`, into which the user enters a name. You need to pass the content of `tbName` to the JavaScript function. Which code snippet will you use?

    a.  ```
        String name = HtmlPage.Window.Invoke("ShowMyName");
        name.sendParameter("Johnny");
        ```

    b. ```
        HtmlPage.Window.Invoke("ShowMyName",Johnny);
        ```

    c.  ```
        HtmlPage.Window.Invoke("ShowMyName","Johnny");
        ```

    d. ```
        HtmlPage.Document.Invoke("ShowMyName","Johnny");
        ```
        ```

Summary

This chapter covered all the ways in which Silverlight enables us to communicate with its host environment. We communicated with the printer to print visuals off Silverlight to the real world; we created an out-of-browser application, which lets us use all the goodies of the OS such as local filesystem, network status, and more. We then discussed the isolated storage mechanism, which allows us to store data securely per application and per user.

We also discussed a second option for loading and saving files in Silverlight using the `OpenFileDialog` and `SaveFileDialog` classes. Using these classes, a user is able to load files from his local computers and save files back to his computer directly in the Silverlight application.

Other subjects we discussed in this chapter were accessing the clipboard, interacting with the HTML DOM, and handling alternative input methods such as the mouse's right button.

We've covered a lot of ground in this chapter and if you don't feel 100 percent comfortable using all of these methods in your application yet, don't worry; some of these concepts take time to sink in.

In the next chapter we are going to discuss how to structure your application correctly. We will discuss how to create and consume resource dictionaries, implant localization and globalization, and handle events at the application level.

7
Structuring Applications

So far, we have covered topics that discuss how to build Silverlight applications. In this chapter we are going to put it aside for a bit and take a look at how to make our code look better and behave better. We will discuss how to utilize sample data while using binding, how to arrange styles in a smart way using resource dictionaries, how to localize an application, and finish off with how to handle events at the application level.

In this chapter we will cover the following topics:

- Creating and consuming resource dictionaries
- Implementing localization and globalization
- Handling application-level events

Creating and consuming resource dictionaries

When we discussed styles in *Chapter 3, Enhancing the User Interface*, we realized that styles can be placed in various scopes throughout our application. Most of the time we will place styles at the global level, which means our App.xaml file may get messy quite fast. A commonly used strategy to enhance the App.xaml file is to place styles and resources that are related to one another into what's called a resource dictionary. When an application uses multiple resource dictionaries, these dictionaries will be merged at compile time.

A nice feature of resource dictionaries is their ability to be used as hosts to sample data at design time.

Utilizing sample data for a item template

When creating an application that uses a custom item template, it's easier to design the template when you can view the data you are designing it for. When you use the binding engine to bind data in Visual Studio, you are usually left in the cold. You can set the properties you bind to, but you can't see the result until you run the application. If you have made a mistake, you need to fix it, compile it, and run it again. This can get tedious quite fast. To get past this issue, sample data was introduced.

By using Microsoft Expression Blend, you can easily create sample data for your templates that will represent the real data you are binding and be viewed at design time.

Create a new Silverlight 4 project in Visual Studio 2010 and name it **Chapter7-SampleData**. Open `MainPage.xaml` and add the following XAML code inside the `LayoutRoot Grid` element:

```
<ListBox x:Name="ProductsList" HorizontalAlignment="Stretch"
VerticalAlignment="Stretch"/>
```

Now that we have a `ListBox` control added, let's add an item template to it. Perform the following steps:

1. In the solution explorer, right-click on **MainPage.xaml** and select **Open in Expression Blend**.

2. On the right-hand side of the screen, you'll see the **Data** tab. Under that tab, we have an option to create new sample data.

3. Click on the tab and then on the **Create Sample Data** button (the left of the two buttons) and select **New Sample Data...**, as shown in the following screenshot:

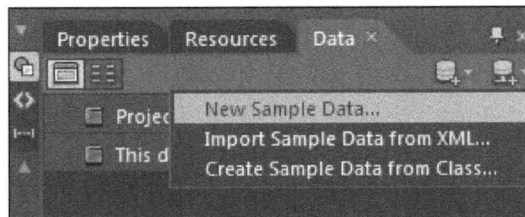

The **New Sample Data** dialog box will pop up, as shown in the following screenshot:

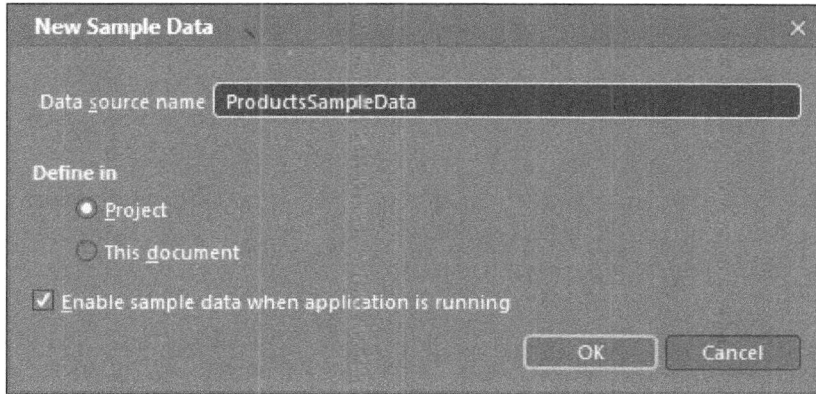

4. Enter **ProductsSampleData** in the **Data source name** field.

5. Under the **Define in section**, we can set what should be the scope of our sample data. If the **Enable sample data when application is running** checkbox is checked, the application will use the sample data while running. If you only design the template using sample data, but have your listbox data bound to real data, you will have to uncheck the box in order for the application to show the real data. For our example, leave the **Define in** section to the default option— **Project**. Click on **OK** to create the new sample data source.

Once the new data source is created, the **Data** window will show the current sample data collection. By default, we have a collection of two properties under the **Collection** section— **Property1**, which is a string and **Property2**, which is a Boolean:

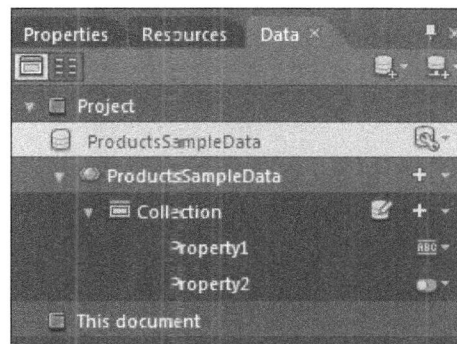

Changing a property's type

To change a property's type, click on the little drop-down arrow beside it and change the type to either string, number, Boolean or image. Each type will have its own properties that you can set. For example, the image type will let you choose a directory with images to show, while the number type will let you set the length of the number. For our demonstration, keep **Property1** a string but change the type of **Property2** to image.

Now that we have the data structure all set up, let's set up the actual data. Click on the little icon next to **Collection**, which is the **Edit Sample Values** button. The following dialog box will appear:

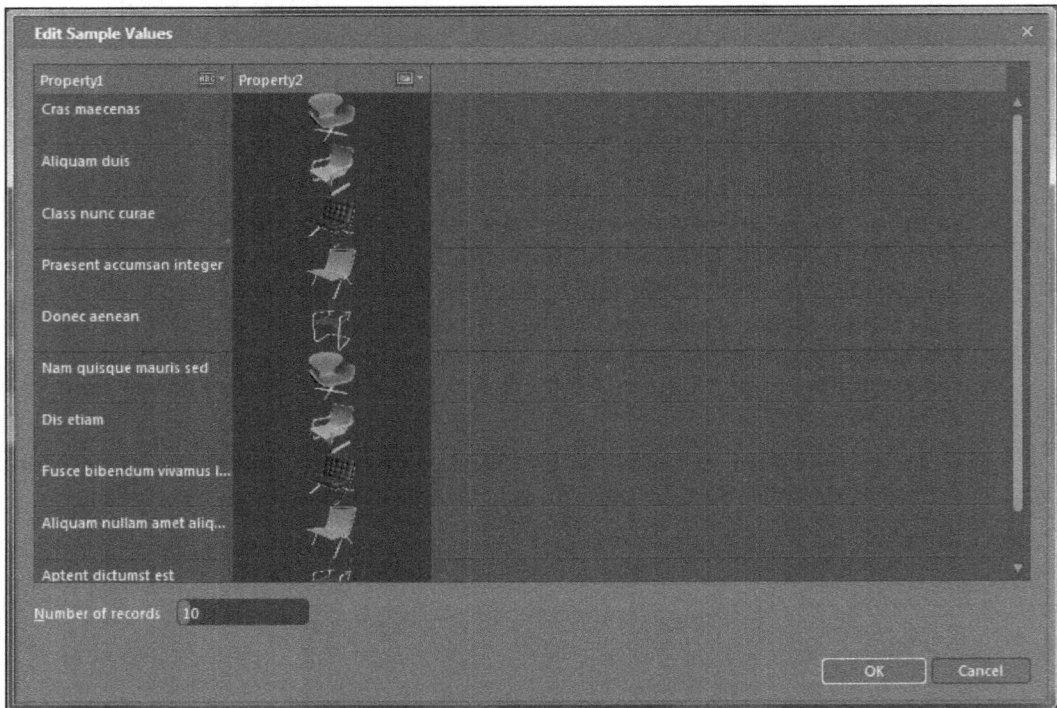

The preceding dialog box allows us to set the number of records we wish to show and change the default form of the properties we have selected.

Leave the default settings and click on the **OK** button.

We have finished setting up all the sample data and it's time to use it with our ListBox control. To add the sample data, simply click on **Collection** from the **Data** window and drag it to the ListBox control. Your ListBox control will now look as follows:

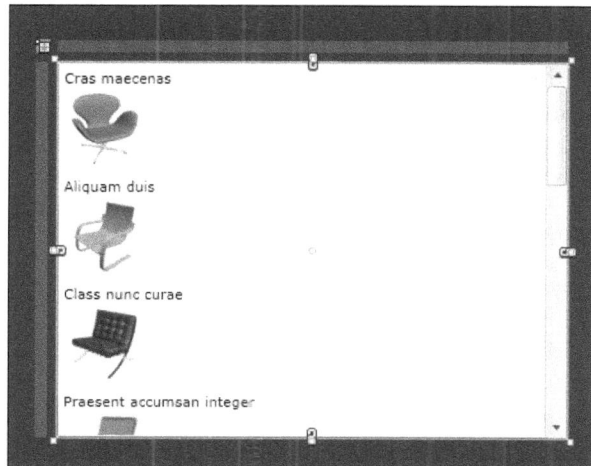

Take a look at the XAML code of MainPage.xaml; you'll notice you have a new item template:

```
<DataTemplate x:Key="ItemTemplate">
    <StackPanel>
        <TextBlock Text="{Binding Property1}"/>
        <Image Source="{Binding Property2}" HorizontalAlignment="Left"
        Height="64" Width="64'/>
    </StackPanel>
</DataTemplate>
```

From here on, you can design your template just as discussed in the previous chapter. The difference now is that you have a visual representation of the data, which makes it easier to design your template.

> If you are curious to see how the sample data is represented in code, take a look at the ProductsSampleData.xaml file located in the ProductsSampleData folder of the project. This is the file that got generated when you built your sample data using the GUI of Blend. The data from this file is bound to the elements of the item template of the ListBox control.

Selecting and merging resource dictionaries

Resource dictionaries are a concept of Silverlight that help you structure and reuse your resources, and styles into the Key type dictionaries of objects. Dictionaries, just like styles, can exist at several positions in an application, such as page level or application level. By separating styles into external dictionaries, we can reuse these dictionaries in other projects by simply importing them into projects. Resource dictionaries are typically used for defining templates for custom-created controls (to create different themes for example, to be packed with the control) or storing animations and storyboards.

An example of a resource dictionary can look as follows:

```
<ResourceDictionary>
    <Style x:Key="MyButtonStyle" TargetType="Button">
        <Setter Property="Background" Value="DarkRed"/>
        <Setter Property="Foreground" Value="#ff000000"/>
        <Setter Property="Padding" Value="13"/>
        <Setter Property="BorderThickness" Value="1"/>
    </Style>
    <Style x:Key="MyButtonStyle2" TargetType="Button"
    BasedOn="{StaticResource MyButtonStyle}">
        <Setter Property="Margin" Value="10"/>
        <Setter Property="Background" Value="DarkBlue"/>
        <Setter Property="FontSize" Value="15"/>
    </Style>
</ResourceDictionary>
```

The preceding resource dictionary holds two styles for Button elements in our application. If we wish to use one of the styles for a button in the application, we will use the following syntax:

```
<Button Content="I'm styled!" Style="{StaticResource MyButtonStyle}"/>
```

When applying the preceding styles to two buttons, the result will be as follows:

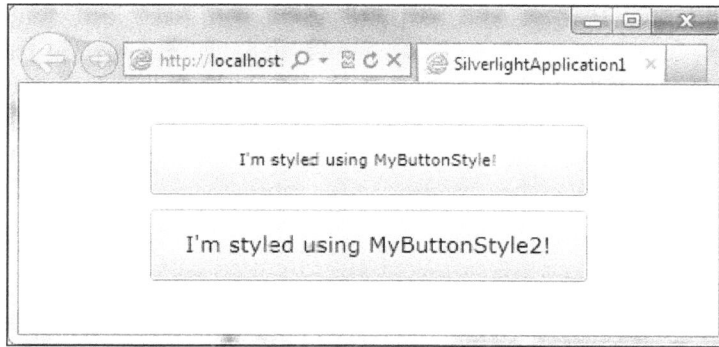

Another use for resource dictionaries is when you style a control template. A template for a control you style might need to appear in more than one project, so it's a good idea to save it in a resource dictionary. Expression Blend makes it easy for us to save a style in a resource dictionary. Open the **Chapter7-RD** project in Expression Blend 4. The project contains a single Button control, which we wish to template. Right-click on the Button control and choose **Edit Template** and then **Edit a Copy...**. The **Create Style Resource** dialog will pop up, as shown in the following screenshot:

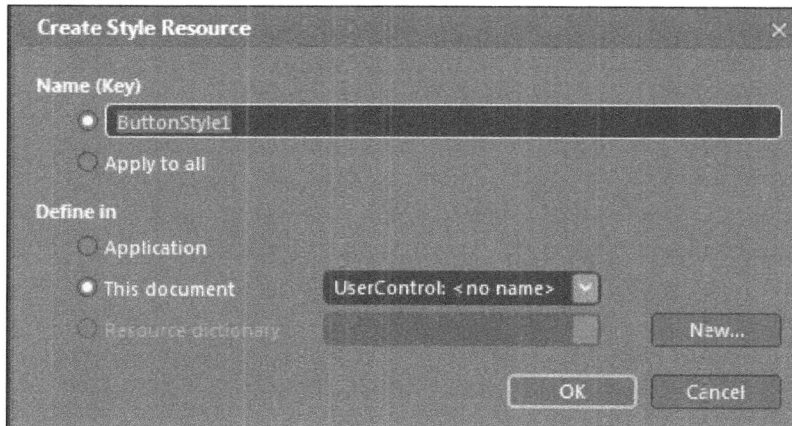

As can be seen from the preceding screenshot, the **Resource dictionary** option is grayed out. This is because we don't have any dictionary added to our project. Click on the **New...** button next to the grayed-out **Resource dictionary** drop-down box. Name the new dictionary **MyButtonDictionary.xaml** and click on OK. Blend will automatically switch to the resource dictionary editing pane and you can now edit the template of the button visually in Blend.

It's important to notice that Blend actually created a new XAML file in our project — the `MyButtonDictionary.xaml` file we specified earlier. Under that file, we have all the styles we specified in Blend. If you open the file in Visual Studio 2010, you'll see this file is nothing more than a XAML file filled with styles, pretty similar to the `App.xaml` file we have discussed earlier.

Merged resource dictionaries

In order to use the resource dictionary, Silverlight will use a feature known as "Merged Resource Dictionaries". The Merged Resource Dictionaries feature provides a way to split up resources into separate files and merge them together for use in an application.

Open the `App.xaml` file of our application in Visual Studio 2010, and you should see the following XAML code:

```
<Application.Resources>
    <ResourceDictionary>
        <ResourceDictionary.MergedDictionaries>
            <ResourceDictionary Source="MyButtonDictionary.xaml"/>
        </ResourceDictionary.MergedDictionaries>
    </ResourceDictionary>

</Application.Resources>
```

The application-level resources (`Application.Resources`) node contains a single `ResourceDictionary` element. Inside that node, we use the attached property — `MergedDictionaries` to define a collection of resource dictionaries. The fact that these resource dictionaries are in different files helps us reuse our styles and have a clean and easy-to-read `App.xaml` file.

> It is also possible to add a resource dictionary that resides in a completely separate assembly (DLL) file. To add an external dictionary, first add a reference to the assembly file the dictionary resides in and then use the following syntax in your `App.xaml` file under the `ResourceDictionary` node:
>
> `<ResourceDictionary Source="/<your assembly>;component/<your dictionary>.xaml" />`
>
> Replace `<your assembly>` with the name of your assembly file (that is `ExternalDictionary`) and `<your dictionary>` with the name of the dictionary file (that is `TextStylesResources.xaml`). If the dictionary file resides inside a folder, don't forget to add it as well!

In *Chapter 3, Enhancing the User Interface*, we have discussed the styles hierarchy and it's important to note that there is a hierarchy within the `ResourceDictionary` node as well. If you add a resource dictionary and decide to override one of its styles, add the desired `Style` node after the closing `ResourceDictionary`. `MergedDictionaries` element. By doing this, you are overriding any style with the same key that is presented in any of the resource dictionaries you added. Just the same, any `ResourceDictionary` element you add to the `MergedDictionaries` node will override a style with the same key that is defined in a previous dictionary under the same `MergedDictionaries` node.

Creating a resource dictionary doesn't have to involve Expression Blend. Creating a dictionary in Visual Studio 2010 is as easy as right-clicking on the project, choosing **Add | New Item**, and then selecting **Silverlight Resource Dictionary**. For our example, follow the steps to create a new dictionary and name it `MyNewResourceDictionary.xaml`.

In order to actually use the dictionary within our application, add a new `ResourceDictionary` element to the `MergedDictionaries` collection in the `App.xaml` file specifying our new dictionary as follows:

```
<ResourceDictionary Source="MyNewResourceDictionary.xaml"/>
```

That's it! You have successfully created a new dictionary and linked it to your project.

Implementing localization and globalization

When building an application, we usually strive to reach as big an audience as possible. Localizing our application to different languages can surely help us boost our audience. Just like most .NET-based applications, localization in Silverlight is done through the use of resource files. **Resource files** are files based on key-value pairs where each pair represents a string, an image, or other types of resources such as audio and icons. We will discuss how to use resource files in just a moment. New to Silverlight 4 is the native support of right-to-left languages such as Arabic or Hebrew, which makes it far easier to localize an application to these languages. Other than strings, resource files can also hold dates or images.

Working with resource files

To get started, open the **Chapter7-RESX** project in Visual Studio 2010. The project can be found in the downloadable content of the book, which is available at www. packtpub.com.

The project's UI is as basic as possible—a TextBox control to hold our localized text and an image. The most important part of the project is the Resources folder. This folder currently contains two resource files—Flags.resx and Flags.de.resx. These two files represent two languages—English and German. The standard naming convention for resource files is ResourceName.Language.resx. If we want to add French for example, the resource file will be named Flags.fr.resx.

Click on either of the files. Both contain the same keys—ImageName for the image URL and WelcomeText for the TextBox control's text.

In order to use the resource file, we first have to tell Silverlight which languages we are going to support. Currently the only way to do so is to manually edit the csproj file (the project file) of the project. To do so, right-click on the project name (**Chapter7-RESX**) and choose **Unload Project**. Now, right-click on it again and choose **Edit Chapter7-RESX.csproj**. Find the SupportedCultures node and add the desired language. In our example, we will simply add German. Your SupportedCultures node should look as follows:

```
<SupportedCultures>
    de
</SupportedCultures>
```

> **Adding more than one language**
> If more than one language is going to be supported, add all the supported languages to the SupportedCultures node separated with a comma.

Next, right-click on the project name and choose **Reload Project**. Now we need to add the resource file as a static resource to the App.xaml file. Open the App.xaml file and add the following XAML code:

```
<resx:Flags x:Key="FlagsResx"/>
```

`Resx` is the namespace for the resource files and `Flags` is the name of the root resource file (`Flags.resx`).

> In the starter project's `App.xaml` file, the `Resx` namespace was already assigned to the right assembly. If you are creating a project from scratch, make sure you add the namespace before trying to access any of its resources.

Now we can bind directly to the strings in the resource file!

Open the `MainPage.xaml` file, and add the following line of code to the `Image` element:

```
Source="{Binding ImageName, Source={StaticResource FlagsResx}}"
```

We are binding the `ImageName` key of the resource file to the `Source` property of the image. Let's do the same for the `TextBox` control but using the `WelcomeText` key instead of `ImageName`:

```
Text="{Binding WelcomeText, Source={StaticResource FlagsResx}}"
```

Build and run the application, and you should get the result, as shown in the following screenshot:

If you were running this same application on a computer, which has German as the local language, you would have seen the following screenshot:

It's important to make sure that the main .resx file we are using (in our example, flags.resx) has its access modifier set to public and its constructor set to public as well (in the Designer.cs file). Failing to have both of them as public will result in an exception being thrown when running the application. Make sure you check for both every time you modify the resource file.

For languages that are written right to left (such as Hebrew and Arabic), Silverlight exposes the FlowDirection property on most of its controls. This property can accept two values — LeftToRight (which is the default) or RightToLeft. Setting this property to RightToLeft will make the control shift to right-to-left mode, meaning the text will flow from right to left.

Forcing local

If you wish to force a specific local on to your application, you can choose in one of the following two ways:

- Using the Silverlight plugin HTML
- Using the binding system's converter

Setting the culture using the Silverlight plugin HTML

The simpler approach is using the plugin HTML, and it's done by adding the following line of code to the Silverlight's `object` tag — `<html>`:

```
<param name="uiculture" value="<your culture>" />
```

Make sure to replace `<your culture>` with your desired culture, that is `de`.

Please note that this method will only work if the language specified for the `uiculture` parameter is already added as a supported culture in the `csproj` file.

Setting the culture using a converter

We've already discussed the use of converters in *Chapter 5, Working with Data*, and culture converters are no different. To set the culture via the binding engine, we need to set the `ConverterCulture` parameter to the desired culture and then use the `resourceManager` class in your converter to read the string from the culture's resource file.

To demonstrate this procedure, we will use the same project as before and set its culture via a converter. Open the **Chapter7-RESX-Converter-Starter** project in Visual Studio 2010.

If you run the project right now, you will get the English version of the application, as shown in the first screenshot under the *Working with resource files* section. We wish to force the application to always show the German version, no matter what is the user's culture.

The first thing we will do is handle the converter. Open the `TextConverter.cs` file under the `Converters` folder. The class has already been set to inherit and implement the `IValueConverter` interface. The method we need to handle is `Convert` and its implementation is as follows:

```
public object Convert(object value, Type targetType, object parameter,
System.Globalization.CultureInfo culture)
{
    ResourceManager resourceManager = new
    ResourceManager("Chapter7_RESX.Resources.Flags", GetType().
Assembly);
        return (string)resourceManager.GetString((string)
        parameter, culture);
}
```

The `Convert` method initializes the `resourceManager` class, passing it the resource file's full namespace (`Chapter7_RESX.Resources` is the namespace where `Flags` is the name of our resource file itself) as the first argument, and the assembly that it resides in as the second argument.

Once initialized, we return a value from the selected resource file based on a key we pass to the `Convert` method as an argument named parameter.

In order to use the converter, we have to first declare it as a resource. To make things easier, the converter is already added in your `App.xaml` file with a key named `textConverter`.

Now for the fun part, open the `MainPage.xaml` file and look for an `Image` element named `FlagImage`. Currently the image's `Source` property is bound to the `ImageName` key of the `Flags` resource file. To set the culture of the binding property to German, change the image's `Source` property as follows:

```
Source="{Binding ImageName,Source={StaticResource FlagsResx},
Converter={StaticResource textConverter},ConverterCulture=de-
DE,ConverterParameter='ImageName'}" />
```

As you can see from the preceding code snippet, we've added two new properties to the binding declaration—`ConverterCulture` and `ConverterParameter`. `ConverterCulture` defines the culture we wish to set. This is passed to the converter's `Convert` method as the culture argument. `ConverterParameter` is a generic object that we can pass to the `Convert` method. In our example, we will pass the name of the key we wish to retrieve from the `.resx` file. Use the same syntax for the `TextBox` element, but change `ConverterParameter` to `WelcomeText`:

```
<TextBlock x:Name="FlagText" HorizontalAlignment="Center"
Text="{Binding WelcomeText,Source={StaticResource FlagsResx},Converter
={StaticResource textConverter},ConverterCulture=de-DE,ConverterParame
ter='WelcomeText'}" />
```

Build and run the application, and you should get the result, as shown in the following screenshot:

Willkommen!

Handling application-level events

Silverlight allows us to handle application-level events. They are the `Startup`, `Exit`, and `UnhandledException` events. These events can be used to hook into the application lifecycle. All of these events are found in the `App.xaml.cs` file.

The `Application_Startup` event is fired as soon as the application is initiated, meaning right after the XAP file is loaded to the user's computer and inspected by the Silverlight runtime engine. By default the `Application_Startup` event is used to load the default visual page into view. Other use of this event is to perform different initialization tasks, such as processing initialization parameters or setting application-wide resources or properties. For example, if you pass `InitParams` from the Silverlight HTML object to the application, you'll have to process them inside this event with code as follows:

```
IDictionary<string, string> iParams = e.InitParams;
```

The `Application_UnhandledException` event enables us to handle uncaught exceptions on the application level. Any exception that hasn't been caught by a `try-catch` block inside the application will be sent to this event. This is the last stop to handle the exception in a graceful way such as logging the error or displaying a message to the user. The event uses an argument, named `e` by default, of the `ApplicationUnhandledExceptionEventArgs` type to give you access to the exception that caused the event to fire. The default implementation of the event is as follows:

```
private void Application_UnhandledException(object sender,
ApplicationUnhandledExceptionEventArgs e)
{
```

```
      if (!System.Diagnostics.Debugger.IsAttached)
      {
      e.Handled = true;
          Deployment.Current.Dispatcher.BeginInvoke(delegate
          { ReportErrorToDOM(e); });
      }
   }
```

Notice the `Handled` property in the preceding code snippet. This Boolean property signals the framework whether the exception has been handled or not. By setting the `Handled` property to `true`, you signal the framework that the exception was handled and that it should continue to run. Leaving the property as `false` however, will cause the Silverlight plugin to unload the application and fire the `OnError` event.

Last, but not least, is the `Application.Exit` event. This is the last stop of an application before it shuts down into the oblivion. This event can be useful for tasks such as logging information or performing last-minute saves. The event is fired whenever a user leaves the application either by exiting it directly, closing the browser or having the Silverlight's `object` tag removed from the page with the help of JavaScript, for example.

The most important thing to remember about this event is that it fires after the browser is closed. Therefore, you cannot manipulate any UI visuals from this event or try to prevent the user from closing the browser.

Test your knowledge

1. You are developing a multilingual Silverlight 4 application. The application UI contains a `StackPanel` control that is used to host content. The content displayed is language aware and needs to support displaying bidirectional languages. Which property should you set for the `StackPanel` control?

   a. `HorizontalAlignment`

   b. `Orientation`

   c. `FlowDirection`

   d. `TextAlign`

2. You are developing an out-of-browser Silverlight 4 application. You need to ensure that whenever a new version of the application is released, the user will be notified. You decided to use the `CheckAndDownloadUpdate` event. Under which application-level event should you place your code?

   a. `Application_DownloadCompleted`

   b. `Application_Start`

c. `Application_UnhandledException`

d. `Application_Exit`

3. You are developing a Silverlight 4 application. You need to ensure that any unhandled exception in the application won't be thrown back to the page. Which code segment should you use?

    a. `e.Handled = true`

    b. `e.Handled = false`

    c. `e.ThrowException = true`

    d. `e.Handled = null`

4. You are developing a Silverlight 4 application that requires a resource dictionary named `StackPanelResources.xaml`, which resides in an assembly file named `AllMyDictionaries.dll`. You reference the DLL file in your project. Which code snippet would you use to declare the external dictionary in your application?

    a. `<ResourceDictionary.MergedDictionaries>`
       `<ResourceDictionary Source="/AllMyDictionaries;component/`
       `StackPanelResources.xaml"/></ResourceDictionary.`
       `MergedDictionaries>`

    b. `<ResourceDictionary.ExternalMergedDictionaries>`
       `<ResourceDictionary Source="/AllMyDictionaries;component/`
       `StackPanelResources.xaml"/></ResourceDictionary.`
       `ExternalMergedDictionaries>`

    c. `<ResourceDictionary.MergedDictionaries>`
       `<ResourceDictionary Source="/AllMyDictionaries/`
       `StackPanelResources;component/StackPanelResources.`
       `xaml"/></ResourceDictionary.MergedDictionaries>`

    d. `<ResourceDictionary.MergedDictionaries>`
       `<ResourceDictionary Source="/AllMyDictionaries /`
       `StackPanelResources.xaml"/></ResourceDictionary.`
       `MergedDictionaries>`

5. You are developing a multilanguage Silverlight 4 application. You notice that when users in France and Netherland use your application, they are seeing it in their own locale while users in Germany don't. You decide to try and force the local to German using Silverlight's `html object` tag using the following line of code:

```
<param name="uiculture" value="de" />
```

Even though your project contains a German resource file the application still shows up in English. What can be the cause?

    a.   You forgot to restart the IIS server running the application.

    b.   You didn't specify German as a supported culture in the `csproj` file.

    c.   You've added the wrong parameter. It should be `langculture` and not `uiculture`.

    d.   You've added the wrong parameter. The value should read German and not `de`.

Summary

This chapter covered some important concepts for structuring our application correctly. We discussed resource dictionaries and how are they used, we dived deep into localization of our application, and we finished off discussing the application-level events that Silverlight offers us.

In the last chapter of this book, we are going to discuss application deployment. We will cover configuration of the Silverlight plugin, we will experiment with dynamically loading application resources, and we will finish off with creating a client access policy.

8
Deploying Applications

So we have built an application using all of the goodies Silverlight offers. Now it's time to deploy our application for users! In this last chapter of the book, we are going to cover everything related to deployment. We will start the chapter with discussing how to configure the Silverlight plugin's object tag. Once done, we will move on to discussing how we can make our application's download size smaller by splitting it up to several files. We will finish things off with discussing the use of a policy file.

In this chapter we will cover the following topics:

- Configuring the Silverlight plugin
- Dynamically loading application resources
- Creating client access policy

Configuring the Silverlight plugin

When we create a new Silverlight solution in Visual Studio 2010, we are given the option to also create an ASP.NET site that will host it. If you inspect the .aspx file in that site, you'll notice that your Silverlight application is hosted in an HTML object element:

```
<object data="data:application/x-silverlight-2," type="application/x-
silverlight-2" width="100%" height="100%">
<param name="source" value="ClientBin/Chapter7-RESX.xap"/>
    <param name="onError" value="onSilverlightError" />
    <param name="background" value="white" />
    <param name="minRuntimeVersion" value="4.0.60310.0" />
    <param name="autoUpgrade" value="true" />
    <param name="initparams" value=
    "ShowNames=true,CurrentUser=local\admin" />
    <a href="http://go.microsoft.com/fwlink/?LinkID=149156
```

```
&v=4.0.60310.0"
    style="text-decoration:none">
        <img src="http://go.microsoft.com/fwlink/?LinkId=161376"
alt="Get
        Microsoft Silverlight" style="border-style:none"/>
    </a>
</object>
```

An HTML `object` tag contains, among other things, several `param` elements. These elements allow us to configure the `object` tag with several predefined properties to better suit our needs. Looking at the preceding code snippet, you'll notice most of the `param` elements have simple values. It's quite obvious how we can change a background color, set the source Silverlight application location, and specify a new error handling function name or enable GPU acceleration (which we discussed in *Chapter 3, Enhancing the User Interface*).

Some of the more advanced parameters we can set for the `object` tag include passing initialization parameters, setting the plugin size, configuring its windowless mode, and even setting a custom splash screen.

Passing initialization parameters

The `initparams` parameter allows us to pass textual initialization parameters to the Silverlight application in the form of key-value pairs. Once the application starts and the `Application_Startup` event fires, these key-value pairs will be read and processed within the application. The `initparams` parameter's value is represented by a typical "key = value" form, separating the pairs with a comma. When handled in Silverlight, the `initparams` collection will be represented as a `Dictionary` object.

An example of the `initparams` parameter might look as follows:

```
<param name="initparams" value="ShowNames=true,CurrentUser=local\
admin" />
```

Reading the values from this collection can be done as follows:

```
private void Application_Startup(object sender, StartupEventArgs e)
{
    this.RootVisual = new MainPage();
        string paramValue = e.InitParams["CurrentUser"];
}
```

Use the IDictionary collection for initparams

It is quite common to have a global object of the IDictionary type, such as IDictionary<string, string>; to hold the initparams collection. By having such a global object and initializing it on the Application_Startup event, you can gain access to the initialization parameters anywhere in your application.

Setting the plugin size

When setting the size attributes (Width and Height) of your Silverlight object tag, you're free to choose between fixed sizing (based on pixels) or relative sizing (based on percentages). The size attributes are set on the root object tag element and affect the way your application is drawn to page. Using fixed sizing, the plugin size will remain the same, regardless of the size of its hosting parent element. If, for example, the parent element's width is smaller than the width specified for the plugin, the plugin will be clipped.

By using relative sizing, the plugin size will change whenever the parent element's size changes. If you specify the plugin's width and height to 50 percent and if the parent element's size is 500x500 pixels, your plugin size will be set at 250x250 pixels. If the browser's size changes all of a sudden to, say 300x300 pixels, your Silverlight application will now resize to 150x150 pixels.

One important thing to note here is that if the Silverlight application itself is set to fixed size, it might get clipped as the parent element's size changes. It's usually not a good idea to have a fixed-size application with a relative-size plugin, as you lose all the flexibility of the relative sizing, so try to avoid it if possible.

The MinHeight and MinWidth properties

The MinHeight and MinWidth properties of a UI control allow you to set the lowest possible boundary for an element size. Setting either of these properties assures that an element cannot scale down to a lower size than the specified value. On the same scale, you have the MaxHeight and MaxWidth properties, which allow you to set the maximum possible size for an element.

These properties are particularly useful when wrapping your controls inside of a ScrollViewer control. ScrollViewer dynamically resizes its child controls according to the available space it has, and setting either of those properties will tell the ScrollViewer control which are the lowest or highest size boundaries of the control.

windowless mode

The `windowless` parameter is a Boolean type of parameter that specifies whether the Silverlight plugin should be "painted" above any HTML element of the hosting page or not. By default, this property is set to `false`, which means that the Silverlight content will appear above any HTML content of the hosting page.

Setting the `windowless` mode to `true` will allow the underlying HTML content to appear through the transparent areas of the plugin, providing you with seamless integration with the HTML host page. This is mostly useful when you wish to create HTML overlays in your application or when you wish to place Silverlight content below flyover menus. Be careful when using the `windowless` mode though. Using it will cause your application to take a performance hit, especially if used in combination with a transparent background. Microsoft recommends using the `windowless` mode only when it's absolutely necessary.

Setting the `windowless` mode to on is quite straightforward, as can be seen from the following line of code:

```
<param name="iswindowless" value="true" />
```

Setting a custom splash page

By default, Silverlight shows its spinning blue circle loading screen while loading the XAP file as follows:

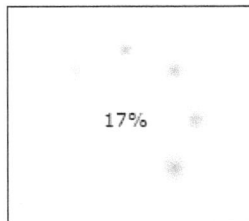

When creating your own application, you might want to change this into something more with the spirit of the application. The process of creating a custom splash screen consists of three steps as follows:

1. Create a XAML page within the website that hosts the application.
2. Integrate the loader with the application.
3. Monitor the progress of the download using JavaScript.

There is a logical explanation for why we are creating the splash screen XAML outside the Silverlight application itself. As the splash page is used while the Silverlight application is being downloaded, it wouldn't make sense to create the splash screen inside of it. There are a few limitations for using custom preloaders as follows:

- You cannot run any managed code in your splash screen. It's JavaScript-only land.

- You cannot use any external libraries.

With that being said, let's go ahead and create our first splash screen.

Creating your own splash screen

Create a new Silverlight project in Visual Studio 2010 and name it **Chapter8-Preloader**. We start off with creating the XAML page of our loader. Right-click on the **Chapter8-Preloader.Web** project, select **Add** and then **New Item**. Select **Silverlight** from the **Installed Templates** menu and select **Silverlight 1.0 Jscript Page**. Name it **MyCustomLoader.xaml** and click on **OK**.

We now have a blank XAML page to use as our loader. Change the content of the page as follows:

```
<Grid xmlns="http://schemas.microsoft.com/winfx/2006/xaml/
presentation"
        xmlns:x="http://schemas.microsoft.com/winfx/2006/xaml"
        Background="#FF2E682E' >
<Grid.Triggers>
        <EventTrigger RoutedEvent="Grid.Loaded">
        <BeginStoryboard>
        <Storyboard x:Name="circle">
            <ColorAnimationUsingKeyFrames
        Storyboard.TargetProperty="(Shape.Stroke).(SolidColorBrush.
        Color)" Storyboard.TargetName="ellipse" AutoReverse="True">
                <EasingColorKeyFrame KeyTime="0" Value="White"/>
                <EasingColorKeyFrame KeyTime="0:0:1"
Value="#FFF5D500"/>
                <EasingColorKeyFrame KeyTime="0:0:2"
Value="#FFFF0017"/>
            </ColorAnimationUsingKeyFrames>
        </Storyboard>
        </BeginStoryboard>
        </EventTrigger>
</Grid.Triggers>
    <Grid>
```

```
        <Ellipse x:Name="ellipse" Margin="130,81,131,81"
  Stroke="White"
        RenderTransformOrigin="0.856,0.406" StrokeThickness="6"/>
        <TextBlock x:Name="ProgressTB" Width="55" Height="20"
            FontFamily="Verdana" FontSize="14" Text="0%"
            TextAlignment="Center" Foreground="White" />
    </Grid>
  </Grid>
```

The first step is complete. We have a nice new graphical representation for our loader. Next, let's integrate the loader with the application. Open the `Chapter8-PreloaderTestPage.aspx` file and add `param` to the `object` tag as follows:

```
<param name="splashscreensource" value="MyCustomLoader.xaml"/>
```

This will change the loader to our custom loader. But that's not all. We also wish to handle the download progress event so that we can update our splash screen. The following line of code will add this support:

```
<param name="onSourceDownloadProgressChanged" value="onSourceDownloadP
rogressChanged" />
```

We have defined a callback for the event, now it's time to define the function itself. Open the `MyCustomLoader.js` file and delete all its content. Add the following code snippet to it:

```
function onSourceDownloadProgressChanged(sender, eventArgs) {
    sender.findName("ProgressTB").Text = Math.round
    ((eventArgs.progress * 1000)) / 10 + "%";
}
```

The preceding function looks for an element in the splash file using the `findName` method and sets its text using the `eventArgs` progress variable.

All that's left to do now is to tell the host ASPX page to load the `MyCustomLoader.js` file. Open the `Chapter8-PreloaderTestPage.aspx` file and add the following line of code to the head element:

```
<script type="text/javascript" src="MyCustomLoader.js"></script>
```

If you run the application now, everything will compile and run, but you won't see your new loader. The reason for that is that the file loads immediately. To simulate low bandwidth conditions, add a big file to the Silverlight project and set its build action to "Content". Run the application now, and you should see your new splash screen in all its glory:

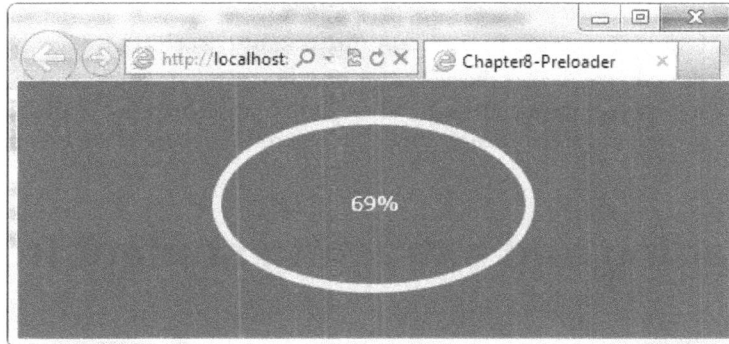

Dynamically loading application resources

When your application is small (in size), everyone is happy. The load on the servers is minimal, the load times for the user fly by instantly, and the user starts to use your application within seconds. As your application gets more complex and more assemblies are used, the size of the application will grow. But what if our application is divided into different projects and each project contains a `Grid` control? Will that mean that each and every time we hit a page, the DLL containing the grid will be loaded to the user? By default, yes.

In order to tackle this issue, we have two options—use assembly caching or create ZIP files ourselves containing assemblies, images, resources and so on.

Using assembly caching

Using assembly caching is straightforward, and we have already discussed it in *Chapter 1, Overview of Silverlight*. To recap, all you have to do is right-click on the Silverlight project in Visual Studio 2010, choose **Properties**, and check the **Reduce XAP size by using application library** checkbox. Now you may ask yourself, "what did I gain from this?" In the end, all the assemblies must be downloaded to the user's computer anyway. The answer lies within the cache. By using this mechanism, you're downloading the assemblies separately from the XAP application. That means that the assemblies are kept in the cache just like the XAP file. Now, let's assume you deploy a new version of your application but keep the same assemblies. A user who revisits the application will only download the new XAP application and not the assemblies. That saves bandwidth!

> **Out-of-browser applications and assembly caching**
> Keep in mind that the assembly caching option is only available for in-browser applications in Silverlight. Out-of-Browser applications are not capable of using this, as they aren't cached in the first place.

Downloading and extracting content from ZIP files

The other option we have to reduce load time is to load external ZIP files with our content. By using the GetResourceStream method of the Application static class, we can return a resource file (be it an image or a XAML page) from a location in a specified ZIP package.

To demonstrate the use of the GetResourceStream method, open the **Chapter8-ExternalResrouces** project in Visual Studio 2010. This project consists of a Silverlight 4 project with some simple UI elements and a web project. Inside the web project, we can find the ClientBin folder. That's where the Silverlight .xap file gets deployed when we build and run our application. In this project however, we have an additional file named ImagesZip.zip. This is a simple ZIP file with two compressed images. The images are called—Nasa1.jpg and Nasa2.jpg. Build and run the application, and you should get the result, as shown in the following screenshot:

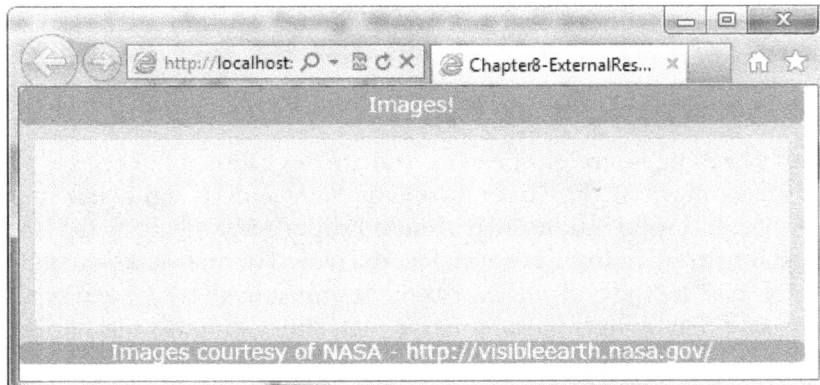

Our goal for this application is to show any of the images in the external ZIP file inside the partly transparent white area of the application. To get started, we first need to tell our Silverlight application to actually download the ZIP file. This is done by using the `WebClient` class, which asynchronously grabs a `Stream` from a given `Uri`. Add the following code snippet to the `MainPage_Loaded` method of the `MainPage.xaml.cs` file:

```
WebClient wClient = new WebClient();
wClient.OpenReadCompleted += new OpenReadCompletedEventHandler(wClie
nt_OpenReadCompleted);
wClient.OpenReadAsync(new Uri("ImagesZip.zip", UriKind.
RelativeOrAbsolute));
```

Nothing spectacular so far. An asynchronous web client call is made to read the content of the ZIP file. Let's add the callback method — `wClient_OpenReadCompleted` to the file:

```
void wClient_OpenReadCompleted(object sender,
OpenReadCompletedEventArgs e)
{
    Stream zipPackageStream = e.Result;
    BitmapImage image = LoadImageFromZipPackage("Nasa2.jpg",
    zipPackageStream);
    wpImage.Source = image;
}
```

The preceding method saves the `Stream` that we get back from `WebClient` to a variable named `zipPackageStream` and then calls the `LoadImageFromZipPackage` method, passing it the name of the image inside the ZIP file we wish to extract and the `Stream` of the ZIP file to get back a `BitmapImage` element, which will be used as the source for the image control in `MainPage.xaml`. The implementation of `LoadImageFromZipPackage` is as follows:

```
public BitmapImage LoadImageFromZipPackage(string uriString, Stream
zipPackageStream)
{
StreamResourceInfo zipPackageSri = new StreamResourceInfo(zipPackageS
tream, null);
    StreamResourceInfo imageSri = Application.GetResourceStream(zipPack
ageSri, new Uri(uriString,UriKind.Relative));

    BitmapImage bi = new BitmapImage();
    bi.SetSource(imageSri.Stream);

    return bi;
}
```

The preceding method accepts two parameters—the name of the image we wish to get (which is really a relative Uri) and the Stream of the ZIP we opened earlier. The method then gets StreamResourceInfo from the ZIP package and then uses the GetResourceStream method of the Application class to extract the stream of the specified image (or any other resource) out of the ZIP package. Finally, the method creates a new BitmapImage control, sets its source to the stream of the extracted image, and returns it. Build and run your application, and you should get the result, as shown in the following screenshot:

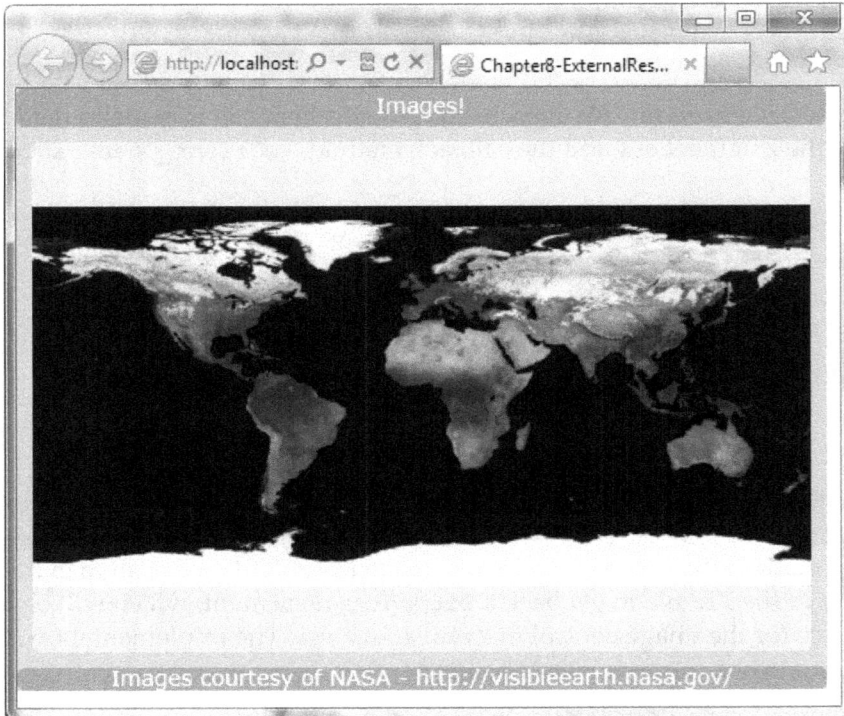

Change the name of the image to any of the other images in the ZIP file (or your own file), and you'll get the image proudly showing within the application.

Loading resources from an external file helps us reduce the size of the application by not containing the resources within the main application file and ultimately reduces the bandwidth (the resource files will get cached as long as they are the same).

Creating a client access policy

We briefly mentioned client access policy in *Chapter 4*, *Implementing Application Logic*, when we discussed cross-domain networking. The reason behind Silverlight's requirement for the client access policy file is to prevent network threats and to give administrators more control over which resources a remote client, such as Silverlight, is allowed to connect to.

Silverlight 5, which was recently released, adds a new feature of creating in-browser trusted applications, which aren't restricted by the security policy (just like trusted out-of-browser applications). In Silverlight 4, the only way to connect to a service, which doesn't expose the client access policy is to create a web service of our own (using WCF or any other technology) on the same domain as the Silverlight application and let it handle the cross-domain call.

Every time Silverlight makes a cross-domain call, either by `WebClient` or by referencing a service, the Silverlight runtime will first try to download the client access policy file—`clientaccesspolicy.xml` from the root of the called domain. If the file is not found, if it has an invalid MIME type, or if its XML is invalid, the Silverlight runtime will fall back to looking for Adobe's Flash policy file named `crossdomain.xml`. If both files fail then the call will not get through and will result in a `SecurityException` of access denied.

A typical implementation of the `clientaccesspolicy.xml` file looks as follows:

```xml
<?xml version="1.0" encoding="utf-8"?>
<access-policy>
    <cross-domain-access>
        <policy>
            <allow-from http-request-headers="SOAPAction">
                <domain uri="*"/>
            </allow-from>
            <grant-to>
                <resource path="/" include-subpaths="true"/>
            </grant-to>
        </policy>
    </cross-domain-access>
</access-policy>
```

Pay attention to the `policy` node. That's where the security action happens. Under the `allow-from` node, we can specify which domains are allowed to access the resource. Specifying a * means everyone, no matter from which domain, can access the resource.

The `grant-to` node provides us a way to specify which resources are affected by the policy file. We can specify a specific resource, such as `/api/items.svc`, and only that web service will be affected by the policy file. Specifying `/` means everything under the root of this domain is affected by this policy file. Make sure that if you do use the general rule of `/`, you should also specify `true` for the `include-subpaths` attribute. If you do not set the attribute to `true`, the policy file will only affect the resource running at the root level of the domain.

The `crossdomain.xml` file is much simpler and easier to understand. A typical implementation of this file is as follows:

```
<?xml version="1.0"?>
<!DOCTYPE cross-domain-policy SYSTEM "http://www.macromedia.com/xml/
dtds/cross-domain-policy.dtd">
<cross-domain-policy>
    <allow-http-request-headers-from domain="*"
    headers="SOAPAction,Content-Type"/>
</cross-domain-policy>
```

`allow-http-request-headers-from` allows us to specify, using the `domain` attribute, which domains are allowed to access the resource. The `headers` attribute allows us to specify what headers are allowed through. For SOAP-based services for example, we will use the `SOAPAction` header.

Don't forget to include either of the files in your project if you are planning to use Silverlight to make cross-domain calls. Always make sure you have the policy files in the root of the domain and not in a subfolder. Checking for these files before deployment will save you a bundle of headaches later.

Test your knowledge

1. You are developing a Silverlight 4 application. The application is hosted on www.myCompany.com. On the same domain, there is a WCF service running on www.myCompany.com/service. Your Silverlight application accesses the service just fine. A vendor has developed a Silverlight application that uses the service as well. Even though you have deployed a `clientaccesspolicy.xml` file, the vendor receives a `SecurityException` while calling the service from his Silverlight application. Which of the following lines from the XML can cause this error?

    a. `<domain uri="8"/>`

    b. `<resource path="/" include-subpaths="true"/>`

    c. `<resource path="/" include-subpaths="false"/>`

    d. `<resource path="/service" include-subpaths="false"/>`

2. You are developing a Silverlight application. You are passing an initialization parameter called `initKey` using the Silverlight's `object` tag `initparam` parameter. How would you retrieve it back in your Silverlight application?

   a. Inside the `Application_Startup` event, use the following line of code—`var key=e.InitParams["initKey"];`

   b. Inside the `Application_Startup` event, use the following line of code—`var key=e.InitParams.initKey;`

   c. Inside the `StartupApp` event, use the following line of code—`var key=e.InitParams["initKey"];`

   d. Inside the `StartupApp` event, use the following line of code—`var key=e.InitParam["initKey"];`

3. You are developing a Silverlight application. The application needs to have a transparent background. You set the `background` parameter of the Silverlight's `object` tag to `transparent`. While testing the application, you notice the background is all white. Which of the following line of code can fix the issue?

   a. `<parameter name="background" value="#00ffffff"/>`

   b. `<parameter name="initparams" value="background=transparent"/>`

   c. `<parameter name="iswindowless" value="true"/>`

   d. `<parameter name="iswindowless" value="false"/>`

Summary

This chapter marks the end of our journey through the Silverlight preparation guide. We covered how to use the Silverlight `object` tag to customize our Silverlight application by setting the right size, passing initialization parameters, or even setting a completely customized splash screen. We discussed how to improve loading time for our application by reading resources externally using the ZIP files and finished off with discussing the client access policy of Silverlight.

I hope this book aided you in your quest to be a Microsoft Certified Professional in Silverlight, and please feel free to contact me for any question you might have about the content of the book.

Test Your Knowledge – Answers

Chapter 2: Laying out Our User Interface

1	2	3	4	5
b	a	c	a	d

Chapter 3: Enhancing the User Interface

1	2	3	4	5
b	c	d	a	d

Chapter 4: Implementing Application Logic

1	2	3	4	5
a	b	a	a	c

Chapter 5: Working with Data

1	2	3	4	5
a	c	b	a	d

Chapter 6: Interacting with the Host Platform

1	2	3	4	5
b	c	a	b	c

Chapter 7: Structuring Applications

1	2	3	4	5
c	b	a	a	b

Chapter 8: Deploying Applications

1	2	3
c	a	c

Index

Thank you for buying
MCTS: Microsoft Silverlight 4 Development (70-506) Certification Guide

About Packt Publishing

Packt, pronounced 'packed', published its first book "Mastering phpMyAdmin for Effective MySQL Management" in April 2004 and subsequently continued to specialize in publishing highly focused books on specific technologies and solutions.

Our books and publications share the experiences of your fellow IT professionals in adapting and customizing today's systems, applications, and frameworks. Our solution based books give you the knowledge and power to customize the software and technologies you're using to get the job done. Packt books are more specific and less general than the IT books you have seen in the past. Our unique business model allows us to bring you more focused information, giving you more of what you need to know, and less of what you don't.

Packt is a modern, yet unique publishing company, which focuses on producing quality, cutting-edge books for communities of developers, administrators, and newbies alike. For more information, please visit our website: www.packtpub.com.

About Packt Enterprise

In 2010, Packt launched two new brands, Packt Enterprise and Packt Open Source, in order to continue its focus on specialization. This book is part of the Packt Enterprise brand, home to books published on enterprise software – software created by major vendors, including (but not limited to) IBM, Microsoft and Oracle, often for use in other corporations. Its titles will offer information relevant to a range of users of this software, including administrators, developers, architects, and end users.

Writing for Packt

We welcome all inquiries from people who are interested in authoring. Book proposals should be sent to author@packtpub.com. If your book idea is still at an early stage and you would like to discuss it first before writing a formal book proposal, contact us; one of our commissioning editors will get in touch with you.

We're not just looking for published authors; if you have strong technical skills but no writing experience, our experienced editors can help you develop a writing career, or simply get some additional reward for your expertise.

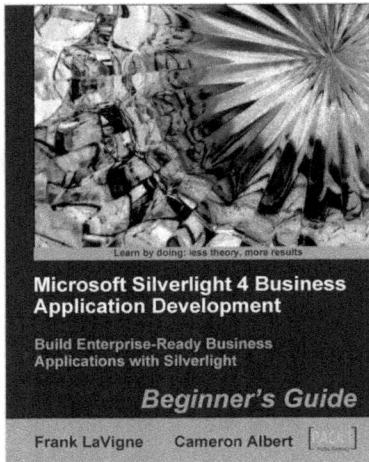

Microsoft Silverlight 4 Business Application Development: Beginner's Guide

ISBN: 9781847199768   Paperback: 412 pages

Build enterprise-ready business applications with Silverlight

1. An introduction to building enterprise-ready business applications with Silverlight quickly.

2. Get hold of the basic tools and skills needed to get started in Silverlight application development.

3. Integrate different media types, taking the RIA experience further with Silverlight, and much more!

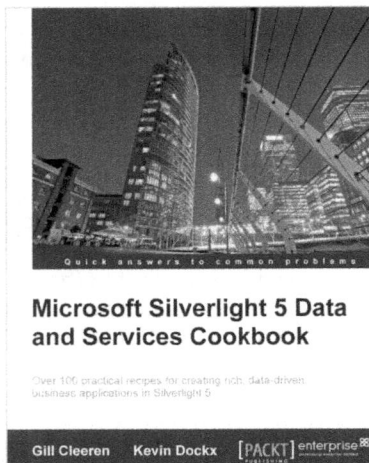

Microsoft Silverlight 5 Data and Services Cookbook

ISBN: 9781849683500   Paperback: 662 pages

Over 100 practical recipes for creating rich, data-driven, business applications in Silverlight 5

1. Design and develop rich data-driven business applications in Silverlight and Windows Phone 7 following best practices using this book and eBook

2. Rapidly interact with services and handle multiple sources of data within Silverlight and Windows Phone 7 business applications

3. Packed with practical, hands-on cookbook recipes, illustrating the techniques to solve particular data problems effectively within your Silverlight and Windows Phone 7 business applications

Please check **www.PacktPub.com** for information on our titles

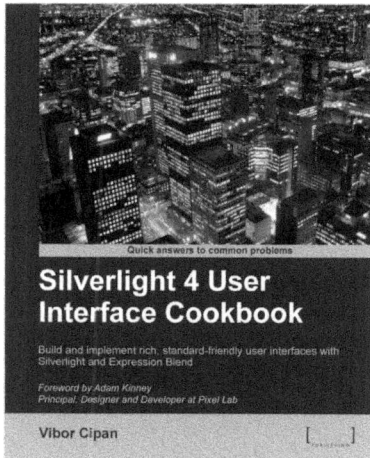

Silverlight 4 User Interface Cookbook

ISBN: 9781847198860   Paperback: 280 pages

Build and implement rich, standard-friendly user interfaces with Silverlight and Expression Blend

1. The first and only book to focus exclusively on Silverlight UI development.

2. Have your applications stand out from the crowd with leading, innovative, and friendly user interfaces.

3. Detailed instructions on how to implement specific user interface patterns together with XAML and C# (where needed) code, and explainations that are easy-to-understand and follow..

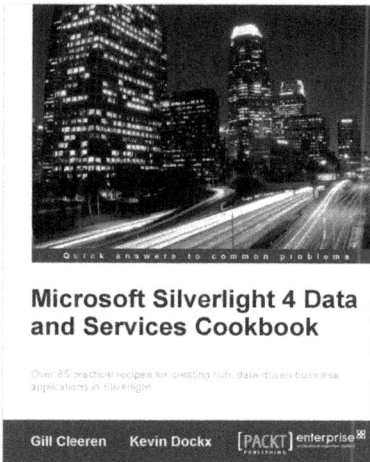

Microsoft Silverlight 4 Data and Services Cookbook

ISBN: 9781847199843   Paperback: 476 pages

Over 85 practical recipes for creating rich, data-driven business applications in Silverlight

1. Design and develop rich data-driven business applications in Silverlight

2. Rapidly interact with and handle multiple sources of data and services within Silverlight business applications

3. Understand sophisticated data access techniques in your Silverlight business applications by binding data to Silverlight controls, validating data in Silverlight, getting data from services into Silverlight applications and much more!

Please check **www.PacktPub.com** for information on our titles

www.ingramcontent.com/pod-product-compliance
Lightning Source LLC
Chambersburg PA
CBHW061346210326
41598CB00035B/5898